BURIED ALIVE

Jack Egan is best known for his work identifying and collecting archival film of Australian cricket and the production of documentary films and books, including *The Bradman Era*, *The Story of Cricket in Australia* and *The Cricket Archives*. *Buried Alive* is the first of a planned series of books on Australian history.

BURIED ALIVE

Sydney 1788–1792

Eyewitness Accounts of the
Making of a Nation

JACK EGAN

ALLEN & UNWIN

First published in 1999 by
Allen & Unwin
9 Atchison Street
St Leonards NSW 1590
Australia
Phone: (61 2) 8425 0100
Fax: (61 2) 9906 2218
E-mail: frontdesk@allen-unwin.com.au
Web: http://www.allen-unwin.com.au

National Library of Australia
Cataloguing-in-Publication entry:

Egan, Jack.
    Buried alive: Sydney 1788–1792: eyewitness accounts
    of the making of a nation.

    Bibliography.
    Includes index.

    ISBN 1 86508 138 8.

    1. Convicts—New South Wales—Sydney—History.
    2. Sydney (N.S.W.)—History—1788–1851. I. Title.

944.41

Set in 11.5/12.5 pt Adobe Garamond by Bookhouse Digital, Sydney
Printed by Australian Print Group, Maryborough, Vic.

10 9 8 7 6 5 4 3 2 1

Contents

Introduction

When the First Fleet arrived in Botany Bay in 1788, George Raper and Henry Waterhouse were 18 years old and their fellow-midshipman Newton Fowell was only a year older. When the *Sirius* ran onto a reef at Norfolk Island in March 1790, Newton Fowell was on board and was one of those who described the disaster. George Raper managed to saving his painting case from the sea and produced two graphic paintings of the wreck.

Detail from The melancholy loss of HMS Sirius,
by George Raper. Natural History Museum, London.

When the governor of the colony, Arthur Phillip, was speared at Manly later in the same year, Henry Waterhouse held him in his arms as they rowed him from Manly to Sydney Cove with the spear still protruding from his back. One of the rowers was Jacob Nagle, a 26-year-old American seaman. Waterhouse and Nagle both wrote about their experiences.

Three of the officers, William Bradley, 29 years old, and David Collins and Watkin Tench, both about 30, wrote detailed reports of the first years of the settlement. Others who wrote first-hand accounts of life at Sydney Cove included the 23-year-old Elizabeth Macarthur; Richard Johnson, a Yorkshireman and chaplain to the settlement; John Easty, a private from the Marine Corps; and the infamous London pickpocket, George Barrington.

It was part of a naval officer's training to learn to draw charts and views. William Bradley and Captain John Hunter were among the settlement's artists and they probably instructed George Raper, who may have been more talented than either of them. Phillip's servant, the eccentric Henry Brewer, despite a heavy workload and a liking for alcohol, is thought to have been one of the settlement's most prolific artists. The convict Thomas Watling, transported for forgery in 1792, was the most accomplished.

Richard Atkins Arrived 'free' in 1792, aged about 47, handsome, educated and well-connected, but battling alcoholism and his creditors in England. He was appointed a magistrate three months after his arrival.

George Barrington A convict from London, he was described as 'tall, approaching to six feet, slender, and his gait and manner bespeak liveliness and activity'. He arrived in October 1791, unmarried and aged about 35.

Arthur Bowes Surgeon of the *Lady Penrhyn*, from Essex, Bowes was unmarried and 37 years old when he arrived in 1788. Questioning and inclined to gossip, he was one of the few writers critical of Governor Arthur Phillip.

William Bradley First lieutenant of the *Sirius*, from Portsmouth, he was married and 29 years old. Bradley was quiet, careful and popular with the seamen—something of a saint in a colony of sinners. He wrote a daily journal with numerous illustrations.

Henry Brewer Phillip's clerk and servant, Brewer arrived with the First Fleet aged about 45. A heavy drinker, he had 'a contracted brow which bespoke him a man soured by disappointment' and was 'always muttering as if talking to himself'. But when he died one of his shipmates wrote: 'If honesty merits heaven, Harry is there'.

Ralph Clark   Second lieutenant of marines and about 33, Clark was homesick, besotted with the wife he had to leave behind at Plymouth, intolerant and dismissive of the convict women, but apparently well-liked by the Aboriginal people. His diary is frequently a catalogue of complaint, but it is nevertheless one of the most compelling of the colony's records.

David Collins   Captain of marines and judge-advocate of the settlement (although he had no legal training or experience), Collins had 'a cheerful and social disposition' and was described as tall and 'remarkably handsome' with 'golden, curly hair and the fine forehead of a scholar'. He was married and 31 years old when the First Fleet arrived. His *Account of the English Colony in NSW* is the most comprehensive book on the first settlement.

John Easty   Private marine, was not married and his age was not known. Laconic but not unemotional, his diary gives the soldier's view of significant events; when six fellow-privates were hanged for theft, he wrote: 'There was hardly a marine present but what shed tears, officers and men'.

Newton Fowell   A 19-year-old midshipman on the *Sirius*, Fowell came from Devon and wrote polished, informative letters to his father. His parents said: 'He excelled most young men of his age both in body and mind'.

John Hunter   Blue-eyed with an open, honest face, the Scotsman John Hunter was described as 'a man devoid of stiff pride'. Second captain of the *Sirius*, at 50, experienced and reliable, he was the oldest of the writers of the first settlement and later became governor of the colony. Hunter had learnt the classics and music as a young man and was said to have 'a pretty turn for drawing'. He produced two books, one of his experiences and another of his sketches.

Richard Johnson   Chaplain to the settlement, aged 32, from Yorkshire, he brought his wife Mary with him. Plump and gloomy, Johnson was one of the unhappiest of the reporters, forever complaining, but through his success as a farmer he made a major contribution to the welfare of the colony.

David Collins, Judge Advocate of New South Wales,
from a miniature by I.T. Barber. Mitchell Library,
State Library of New South Wales.

Philip Gidley King   The son of a draper from Cornwall, a close friend of Governor Phillip's and second lieutenant in the *Sirius*, King was unmarried and aged 29 when he arrived. He was described as one of the navy's 'most promising young men' and 'a pleasant companion, because full of information, having travelled and read a good deal'.

Elizabeth Macarthur   Born Elizabeth Veale in Devon, the daughter of a farmer, and married to a lieutenant in the New South Wales Corps, she arrived with the Second Fleet in June 1790, aged 23, with a one-year-old son. Energetic and inquisitive, she was soon studying botany and astronomy and learning to play the piano. Later she played a major part in bringing productive farming methods to the colony.

Jacob Nagle   An American seaman who had been a prisoner of war of the English during the War of Independence, Nagle was aged 26 when he arrived in the *Sirius*. He had a squint and wore his hair long, tied behind his head, but he took pride in his appearance and his competence as a seaman. 'In the governor's barge' and frequently employed in rowing Phillip around the harbour, Nagle was one of the few men of his rank who could read and write.

Mary Ann Parker   Wrote a book about her experiences travelling around the world as the wife of the captain of HMS *Gorgon*, which brought provisions to the settlement in 1792.

Arthur Phillip   Governor of the colony, from London, was divorced and aged 49 when he arrived in Botany Bay in 1788. Slightly built, but with a 'sharp and powerful' voice, Phillip had a blend of authority and experience and a humane outlook which served him well in the task of founding a colony in an unexplored continent at least six months by sea from its home base, with 700 thieves as the colonists.

George Raper   Born in London, although he was from a prominent Yorkshire family, and aged 18 when he arrived with the First Fleet as a midshipman in the *Sirius*. Although he was praised for his 'diligence and sobriety', Raper's early life at sea was unremarkable. There is evidence that he suffered poor health and that his 'passion was drawing rather than the sea'.

James Scott   Sergeant of marines, age unknown, he arrived with his wife Jane and daughter Elizabeth, born on the voyage out. Scott seems to have been a conscientious and reliable member of the marines. His handwriting is large and legible and his spelling is reasonable, but his punctuation was described as 'even more excessive and erratic than his capitalisation'.

Daniel Southwell   Master's mate on the *Sirius*, from London, he was unmarried and aged about 22. His time at Port Jackson was soured by a long period of service at the lookout at South Head, where he felt excluded from the action and ignored by senior officers who might be influential in his promotion. His reports come from a journal and letters to his mother and an uncle.

Watkin Tench   Captain of marines, unmarried, and aged about 30, wrote the most literary of the contemporary accounts. Of medium build with a neat, calm appearance, Tench was described as having a 'candid and liberal' mind. He and Collins were well aware of the effect of the

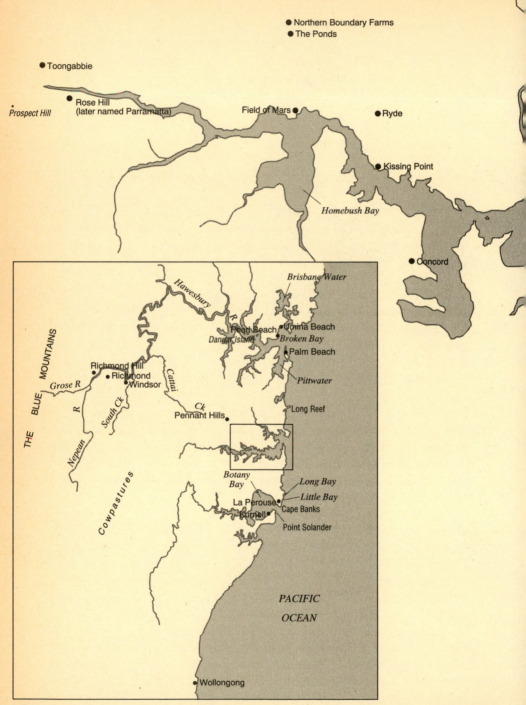

This page and opposite: Map showing the main features of the early settlement: Botany Bay, Port Jackson, Broken Bay, the Hawkesbury and Nepean Rivers, Sydney, Parramatta, Prospect, Toongabbie and Richmond.

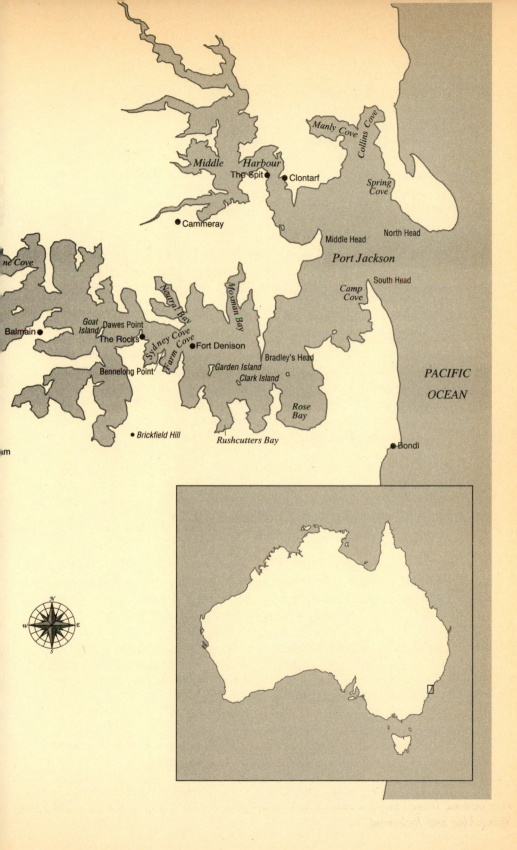

settlement on the Aboriginal people and took a lively interest in their customs and welfare.

Henry Waterhouse   Midshipman in the *Sirius*, from London and aged about 18 when he arrived, was referred to by Daniel Southwell as Phillip's 'young lieutenant, his favourite, his darling'. Waterhouse often acted as an aide to the governor, accompanying him on journeys around the settlement.

Thomas Watling   Arrived in October 1792, from Scotland, aged about 30. Transported for forgery, Watling faced a death sentence, but the Lord Advocate said of him: 'He is a young man, unmarried, and an ingenious artist; he will be an acquisition to the new colony at Botany Bay'.

John White   Surgeon to the First Fleet, was unmarried and aged about 32. Irish, with a peppery temperament, White fought a duel with his understudy, William Balmain, and in the early days of the settlement was scathing about its prospects. But he adopted an Aboriginal boy when smallpox struck the Aboriginal people in 1789; he coped with appalling conditions—as many as 600 sick after the arrival of the Third Fleet—and he changed his mind about the outlook for the colony.

George Worgan   Surgeon of the *Sirius*, from London, 30 years old and unmarried, he brought a piano with him to the new settlement. Worgan had a sharp eye and a sense of humour; his report is taken from a long letter to his brother in England.

If it was an incomparable, exotic experience for the Europeans, it was no less amazing for the people who already lived there. The Europeans knew about native civilisations in other parts of the world, but the Aboriginal people had no concept of the world outside the land they lived in. The coming of people from another civilisation to live in and on their land must have been so alien as to be almost incomprehensible. It is not surprising that it took some time for them to become involved with the settlement, but eventually many of them did, in some cases not of their own volition.

Arabanoo was captured in December 1788 and died of smallpox in May the following year. Tench said he was thoughtful and gentle, but 'impatient of indignity and allowed of no superiority on our part'; Newton Fowell wrote that he 'was much regretted by everyone, as it

Nanbaree, *pencil portrait by Thomas Watling.*
Natural History Museum, London.

was supposed he would have been of infinite service in reconciling the natives to us'.

Abaroo and **Nanbaree** came to the colony as children in April 1789, when their parents died of smallpox; the girl Abaroo was taken over by Mary Johnson, the clergyman's wife, and lived with his family; the boy Nanbaree lived with the surgeon-general, John White, and later worked in the settlement as a 'gamekeeper' and as a seaman.

Colbee and **Bennelong** were captured in November 1789. Colbee escaped within a few weeks, although he was later quite close to the colony and received two grants of land—the irony of which may not have been appreciated at the time. Bennelong, intelligent and passionate, had a love–hate relationship with the settlement and its governor, and travelled to England with Phillip when he left the settlement in 1792.

Daringa and Barangaroo, described as the wives of Colbee and Bennelong, demonstrated the cultural differences between the old and new settlers, and themselves had very different personalities. When Phillip ordered that a convict who had been caught stealing Daringa's fishing lines should be flogged in front of the Aboriginal people, they found the punishment abhorrent; 'Daringa shed tears and Barangaroo, kindling into anger, snatched a stick and menaced the executioner'.

Others who came into the settlement included **Yemmerrawannie**, a 'good-tempered lively lad' who lived with the governor; he went to England with Bennelong and Phillip in 1792. **Boladeree** ran foul of the settlers when he sought revenge after his canoe had been senselessly destroyed, although Collins said, 'Among his countrymen we had nowhere seen a finer young man.' Another was **Gooreedeeana**, described by Tench as 'this elegant timid female' who 'excelled in beauty all their females I ever saw'.

1788
Birth of a Thief Colony

18 January	The *Supply* arrived in Botany Bay.
19 January	'A great many Indians…came down to the shore and shouted at us.'
26 January	The fleet moved to Port Jackson.
29 January	First meeting with Aboriginal women.
15 February	The *Supply* sailed to establish a settlement at Norfolk Island.
27 February	The convict Thomas Barrett hanged for stealing provisions.
2 March	Phillip led an expedition to Broken Bay.
22 April	Phillip became ill on an expedition west from the harbour.
30 May	Convicts William Okey and Samuel Davis killed while cutting rushes.
1 June	A gathering estimated at 300 Aboriginal people seen near Botany Bay.
7 August	The brick kiln and many other buildings damaged by heavy rain.
24 August	An encounter between Aboriginal groups observed at Manly.
2 October	The *Sirius* sailed for Cape Town to obtain provisions for the colony.
2 November	A settlement established at Rose Hill.
30 December	Capture of Arabanoo.

JANUARY

Friday 18th

Second lieutenant Philip Gidley King We hauled in for the harbour at a quarter past two in the afternoon…at three, the boats were hoisted out and Governor Phillip and some officers belonging to the *Supply*, with Lieutenant Dawes and myself, landed on the north side of the bay and just looked at the face of the country which is, as Mr Cook remarks, very much like the moors in England except that there is a great deal of very good grass and some small timber trees. We went a little way up the bay to look for water but finding none, we returned abreast of the *Supply*, where we observed a group of the natives.

We put the boats on shore near where we observed two of their canoes lying. They immediately got up and called to us in a menacing tone and at the same time brandishing their spears or lances. However, the governor showed them some beads and ordered a man to fasten them to the stem of the canoe. We then made signs that we wanted water, when they pointed round the point on which they stood and invited us to land there. On landing, they directed us by pointing to a very fine stream of fresh water.

Governor Phillip then advanced toward them alone and unarmed, on which one of them advanced towards him but would not come near enough to receive the beads which the governor held out for him, but seemed very desirous of having them and made signs for them to be lain on the ground, which was done.

He (the native) came on with fear and trembling and took them up, and by degrees came so near as to receive looking glasses etc and seemed quite astonished at the figure we cut in being clothed. I think it is very easy to conceive the ridiculous figure we must appear to these poor creatures, who were perfectly naked. We soon after took leave of them and returned on board.

Saturday 19th

King At daylight we went on shore to haul the seine [net] on the north side, but caught very few fish; just as we were going on board the natives came down and were much more confident than they were the night before. At eight o'clock we were very agreeably surprised with the appearance of the *Alexander, Scarborough* and

Friendship coming round Point Solander. They anchored about 10 o'clock, when Major Ross, the lieutenant-governor, came on board.

Ralph Clark, second lieutenant of marines, on board *Friendship*, **wrote to his wife** At half past ten came to an anchor and found riding here the *Supply* who only had got in yesterday at two o'clock. The *Supply's* boat came on board with some hay for the sheep which I am very glad of, for the poor sheep that had her lambs taking from her died in the night. The *Supply* boat has been on shore often; had intercourse with the natives who they say are very friendly, but I will not trust them.

Private John Easty of the marines Saw several fires made by the Indians on Cape Banks. Saw a great many Indians on Point Solander. Came down to the shore and shouted at us and held up their weapons over their heads and shaked them at us. They seem all to be naked and of black colour.

Sunday 20th

King At eight in the morning we were again gratified with seeing the *Sirius* and all her convoy coming round Point Solander, and they anchored in the bay at half past nine.

David Collins, captain of marines and judge-advocate of the colony Thus, under the blessing of God, was happily completed, in eight months and one week, a voyage which, before it was undertaken, the mind hardly dared venture to contemplate...for in the above space of time we had sailed five thousand and twenty-one leagues, had touched at the American and African continents, and had at last rested within a few days sail of the antipodes of our native country, without meeting any accident in a fleet of 11 sail, nine of which were merchantmen that had never before sailed in that distant and imperfectly explored ocean.

Phillip had transferred from *Sirius,* the flagship, to *Supply* and, with the transports *Alexander, Friendship* and *Scarborough* had gone ahead of the rest of the fleet to Botany Bay, so that he could 'make his observations on the place, whether it is a proper spot for the settlement or not'. But as it happened, the ships they left behind had arrived within two days; the fleet comprised the naval escorts *Sirius* and *Supply* and six convict transports—*Alexander, Charlotte, Friendship, Lady Penrhyn,*

Prince of Wales and *Scarborough*—supported by three storeships—*Borrowdale*, *Fishburn* and *Golden Grove*.

Jacob Nagle, seaman in *Sirius* We out boats and went on shore with the governor and a number of officers...The natives came down to us and appeared as though they did not approve of our visit. When we were going on board the governor attempted to be very friendly with them, but they came with spear in hand and a bark shield. When we were all in the boats excepting Captain Ball, they begin to be mischievous with him, but he took one of their shields and set it up against an old stump of a tree and fired one of his pistols at it, which frightened them when they heard the report, but much more when they saw the ball went through the shield.

King They wanted to know of what sex we were, which they explained by pointing where it was distinguishable. As they took us for women, not having our beard grown, I ordered one of the people to undeceive them in this particular, when they made a great shout of admiration, and pointing to the shore, which was but 10 yards from us, we saw a great number of women and girls, with infant children on their shoulders, make their appearance on the beach...

Those natives who were round the boats made signs for us to go to them and made us understand their persons were at our service. However, I declined this mark of their hospitality but showed a handkerchief, which I offered to one of the women, pointing her out. She immediately put her child down and came alongside the boat and suffered me to apply the handkerchief where Eve did the fig leaf; the natives then set up another very great shout and my female visitor returned on shore.

Arthur Bowes Smyth, surgeon of *Lady Penryhn* This evening I went on shore in the boat with some of the ship's company to the north side of the bay to haul the seine and caught a great many fish, all excellent eating. Upon first sight one would be induced to think this a most fertile spot, as there are great numbers of very large and lofty trees reaching almost to the water's edge and every vacant spot between the trees appears to be covered with verdure. But upon a nearer inspection, the grass is found long and coarse, the trees very large and in general hollow, and the wood itself fit for no purposes of building or anything but the fire. The soil to a great depth is nothing but a black sand. Add to this, that every part of the ground is in a manner covered with black and red ants of a most enormous size.

John Hunter, second captain of *Sirius* I went with the governor to examine the south shore, in order to fix on a spot for erecting some buildings, but we found very little fresh water and not any spot very inviting for our purpose...We sounded the bay all over and found a considerable extent of anchorage in four, five, six and seven fathoms water, but wholly exposed to easterly winds, and no possibility of finding shelter from those winds in any part of the anchorage.

Captain Arthur Phillip, governor of the colony Several runs of fresh water were found in different parts of the bay, but there did not appear to be any situation to which there was not some very strong objection...Smaller numbers might indeed in several spots have found a comfortable residence, but no place was discovered in the whole circuit of Botany Bay which seemed at all calculated for the reception of so large a settlement.

Arthur Phillip was the son of Elizabeth Breach and Jacob Phillip, a German, probably Jewish, who had left Frankfurt to settle in London, where he taught languages. At 16, Arthur went to sea with the merchant navy, working as a cabin boy and then as a seaman. When he joined the Royal Navy as a lieutenant in 1761, he was 23 years old. He saw action in the West Indies and Havana, but the end of the Seven Years War made jobs scarce for naval officers and Phillip was retired on half pay. In 1763 he married a wealthy widow, Margaret Denison, and for several years he ran a farm which she owned in the New Forest, where they lived near the then Under-Secretary of the Treasury, George Rose.

The Phillips separated in 1769. Phillip served for a time with the Portuguese navy, where his duties included transporting convicts to Brazil and in 1778, when England resumed its war with France, Phillip rejoined the British navy as first lieutenant in HMS *Alexander*. The following year he was master and commander of HMS *Basilisk*, in 1781 he was post-captain of the frigate *Ariadne*, and in 1783 he commanded the 64-gun ship *Europe* on a voyage to the East Indies. During 1784 and 1785 he travelled in France, gathering information about the French navy for the British Admiralty.

When the decision was made to form a settlement in New South Wales, Phillip was known by many of the officials involved and had a suitable blend of experience and temperamant. George Rose was by that time Treasurer for the Navy and may have been influential in his appointment as governor. Born in October 1838, he was nearly 50 years old when the fleet arrived in Botany Bay.

On the voyage out, Phillip's concern for the seamen made an impression on Jacob Nagle. 'The governor thought fit to put us into three watches, as it would be much comfortabler', Nagle wrote, and he reported Phillip's response to the discovery that an officer named Maxwell had flogged some sailors for no good reason:

> The governor ordered every officer on board the ship to appear in the cabin, even to a boatswain's mate, and told them all if he knew any officer to strike a man on board, he would break him immediately. He said 'Those men are all we have to depend upon, and if we abuse those men that we have to trust to, the convicts will rise and massacre us all. Those men are our support. We have a long and severe station to go through in settling this colony; at least we cannot expect to return in less than five years. This ship and her crew is to protect and support the country and if they are ill-treated by their own officers, what support can you expect of them? They will be all dead before the voyage is half out, and who is to bring us back again?' So he dismissed them, and would not allow any officer, boatswain or his mates to carry a stick to strike any man with.

Portraits show that Phillip had a high forehead, a long nose, dark eyes and an olive complexion. He had a slight figure with sloping shoulders, but his voice was described as 'sharp and powerful'.

The new colony on the other side of the world, with its wild inhabitants, unique plants, and animals which defied the imagination, was a source of fascination in England and Europe; from the very beginning there was a rush to publish accounts of the voyage and the settlement. Surgeon-General White, Captain Watkin Tench and the judge-advocate, David Collins, kept journals specifically for publication.

There is evidence that Phillip kept a journal, too; in 1791, in a letter to Evan Nepean, who was Under-Secretary of State in the Home Department and responsible for the administration of the settlement, Phillip wrote: 'I have now, as usual, enclosed an extract from a book in which the occurrences of the day are set down...they never were intended, so they certainly are not calculated, for the eye of the public, having been put down in haste, and merely for the information of a friend'.

Phillip's journal has not been found, but he was constantly writing despatches and accounts of the colony's progress and providing other information to officials in London. John Stockdale of Piccadilly was an enterprising London publisher with an established clientele for books

Arthur Phillip on the eve of the First Fleet's
voyage to Botany Bay. *Portrait by
Francis Wheatley. Dixson Galleries, State
Library of New South Wales.*

of discovery. His firm, with the sanction of colonial officials, compiled
The Voyage of Governor Phillip to Botany Bay from the various accounts
from the colony.

About 1500 copies of the book had been ordered before it was published late in 1789; subscribers included the prime minister, William
Pitt, and Sir Joseph Banks. It quickly ran to three editions and was
translated into French and German. The title of the book is abbreviated to *Phillip* in attributing quotations.

Monday 21st

John Worgan, surgeon in *Sirius* During our stay at Botany Bay the
governor had made himself well acquainted with the situation of
the land, nature of the soil etc etc which he not finding so eligible

as he could wish for the purpose of forming a settlement, he determined, before he fixed on it, to visit an inlet on the coast about 12 miles to the northward of this bay which our great circumnavigator, Captain Cook, discovered and named in honour of one of the then commissioners of the navy, Port Jackson.

Collins   The governor set off on Monday the 21st, accompanied by Captain Hunter, Captain Collins (the judge-advocate), a lieutenant, master of the *Sirius*, with a small party of marines for their protection, the whole being embarked in three open boats. The day was mild and serene and there being but a gentle swell without the mouth of the harbour, the excursion promised to be a pleasant one. Their little fleet attracted the attention of several parties of the natives as they proceeded along the coast, who all greeted them in the same words, and in the same tone of vociferation, shouting everywhere: 'Warra, warra, warra', words which, by the gestures that accompanied them, could not be interpreted into invitations to land or expressions of welcome. It must however be observed that at Botany Bay the natives had hitherto conducted themselves sociably and peaceably toward all the parties of our officers and people with whom they had hitherto met, and by no means seemed to regard them as enemies or invaders of their country and tranquillity.

The coast, as the boats drew near Port Jackson, wore so unfavourable an appearance that Captain Phillip's utmost expectation reached no farther than to find what Captain Cook, as he passed by, thought might be found, shelter for a boat. In this conjecture, however, he was most agreeably disappointed, by finding not only shelter for a boat, but a harbour capable of affording security to a much larger fleet than would probably ever seek for shelter or security in it.

Jacob Nagle was one of the seamen who rowed Phillip's party from Botany Bay to Port Jackson:

> We arrived in the afternoon and run up Middle Harbour to the westward and then a circular round to a bay on the north side, which Governor Phillip called Manly Bay, and surveyed round till we came into the south-west branch...It coming on dark, we landed on a beach on the south side and there pitched our tents for the night. This was called Camp Cove. The marines were put on their posts. The sailors were variously employed, some kindling fires and some shooting the seine for fish, others getting

out utensils for cooking. By the time we got our suppers, was late in the night.

———

Jacob Nagle, who had been a prisoner of war of the English during the American War of Independence and had later joined the British navy, was at Spithead in the *Ganges* when Phillip arrived in *Supply*, recruiting for the expedition to Botany Bay. 'Seven of us turned out, belonging to the boat from the *Ganges*', he wrote in his journal. 'I was put into the governor's barge.'

Nagle, whose father had been a colonel in the American army, was probably better educated than most of his fellow-seamen; 26 years old when the First Fleet sailed, he was slim, strong and adventurous, a highly professional seaman. At a time when people were judged by their rank, Nagle judged them by how they did their job, and he took great pride in his own competence and appearance. He had a cast in his left eye, but he wore his hair long, tied at the back of his head, and when he was dressed to go ashore he wore a silk scarf round his neck, a tailored coat and gold brooch, rings and watch.

It seems from his writing that Nagle kept a journal of some sort throughout his seafaring life. As a prisoner of the British during the War of Independence, he wrote that his fellow prisoners persuaded him to destroy his journal, for fear that he might be hanged as a spy, and later he notes that he lost the journal of his experiences in Australia. The journal which has survived is a 'near-final draft', apparently written over a relatively short period. It was probably written after he retired from the sea in 1825 and some if not all of it must have been written from recollection of events some 40 years past. The *Journal's* editor, John C. Dann of the University of Michigan, wrote: 'The vast majority of his facts are confirmable in other contemporary sources, and those that are not have the ring of authenticity about them'.

Tuesday 22nd

Nagle By four in the morning we had everything in the boats again and on our oars... We eat our breakfasts on our seats and pulled all day. The harbour was large and extensive and the governor anxious to get to the head of the harbour, but we could not, but we got as far as where the town is now called Sydney Cove, about seven miles from the entrance of the harbour. We landed on the west side of the cove. Along shore was all bushes, but a small distance at the head of the cove was level and large trees, but scattering and no underwood worth mentioning and a run of fresh water running down into the centre of the cove. The governor, officers and seamen went up to see it.

I being boat-keeper, I had to remain in the boat. I hove my line over, being about four or five fathom water alongside of the rocks. I hauled up a large black bream and hove it into the stern sheets of the boat. The governor coming down, very much pleased with this cove and a situation for a town, he was determined to settle in this cove. Coming into the barge, he observed the fish I had catched and asked who had caught that fish. I informed him that I had. 'Recollect,' said he, 'that you are the first white man that ever caught a fish in Sydney Cove where the town is to be built.'

Phillip wrote to Lord Sydney The boats, in passing near a point of land in the harbour, were seen by a number of men and 20 of them waded into the water unarmed, received what was offered them, and examined the boats with a curiosity which gave me a much higher opinion of them than I had formed from the behaviour of those seen in Captain Cook's voyage, and their confidence and manly behaviour made me give the name of Manly Cove to this place...

The different coves were examined with all possible expedition. I fixed on the one that had the best spring of water and in which the ships can anchor so close to the shore that at a very small expense quays may be made at which the largest ships may unload. This cove, which I honoured with the name of Sydney, is about a quarter of a mile across at the entrance, and half a mile in length.

This despatch, completed on 15 May, was the first sent from the settlement. Thomas Townshend, Viscount Sydney, a friend of Arthur Phillip's, was Home Secretary in William Pitt's cabinet, and it was under his administration that the colony was established.

Wednesday 23rd

John White, surgeon-general of the colony While the people were employed on shore, the natives came several times among them and behaved with a kind of cautious friendship. One evening while the seine was hauling, some of them were present and expressed great surprise at what they saw, giving a shout expressive of astonishment and joy when they perceived the quantity that was caught. No sooner were the fish out of the water than they began to lay hold of them, as if they had a right to them, or that they were their own; upon

Thomas Townshend, Viscount Sydney.
Portrait by Gilbert Stuart. Dixson Galleries,
State Library of New South Wales.

which the officer of the boat, I think very properly, restrained them, giving, however, to each of them a part. They did not at first seem very well pleased with this mode of procedure, but on observing with what justice the fish was distributed they appeared content.

James Scott, sergeant of marines   The commodore…on his return at p.m. made the signal for all masters and gave orders to sail for Port Jackson tomorrow morning, as he approved of it better than Botany Bay.

Thursday 24th

Watkin Tench, captain of marines   I rose at the first dawn of the morning. But judge of my surprise on hearing from a sergeant, who ran down almost breathless to the cabin where I was dressing, that a ship was seen off the harbour's mouth. At first I only laughed, but knowing the man who spoke to me to be of great veracity, and hearing him repeat his information, I flew upon deck, on which I had barely set my foot, when the cry of 'Another sail' struck on my astonished ear. Confounded by a thousand ideas which arose in my mind in an instant, I sprang upon the barricado, and plainly descried two ships of considerable size standing in for the mouth of the bay. By this time the alarm had become general and every one appeared lost in conjecture. Now they were Dutchmen sent to dispossess us, and the moment after storeships from England with supplies for the settlement. The improbabilities which attended both these conclusions were sunk in the agitation of the moment. It was by Governor Phillip that this mystery was at length unravelled, and the cause of the alarm pronounced to be two French ships, which, it was now recollected, were on a voyage of discovery in the southern hemisphere.

King wrote that one of the ships flew a 'pennant from which we conclude them to be *La Boussole* and *l'Astrolabe* under the orders of Monsieur De la Pérouse, on discoveries; but the wind blowing strong from nor-nor-east prevented their getting in, or our going out. At four in the afternoon they were out of sight'.

Friday 25th

White   The governor, with a detachment of marines, sailed in the *Supply* tender for Port Jackson, leaving instructions with Captain Hunter to follow him, with all the transports and victuallers, as soon as the wind and weather would permit.

Clark   It blows very hard and a great sea rolling into the bay. The rest of the fleet had to wait in Botany Bay.

Saturday 26th

The French ships had not been able to enter the harbour and were not seen on the 25th. On the 26th, Tench wrote: 'They reappeared in their former situation, and a boat was sent to them with a lieutenant of the navy in her to offer assistance and point out the necessary marks for entering the harbour.'

Clark, in the *Friendship* At eight o'clock got under way...There being little wind and the place very narrow and the wind quite against us, the *Prince of Wales* and us got foul of each other; they carried away our jib boom but what damage we did her I cannot say... soon after the *Charlotte* ran foul of us and shook us very much. I was more frightened than I was when the *Prince of Wales* was foul of us; if it had not being by the greatest good luck we should have been both on shore on the rocks and the ships must must have been all lost and the greater part if not the whole on board drowned, for we should have gone to pieces in less than a half of an hour.

Bowes, in the *Lady Penrhyn* At last the whole fleet got clear of the harbour's mouth without any further damage being sustained, everyone blaming the rashness of the governor in insisting upon the fleet working out in such weather and all agreed it was next to a miracle that some of the ships were not lost, the danger was so very great. We reached the mouth of Port Jackson about seven o'clock p.m. and sailed about eight miles up to Sydney Cove where the settlement is made...The ships, many of them, lie so near the shore that they might with ease be fastened with ropes to the trees instead of putting down their anchors.

Scott, in the *Prince of Wales* Came to an anchor at half past six o'clock in Port Jackson close to the new town which was christened this day and four volleys of small arms fired.

White In the evening, when all the ships had anchored, the English colours were displayed and at the foot of the flagstaff his Majesty's health and success to the settlement was drunk by the governor, many of the principal officers, and private men who were present upon the occasion.

Sunday 27th

King The shore on each side is bounded by rocks, within which there is a very fine soil, and full of trees which will require some time and labour to clear away. The marines and convicts are to be encamped on the west side, and the governor and staff, with his guard and a small part of the convicts, on the east side of the rivulet.

Collins Sufficient ground was cleared for encamping the officer's guard and the convicts who had been landed in the morning.

The spot chosen for this purpose was at the head of the cove, near the run of fresh water which stole silently along through a very thick wood, the stillness of which had then, for the first time since the creation, been interrupted by the rude sound of the labourer's axe.

A list of 'Articles sent by the First Fleet to Botany Bay' included 700 felling axes, 700 hatchets, 80 carpenters' axes, 700 steel spades, 700 iron shovels, 700 garden hoes, 40 wheelbarrows, 6 carts, harness for 6 horses, 12 ploughs, 5,448 squares of crown glass, 175 claw hammers, 175 handsaws, 20 pit saws, 20 adzes, 300 chisels, 14 fishing nets, 8000 fish hooks and 48 dozen lines, 10 blacksmiths' forges, 800 sets of bedding, 44 tons of tallow and 420 dozen candles.

Worgan The boats that were sent to haul the seine were very successful. They met with some of the natives who behaved very friendly, even helped them to haul the seine on shore, for which kind office they were liberally rewarded with a portion of the fish. The governor gave strict orders that the natives should not be offended or molested on any account and advised that, wherever they were met with, they were to be treated with every mark of friendship. In case of their stealing anything, mild means were to be used to recover it, but upon no account to fire at them with ball or shot.

Clark I am much charmed with the place. Oh, that if you was only here and our dear boy, my Alicia, I should not wish to come home, if the place agreed with our health; but without you I would not stay if it was the best place under the face of heaven, no, that I would not, my dear beloved wife, for without you I cannot live. The tents look pretty amongst the trees; I hope to be on shore tomorrow.

When Ralph Clark volunteered for service with the First Fleet, he was apparently under the impression that he would be able to take his wife Betsey Alicia and his young son, Ralph, with him to New South Wales. He wrote to Phillip on 3 April 1787: 'Being one of the officers of the detachment of marines going to Botany Bay under your command I will be much obliged to you to inform me if you have any objection or if there is any impropriety for me to take my family out with me'.

Permission was refused. Phillip replied: 'Your request depended on the minister and if Lord Sydney had consented I certainly should not have made any objections. As it is I think when you reflect on the many inconveniences that must have attended it, you will be satisfied of the propriety of the refusal.'

At sea during the voyage, Clark had been desperately unhappy and 'exceedingly seasick'. On 16 May he wrote in his journal: 'Going every moment from all that my soul holds dear; I wish to God that I was once so near home to them again, then I should be a happy man'. For all his obvious affection for his wife and son, Clark was intolerant of the convicts, especially the women; on the same day he wrote: 'I never could have thought that there were so many abandoned wretches in England; they are ten times worse than the men convicts'.

It is thought that Ralph Clark kept a personal diary from the time he left England in May 1787 until he arrived back in June 1792, in three notebooks, the second of which, covering the period 11 March 1788 to 14 February 1790, was lost. Clark's papers were purchased by the Mitchell Library in 1914. *The Journal and Letters of Lieutenant Ralph Clark, 1787–1792* was published by the Australian Documents Library in 1981.

Monday 28th

Scott   The whole detachment of marines, wives and children disembarked and encamped immediately. The male convicts employed in clearing away the ground.

Bowes   This day Lieutenants G. Johnston and William Collins took their leave of the ship and pitched their tents on shore: very hot. The governor has appointed several coves for the different ship's boats to go to, to haul their seines, upon first calling on board the *Sirius* to let them know the boat is going and either the master himself or one of the mates must be in the boat. In general, the boats were very successful in catching a great number of fish of variety of sorts. All the rock near the water are thick covered with oysters, which are very small but very finely flavoured; they also adhere to the branches of the mangrove trees.

Bradley   Went with Captain Hunter, the master and one of the mids about surveying the harbour. On a point of land in the lower part of the harbour between Middle Head and Bradley Point we saw several of the natives on the upper part of the rocks, who made a great noise and waved to us to come on shore; there being a great surf we could not land at the point we wished, which they observing, pointed to the best place to land and came down unarmed to meet us. We of course landed unarmed, taking care that arms were ready for us at a moment's notice...

On our landing we observed some women at the place the men came down from; they would not come near us, but peeped from behind the rocks and trees. When the boats put off, the men began dancing and laughing and when we were far enough off to bring the place the women were at in sight, they held their arms extended over their heads, got on their legs and danced till we were some distance, then followed us upon the rocks as far as the boats went along that shore.

Nagle Eight of us that belonged to the governor's barge pitched our tent by the water side on a rock near the landing place and the boat in view. The convicts were immediately employed in cutting down timber and clearing to build log houses for the officers and soldiers on the west side and fencing in ground, and the women employed carrying the stones away into the corners of the fences.

The *Sirius* having the stock on board, laying at the entrance of the cove, we landed the cattle on the east side, being a flat point, and all the other stock that was for the settlement.

Clark Got up early this morning and sent all the convicts on shore except them that were sick. Thank God that they are all out of the ship, hope in God that I will have nothing to do with them any more. At 10 debarked with all the marines and their baggage, except my own. I never saw so much confusion in all the course of my life as there was in the three companies disembarking.

Tuesday 29th

King A great deal of work has been done in clearing away, but much remains to be done. Some carpenters preparing for fixing the governor's portable house—£125—a number of the convicts digging up the ground for a garden.

White The laboratory and sick tents were erected, and, I am sorry to say, were soon filled with patients afflicted with the true camp dysentery and the scurvy. More pitiable objects were perhaps never seen. Not a comfort or convenience could be got for them, besides the very few we had with us.

His Excellency, seeing the state these poor objects were in, ordered a piece of ground to be enclosed for the purpose of raising vegetables for them... The sick have increased since our landing to such a degree that a spot for a general hospital has been marked out and artificers already employed on it.

Collins   The tents for the sick were placed on the west side, and it was observed with concern that their numbers were fast increasing. The scurvy, that had not appeared during the passage, now broke out, which, aided by a dysentery, began to fill the hospital, and several died. In addition to the medicines that were administered, every species of esculent plants that could be found in the country were procured for them; wild celery, spinach and parsley fortunately grew in abundance about the settlement. Those who were in health, as well as the sick, were very glad to introduce them into their messes and found them a pleasant as well as wholesome addition to the ration of salt provisions.

Bradley was surveying the harbour with Hunter   As we were going into…Spring Cove [between Manly and North Head] we were joined by three canoes, with one man in each. They hauled their canoes up and met us on the beach, leaving their spears in the canoes. We were soon joined by a dozen of them and found three of them with trinkets hanging about them that had been given to them a week before by the governor on his first visit to this place. Our people and these mixed together and were quite sociable, dancing and otherwise amusing them. One of our people combed their hair, with which they were much pleased…

We had here an opportunity of examining their canoes and weapons. The canoe is made of the bark taken off a large tree, of the length they want to make the canoe, which is gathered up at each end and secured by a lashing of strong vine which runs amongst the underbush. One was secured by small line. They fix spreaders in the inside. The paddles are about two feet long, in shape like a pudding stirrer. These they use one in each hand and go along very fast, sitting with their legs under them and their bodies erect, and although they do not use outriggers, I have seen them paddle through a large surf without oversetting or taking in more water than if rowing in smooth water. From their construction they are apt to leak when any weight is in them. The man nearest that part of the canoe where the water lies heaves it out behind him with a piece of wood in the hollow of his hand, still keeping his body erect as when rowing. They are by far the worst canoes I ever saw or heard of. I have seen some so small as eight feet long and others twice that length. In these canoes they will stand up to strike fish, at which they seem expert.

Hunter We observed at a distance a number of women who were peeping from their concealments, but durst not gratify their natural curiosity by appearing openly and conversing with us, as the men appeared here to be very absolute. I signified to the men that we had observed the women, and that I wished to make them some presents, if they might be permitted to come forward and receive them. The men seemed unwilling to suffer them to advance, for we had frequently observed that they took particular care upon every occasion to keep the women at a distance, and I believe wholly from an idea of danger. They desired to have the presents for the women and they would carry and deliver them, but to this proposal I positively refused to agree, and made them understand that unless they were allowed to come forward they should not have any.

Finding I was determined, an old man who seemed to have the principal authority directed the women to advance, which they did immediately with much good humour and during the whole time that we were decorating them with beads, rags of white linen and some other trifles, they laughed immoderately, although trembling at the same time, through an idea of danger. Most of those we saw at this time were young women, who I judged were from 18 to 25 years of age. They were all perfectly naked, as when first born.

The women in general are well made, not quite so thin as the men, but rather smaller limbed. As soon as the women were ordered to approach us, about 20 men, whom we had not before seen, sallied from the wood, completely armed with lance and shield; they were painted with red and white streaks all over the face and body, as if they intended to strike terror by their appearance. Some of them were painted with a little degree of taste, and although the painting on others appeared to be done without any attention to form, yet there were those who, at a small distance, appeared as if they were accoutred with cross-belts. Some had circles of white round their eyes, and several a horizontal streak across the forehead, others again had narrow white streaks round the body, with a broad line down the middle of the back and belly and a single streak down each arm, thigh, and leg.

These marks, being generally white, gave the person, at a small distance, a most shocking appearance, for upon the black skin the white marks were so very conspicuous that they were exactly like so many moving skeletons. The colours they use are mostly red and white, the first of which is a kind of ochre, or red earth, which is found here in considerable quantities; the latter is a fine pipe-clay. The bodies of the men are much scarified, particularly their breasts and shoulders; these scarifications are considerably raised above the skin, and although they are not in any regular form, yet they are certainly considered as ornamental.

The men, thus armed and painted, drew themselves up in a line on the beach, and each man had a green bough in his hand as a sign of friendship; their disposition was as regular as any well-disciplined troops could have been and this party, I apprehend, was entirely for the defence of the women, if any insult had been offered them. We also observed at this interview that two very stout armed men were placed upon a rock, near to where our boats lay, as sentinels, for they never moved from the spot until we left the beach; I therefore suppose they were ordered there to watch all our motions. We left these people, after a visit of about four hours, both parties apparently well satisfied with all that passed...

Many of the women want the two lower joints of the little finger of the left hand, which we have not as yet been able to discover the reason or meaning of. This defect of the little finger we have observed in old women, and in young girls of eight or nine years old; in young women who have had children, and in those who have not, and the finger has been seen perfect in individuals of all the above ages and descriptions.

They have very good teeth in general; their hair is short, strong, and curly, and as they seem to have no method of cleaning or combing it, it is therefore filthy and matted. The men wear their beards, which are short and curly, like the hair of the head. Men, women, and children go entirely naked, as described by Captain Cook.

Phillip observed that 'most of the men want the right front tooth in the upper jaw...On my showing them that I wanted [lacked] a front tooth it occasioned a general clamour and I thought gave me some little merit in their opinion.'

Newton Fowell, second lieutenant of the *Sirius*, described the fishing and hunting weapons:

All of them have a spear made of hard wood and sharpened by scraping it with a shell. It is about 12 feet in length and joined in several places with gum. They can throw them about 70 yards. This sort of spear we afterward found to be the war spear; another sort they have for fishing, which is about the same length, having four prongs at the end, and at the end of each prong is a fish's tooth, very nicely fastened with gum and bearded with the same.

The other they throw with a stick about three feet long that has a crook at one end which they hook in the end of the spear and throw it with great exactness. At the other end is a shell they use for scraping their spear and opening oysters.

Most of the diarists also described a form of sword or scimitar. Bradley said it was 'somewhat the shape of the common hanger, with the handle or hilt carved so as to give them a good hold of it. It is made of very hard wood, smooth and sharp at both edges, coming to a tolerable sharp point. They are from two to three feet long and as many inches broad, or more'. Various forms of wooden swords were used and there is some dispute as to whether a similar weapon was in fact a boomerang. It has been suggested that the boomerang was not understood by the settlers, but there does not seem to be a record of this type of implement being used in the Sydney region.

Thursday 31st

Clark What a terrible night it was last of thunder lightning and rain; was obliged to get out of my tent with nothing on but my shirt to slacking the tent poles. Dreamt of you my dear sweet woman and that I was in bed with you...Remarkably hot; have nothing to sleep [in] but a poor tent and a little grass to sleep on.

∽

A total of about 1500 people arrived with the First Fleet. Of this number, 1373 have been identified, including 732 convicts, 306 ships' crew and 245 marines. There were 22 children of convicts, 23 marines' children, 31 wives of marines and 14 other officials and passengers. Almost all of the 732 convicts had been convicted for theft; 189 were women. There would have been a further hundred or more seamen on the transports, for whom no records have been found.

Some 20 nationalities were represented; apart from the English, there were 83 Irish, 33 Scots (of whom only one was a convict), nine Welsh, and 14 from North America (including four convicts).

Other nationalities included Dutch, French, German, Indian, Jamaican, Madagascan, Norwegian, Portuguese and Swedish. About a dozen black men of various nationalities came with the fleet, and there was probably a similar number of Jewish men and women.

Most were young; incomplete statistics suggest that at least two-thirds were aged 30 or younger.

Only the chaplain, the Reverend Richard Johnson, and the 'other ranks' of the marines—the privates, corporals and sergeants—were allowed to bring their wives to the colony with them. Richard Howe, First Lord of the Admiralty, said that permission was denied the officers because the extent of their duties would be 'as if they were at war'.

Thirty-two of the marines' wives left England with the fleet. One of them, Mary Cook, wife of the drum-major, died of a fever at the Cape of Good Hope. They arrived with 23 children, ranging in age from Joseph Cox, who was old enough to become a drummer with the marines in June 1788, down to eight children who were born on the voyage.

Twenty-two children came with the convicts, 11 boys and 11 girls. Joseph Harrison was about 16 and Jane Jones was about 10; the others were at most three or four years old.

Two other children and two other wives came with the First Fleet. Alexander Ross, the son of Major Robert Ross, commander of the marines, was about eight years old when he embarked, recorded as a volunteer without pay in the marines. James Campbell, a cousin of Captain James Campbell of the marines, was about 12 years old. Both came in the *Lady Penrhyn*. Mary Johnson, wife of the chaplain, came with her husband in the *Golden Grove*; Deborah Brooks was recorded as the wife of Thomas Brooks, the bosun of the *Sirius*.

A British seaman, Edward Spain, who had served with Arthur Phillip in HMS *Europe*, mentioned in his journal an episode involving Phillip and Thomas and Deborah Brooks on a voyage to the East Indies in 1783. Spain wrote that Phillip had 'granted leave to four women to go to sea in the ship. But don't imagine that it was out of any partiality to any of them, except one, which one he had a sneaking kindness for and had he given permission to her alone the reason would have been obvious to the officers and the ship's company'.

The woman known as Deborah Brooks came aboard with Thomas Brooks, the boatswain's mate. Spain wrote: 'The woman that Brooks brought with him had eloped from her husband, who was a house carpenter in Plymouth dock. She it was that our noble commander had a partiality for, and through her the man.'

Phillip, according to Spain, plotted with the master of the ship to have him demoted: 'The captain by this manoeuvre between him and the master had an opportunity of giving Brooks an order to officiate in my station, and so ingratiate himself in favour with the woman, who had free access in and out of the great cabin'. However, 'the admiral no doubt saw through the scheme,' Spain wrote, which 'ended the business, and Brooks, the fancy-woman's gallant, was fain to stay on board our ship in his old station as boatswain's mate'.

———

The journals and records from which this book has been compiled were written and published at different times and using different conventions for presentation. The published version of Bradley's *A Voyage to New South Wales*, for example, is a facsimile (or photocopy) edition of the original which Bradley completed in May 1792, while *The Nagle Journal* was first published in 1988, in print and with the benefit of an expert editor to explain abbreviations and clarify meanings where appropriate. As noted in the introduction to Scott's *Passage to Botany Bay*, Scott scatters 'initial capitals so liberally and inconsistently…that it is sometimes impossible to be sure how he meant them to be taken. His punctuation is even more excessive and erratic than his capitalisation'. In this compilation, the words have generally been left as they were in the original, while uniform, modern punctuation, spelling and capitalisation have been used throughout, with the intention of retaining the character of the original work, while making it easy to read and understand.

Some words were spelled differently 200 years ago—clothes were *cloaths*, a musket was a *musquet*, shallow was *shoal*, trousers were *trowsers* and King still used *ye* for the. Words which were new to the language produced a variety of spellings; Bennelong, as it is generally spelled now, was spelled *Bannelong* by Hunter, *Baneelon* by Tench, *Benallon* by Bradley, *Benelong* by Johnson, and *Benalong* by Fowell.

The kangaroo created even more confusion: Phillip spelled it *kangurroo*; Clark spelled it *kankeroo*; Collins and White spelled it 'correctly'; but other correspondents used *cangaroo*, *congaroo*, *kanguroo*, *kangooroo* and *kangurroo*. Mary Ann Parker, a latecomer on the scene, wrote that she had 'often ate part of a kingaroo with as much glee as if I had been a partaker of some of the greatest delicacies of this metropolis, although latterly I was cloyed with them and found them very disagreeable'.

In fact, the Aboriginal people around Port Jackson called the the grey kangaroo *bangaray* and the red kangaroo *patagarang*. The word 'kangaroo' comes from the Aboriginal people of the Endeavour River region in North Queensland, where Captain James Cook was forced ashore when his ship was holed on the reef in June 1770. Tench observed of the Aboriginal people in the Sydney region that 'Kangaroo was a name unknown to them for any animal, until we introduced it. When I showed Colbee the cows brought out in the *Gorgon*, he asked me if they were kangaroos.' Thus are icons created.

FEBRUARY

Friday 1st

Clark Captain Meredith and Davey came over last night and stayed supper with me; Meredith sent me some fish which I had boiled. In all the course of my life I never slept worse, my dear wife, than I did [last] night; what with the hard cold ground, spiders, ants and every vermin that you can think of was crawling over me. I was glad when the morning came.

For reasons which are still not clear, no overseers to supervise the work of the convicts had been sent with the expedition. It may have been assumed that the marines would take on the role, but they were trained as 'sea soldiers', to fight on ships, and they took the view that they were sent to defend the settlement, not to superintend the convicts. Phillip wrote to Lord Sydney:

> The officers who compose the detachment are not only few in number but most of them have declined any interference with the convicts, except when they are employed for their particular service. I requested soon after we landed that officers would occasionally encourage such as they observed diligent and point out for punishment such as they saw idle or straggling into the woods. This was all I desired, but the officers did not understand that any interference with the convicts was expected and that they were not sent out to do more than the duty of soldiers.

So the bosses had to be drawn from the ranks of the convicts. Worgan wrote:

> The governor had on the passage made himself acquainted with the trade and occupations of each; accordingly, when they were landed, the men that could be spared from the principal business of clearing the ground were set at their respective employments as occasion required, such as the carpenters, sawyers, shingle makers, stone cutters, masons, brick makers,

blacksmiths etc. These were divided into parties and one of the most promising among the party was made an overseer to the rest.

Clearing and cultivation of the ground at the head of Farm Cove was begun under the supervision of Henry Edward Dodd, a servant of Phillip's since his days as a farmer in the New Forest. Walter Brody, a 21-year-old seaman from the *Sirius*, was set up on shore as a blacksmith. Tools were taken ashore including the blacksmith's forge and bellows, crosscut saws and splitting wedges.

Tench Business now sat on every brow and the scene to an indifferent spectator, at leisure to contemplate it, would have been highly picturesque and amusing. In one place, a party cutting down the woods, a second setting up a blacksmith's forge, a third dragging along a load of stones or provisions; here an officer pitching his marquee with a detachment of troops parading on one side of him and a cook's fire blazing upon the other. Through the unwearied diligence of those at the head of the different departments, regularity was, however, soon introduced, and as far as the unsettled state of matters would allow, confusion gave place to system.

Saturday 2nd

King At two in the morning Lieutenant Dawes of the marines and myself set off in a cutter for Botany Bay to visit Monsieur De La Pérouse on the part of Governor Phillip and to offer him whatever he might have occasion for. We got down to the harbour's mouth at daylight; finding a light air from the southward, we were obliged to row all the way and arrived on board the *Boussole* at 11 o'clock in the morning, where we were received with the greatest politeness and attention by Monsieur De La Pérouse and his officers...

Monsieur De La Pérouse informed me that a number of the convicts had been to him and offered to enter, but he had dismissed them with threats and gave them a day's provision to carry them back to the settlement. As the wind came on to blow fresh from the northward, I yielded to the solicitations of the French commodore and consented to dine with him and stay the remainder of the day and return to Port Jackson next morning...

After dinner I attended the commodore and other officers on shore where I found him quite established, having thrown round his tents a stockade, guarded by two small guns, in which he is setting up two long boats which he had in frame. An observatory tent was also fixed here, in which was an astronomical quadrant, clocks etc.

Sunday 3rd

The Reverend Richard Johnson conducted the first church service. Tench wrote that it was conducted 'under a great tree…in the presence of the troops and convicts, whose behaviour on the occasion was equally regular and attentive'. James Thomas, son of Private Samuel Thomas and Ann Thomas, was baptised during the service, the first person to be baptised in the colony. The identity of the first child born in the colony is not known.

Tuesday 5th

Bradley   We found fish plenty although the harbour is full of sharks. There is a great quantity of shell fish in the coves that have mud-flats at the bottom. Oysters very large. We found wild spinach, samphire and other leaves of bushes which we used as vegetables. An island near a mile below the settlement was granted for the use of the *Sirius* to make a garden of.

Wednesday 6th

Bowes   At five o'clock this morning, all things were got in order for landing the whole of the women, and three of the ships long-boats came alongside us to receive them; previous to their quitting the ship a strict search was made to try if any of the many things which they had stolen on board could be found, but their artifice eluded the most strict search and at six o'clock p.m. we had the long wished for pleasure of seeing the last of them leave the ship. They were dressed in general very clean and some few amongst them might be said to be well dressed.

The men convicts got to them very soon after they landed, and it is beyond my abilities to give a just description of the scene of debauchery and riot that ensued during the night. They had not been landed more than an hour, before they had all got their tents pitched or anything in order to receive them, but there came on the most violent storm of thunder, lightning and rain I ever saw.

The lightning was incessant during the whole night and I never heard it rain faster. About 12 o'clock in the night one severe flash of lightning struck a very large tree in the centre of the camp, under which some places were constructed to keep the sheep and hogs in. It split the tree from top to bottom, killed five sheep belonging to Major Ross and a pig of one of the lieutenants.

Bowes was the least inhibited of the contemporary writers. Collins referred to 'the hurry and tumult necessarily attending the disembarkation'. Bradley described only the thunder and lightning, adding that 'the sentinel on post near the tree was knocked down and lost his sight'. Tench observed that 'while they were on board ship, the two sexes had been kept most rigorously apart, but, when landed, their separation became impracticable and would have been, perhaps, wrong; licentiousness was the unavoidable consequence'.

Arthur Bowes Smyth, known in the colony as Bowes, was born in Tolleshunt, Essex in 1750 and practised there as a surgeon before being appointed as surgeon to the ship's company on the transport *Lady Penrhyn* in 1787 as she prepared for the voyage to Botany Bay. Bowes had a sharp mind and took a considerable interest in the events at the settlement and in its plants and animals. He wrote in a neat hand in a large journal, which included several sketches. *The Journal of Arthur Bowes Smyth* was among the 60 000 books and manuscripts (along with £70,000) given to the Public Library of New South Wales by David Scott Mitchell and was first published in 1979 by the Australian Documents Library.

Bowes, who left Port Jackson in the *Lady Penrhyn* in May 1788, was virtually alone among the writers of the First Fleet in expressing criticism of Phillip, calling the decision to separate the fleet as they approached Botany Bay an 'abortion of the brain', blaming Phillip's 'rashness' for the near disaster when the fleet left Botany Bay for Port Jackson and later castigating him for lack of respect for the captains of the transports and storeships after the reading of the governor's Commission.

Thursday 7th

It was a fine, clear day, with light winds. Bowes wrote:

> The marines were all under arms and received the governor with flying colours and a band of music. He was accompanied by the judge-advocate, lieutenant-governor, clergyman, surveyor-general,

surgeon-general etc. After taking off his hat and complimenting the marine officers, who had lowered their colours and paid that respect to him as governor which he was entitled to, the soldiers marched with music playing, drums and fifes, and formed a circle round the whole of the convicts, men and women who were collected together. The convicts were all ordered to sit down on the ground; all gentlemen present were desired to come into the centre, where stood the governor, lieutenant-governor, judge-advocate, clergyman, surgeon etc etc. A camp table was fixed before them, and two red leather cases laid thereon, containing the Commissions etc which were opened and unsealed in the sight of all present, and read by the judge-advocate (Captain Collins).

Phillip's *Commission and Instructions* under the *Act of Parliament Establishing the Colony* set out the procedures for civil and criminal courts and gave Phillip wide powers to appoint public officials. He had the power to pardon criminals except for murder, where the royal assent was required. He was instructed to commence cultivation, especially of the flax plant, and to establish a settlement at Norfolk Island as soon as possible. He was authorised to emancipate convicts for good behaviour and industry and to grant land to them, but he was not given the power to grant land to the marines. His instructions in respect of the Aboriginal people were:

> To endeavour by every possible means to open an intercourse with the natives, and to conciliate their affections, enjoining all our subjects to live in amity and kindness with them. And if any of our subjects shall wantonly destroy them, or give them any unnecessary interruption in the exercise of their several occupations, it is our will and pleasure that you do cause such offenders to be brought to punishment.

Phillip Governor Phillip advanced and addressing first the private soldiers, thanked them for their steady good conduct on every occasion, an honour which was repeated to them in the next general orders. He then turned to the convicts and distinctly explained to them the nature of their present situation. The greater part, he bade them recollect, had already forfeited their lives to the justice of their country; yet, by the lenity of its laws they were now so placed that, by industry and good behaviour, they might in time regain the advantages and estimation in society of which they had deprived themselves...

He particularly noticed the illegal intercourse between the sexes as an offence which encouraged a general profligacy of manners and was in several ways injurious to society. To prevent this, he strongly recommended marriage and promised every kind of countenance and assistance to those who, by entering into that state, should manifest their willingness to conform to the laws of morality and religion.

Governor Phillip concluded his address by declaring his earnest desire to promote the happiness of all who were under his government and to render the settlement in New South Wales advantageous and honourable to his country. This speech, which was received with universal acclamations, terminated the ceremonial peculiar to the day.

Tench observed that the British government had not been 'backward in arming Mr Phillip with plenitude of power', and that 'no mention is made of a council to be appointed, so that he is left to act entirely from his own judgment'.

Bowes reported that, after the speeches, 'The governor retired to a cold collation under a large tent erected for that purpose to which the general officers only were invited and not the least attention whatever was paid to any other person who came out from England. The master of the different ships paid him the compliment of attending on shore during the reading of the Commission, which they were not under any obligation to do, notwithstanding which there was no more notice taken of them, or even to provide the slightest accommodation for them, than for the convicts themselves.'

Clark had the last word on this historic day: 'I never heard of any one single person having so great a power invested in him as the governor has by his Commission. All the officers dined with him on a cold collation; but the mutton which had been killed yesterday morning was full of maggots. Nothing will keep 24 hours in this country, I find.'

Friday 8th

Bradley The captain of the *Astrolabe* came round from Botany Bay to pay respects to Governor Phillip and and leave the French commodore's dispatches for Europe to go by our transports. We found that they had been obliged to fire on the natives at Botany Bay to keep them quiet.

Collins wrote that Hunter had completed a survey of the harbour and found it to be 'far more extensive to the westward than was at first imagined, and Captain Hunter described the country as wearing a much more favourable countenance toward the head or upper part, than it did immediately about the settlement'.

Saturday 9th

Marines who were charged with crimes were tried by a court-martial, made up of officers of the Marine Corps. Clark wrote:

> Sat, my dear wife, as one of members of the court-martial to try prisoners, when Brimage [Thomas Bramwell] was sentenced to receive 200 lashes on his bare back for striking one of the convict women because she would not go up into the woods with him.

Sunday 10th

The first weddings were celebrated by the Reverend Richard Johnson. William Parr was married to Mary McCormack, William Bryant to Mary Braund, Simon Burn to Frances Anderson, William Haynes to Hannah Green, and Henry Kable to Susannah Holmes. All five couples were convicts and only three of the 10 people could write their names in the register, the others signing with a cross.

Susannah Holmes was 14 years old when she was sentenced to death for theft in 1784; she was reprieved to 14 years' transportation and was being held in the castle at Norwich when she and Henry Kable met. They had a child, born in the prison in 1786, and their situation attracted some public attention and sympathy. Kable, also known as Cable or Cabell, had been convicted in 1783 of breaking into a house with his father and another man. It was alleged that they 'stripped it of every movable'. The two older men were hanged; Henry, aged about 17, was reprieved to seven years' transportation. Henry and Susannah, with their child, left England together in the *Friendship* but were separated at the Cape of Good Hope when the women and children were moved to the *Charlotte* to make way for livestock.

The criminal court heard cases involving convicts and men from the ships. King described its workings:

> The judge-advocate issues his precept [order] for the three senior naval officers and three military officers to assemble at the time

appointed, dressed in their uniforms and their side arms... the prisoner is then asked whether he is guilty or not, and, as the general answer is, 'Not guilty', the accusations against him are read and witnesses are examined on oath to support or prove the charge, after which the prisoner enters on his defence and brings evidence to prove his innocence. The court is then cleared and the members consider what sentence to pronounce; if it be death, five out of the seven must concur in opinion. The governor can respite a criminal condemned to die, and the legislature has fully empowered him to execute the sentence of the law, or to temper it with mercy.

There was also a magistrates' court, consisting initially of Collins and the surveyor-general, Augustus Alt. Alt was appointed a Justice of the Peace for this purpose and Collins wrote that the role of the court was 'to examine all offences committed by the convicts and determine on and punish such as were not of sufficient importance for trial by the criminal court'.

Phillip had appointed Henry Brewer provost-marshal; his duties, Collins wrote, were to 'cause the judgment of the court to be executed according to the governor's warrant under his hand and seal'. In a prison colony without a prison, the sentence was usually, of necessity, death or the lash.

Henry Brewer had first served with Phillip in *Alexander*, which he joined as a 'landsman', and he followed Phillip to the fireship *Basilisk* as his clerk, and later to *Ariadne* and *Europe*. Edward Spain, who was bosun of *Europe* when Phillip and Brewer joined that ship, left in his journal an account of his first meeting with them:

> They joined us on Christmas day and Harry had drunk pretty freely, to show his attachment to the Christian religion without doubt. After the lights were extinguished he got upon the gun deck where he lost himself and instead of going aft to the gun-room where his berth was, he got forward abreast of the fore hatchway, which being open he pitched down head foremost upon the orlop gratings, within a few inches of an iron pitch for which had his head come in contact with in all probability would have finished him. Here he lay, calling for help till the master at arms coming round to see that the lights were all out, he helped him up and conducted him to his hammock.

'Figure to yourself a man about 50 years of age', Spain wrote, of coarse harsh features, a contracted brow which bespoke him a man soured by disappointment, a forbidding countenance always muttering as if talking to himself. How shall I describe his dress-a blue coat of the coarsest cloth, a wool hat about three shillings price, cocked with three sixpenny nails, a tolerable waistcoat, a pair of corduroy breeches, purser's stockings and shoes, a purser's shirt, none of the cleanest.

But Spain also wrote: 'I cannot omit wishing that some stewards in higher life had the integrity and disinteredness of Henry Brewer; if that were the case we should not see so many gilt equipages.' According to Spain, Brewer was 'bred a house carpenter and having learnt architecture he was clerk to some great concern in the building line...he was just such a man as the governor wanted; what excellent plans, drafts and views of places he could draw, which I can send home to my patrons. Harry was accordingly appointed, and sailed with his old captain to New South Wales, where he was appointed provost-marshal.'

Monday 11th

Easty   The sentence of the court-martial held on Saturday put into execution. Bramwell sentenced 200 lashes, received 100, sent to the hospital.

John Tenhel (also known as James Tenhel and Thomas Hill) was also tried on the 11th, charged with stealing twopence worth of bread from another convict. In his defence, Tenhel, aged about 21, said he took the bread because he was hungry.
Ralph Clark wrote to the judge-advocate, David Collins,

To inform you that Jas Tennehill [John Tenhel] a convict, now a prisoner in charge of the quarter guard, has beg of me to speak to you respecting his behaviour while on board the *Friendship* transport. If his good behaviour...can have any weight in mitigating the punishment that may be inflicted for the crime for which he now stands charged with, I can only say on his behalf that for these last nine months past, that he behaved himself remarkably peaceably and obedient always to command.

Perhaps Clark's reference helped Tenhel to avoid the lash; Collins wrote that he was 'sentenced to a week's confinement on bread and water on a small rocky island near the entrance of the cove'. The small rocky island is now known as Fort Denison, or Pinchgut.

Many convicts used more than one name, and the spelling of names was highly variable; names and spelling throughout this book are as used in *The Founders of Australia*, by Mollie Gillen, and *The Second Fleet*, by Michael Flynn, which have entries for every person who came with those fleets, and a vast amount of additional information besides. To add to confusion in the courts, the convicts had their own language. Tench wrote:

> A leading distinction, which marked the convicts on their outset in the colony, was an use of what is called the 'flash', or 'kiddy' language. In some of our early courts of justice, an interpreter was frequently necessary to translate the deposition of the witness and the defence of the prisoner.

Clark   Several of the convicts were married yesterday and amongst them that were have left wives and families at home. Good God what a scene of whoredom is going on there in the woman's camp; no sooner has one man gone in with a woman but another goes in with her. I hope the almighty will keep me free from them as he has hitherto done but I need not be afraid, as I promised you my tender Betsey I will keep my word with you. I never will have any thing, any woman whatever except yourself, my dear wife, I will be true to my Betsey, my love for you will keep me so.

Tuesday 12th

Bowes   Our carpenter, one of our sailors and a boy belonging to the *Prince of Wales* were caught in the women's tents. They were drummed out of the camp with the *Rogue's March* playing before them, and the boy had petticoats put upon him. They had all of them their hands tied behind 'em. The anarchy and confusion which prevails throughout the camp and the audacity of the convicts, both men and women, is arrived to such a pitch as is not to be equalled, I believe, by any set of villains in any other spot upon the globe.

Friday 15th

Clark   Early sailed His Majesty's Brig *Supply* with several male and female convicts for Norfolk Island under Lieutenant King of the navy to settle there. Lieutenant King is appointed governor of the same island; there are no inhabitants on the island.

Cook in 1774 had noted the presence of pine trees and flax on Norfolk Island. These were important items because of the navy's demand for ships' masts and canvas. Phillip's instructions regarding Norfolk Island were, 'as soon as circumstances will permit of it, to send a small establishment thither to secure the same to us, and prevent it being occupied by the subjects of any other European power'.

Collins Lieutenant King took with him one surgeon (Mr Jamison, surgeon's mate of the *Sirius*), one petty officer (Mr Cunningham, also of the *Sirius*), two private soldiers, two persons who pretended to some knowledge of flax-dressing, and nine male and six female convicts, mostly volunteers. This little party was to be landed with tents, clothing for the convicts, implements of husbandry, tools for dressing flax etc and provisions for six months, before the expiration of which time it was designed to send them a fresh supply.

George Nelson, the cook of the *Prince of Wales*, who was a Negro, probably from Jamaica, was going ashore hand over hand on the ship's hawser, which was tied to the rocks, when two boys on the ship began to shake the rope. It may have been meant in fun, but, as Bowes wrote, they 'shook him off the rope, and the poor fellow sunk down and was drowned, not being able to swim. Many sailors jumped overboard to save him, but he sunk and did not come up again'.

Captain Shea shot a kangaroo and Clark described its peculiarities:

> They are the most extraordinary animal that I ever saw, for they have a pocket at the bottom of their belly where they carry their young in case of danger, where the teats comes. The first I kill I will have it stuffed and sent home to you, my dear beloved Alicia.

Bowes reported that he had 'a young one preserved in spirits' and added:

> I have several times tasted the flesh of this animal cooked in different ways and at such a place as Port Jackson, where fresh meals are a great rarity, it is thought a luxury; but I cannot be so partial as to say it equals venison, as some gentlemen reported, or that it is even so good as mutton. It is totally destitute of fat and the flesh as dark coloured as venison.

Sunday 17th

Clark This being the Lord's day, got up early and kissed your dear sweet image as usual on this day. Major Ross sent down to ask me [if] I would be so good as to let the governor have our marquee to take sacrament in, which I could not refuse and I am happy that it is to be in my marquee. Never did it receive so much honour.

Monday 18th

Clark Was very ill with the toothache all last night. Got up early and went to the hospital and had it out by Mr Considen. Oh, my God what pain it was. It was so fast in, and the jaw bone very fast to one of the prongs, the tooth would not come out without breaking the jaw bone, which he did. I thought that half my head would have come off; there is a piece of the jawbone remaining to the tooth. The pain was so great, my dear wife, that I fainted away and was very ill the remainder of the day, but I would not let Considen report to Major Ross that I was ill but would go on picket. My gum kept bleeding all the day.

Tuesday 19th

Bradley Several of the natives came down the harbour and slept in a bay near the ships. Seven of them in four canoes passed through the cove between the *Sirius* and transports and went close past one of our boats with great confidence. One of them landed on the east point of Sydney Cove to meet some of our people who were there. From this they went to our garden island and found means to steal two iron shovels and a pickaxe. The pickaxe the gardeners obliged them to bring back and lay it themselves in the very spot they had taken it from. The shovels they escaped with, but not without their shins being well peppered with small shot.

Clark Having the picket, lay with my clothes on and had but little sleep, as my jaw pained me very much, but in the course of the little I did sleep I dreamt that I was with you, my tender woman, and I thought that I saw your head was dressed out and small sparks of fire in your hair that you often told me was malice.

Wednesday 20th

Bowes This day in the hospital tent the temperature was up to 105 degrees.

Clark Got but little sleep on guard: my jaw pained, and does now very much, and bleeds every now and then afresh. The governor asked me to breakfast, but my face is so much swelled that I would not go.

Thursday 21st

Bradley Some of the officers of the *Boussole* came from Botany Bay to visit the governor; they inform us that the natives are exceedingly troublesome there and that wherever they meet an unarmed man they attack him.

Tuesday 26th

Collins Each male convict was that day put upon the following weekly ration of provisions, two-thirds of which was served to the female convicts, viz. seven pounds of biscuit [bread], one pound of flour, seven pounds of beef or four pounds of pork, three pints of [dried] peas and six ounces of butter.

Collins noted that 'the convict saw the same proportion of provision issued to himself that was served to the soldier and the officer, the article of spirits only excepted'. Like the female convicts, the wives of the marines received two-thirds of the men's ration.

Wednesday 27th

Thomas Barrett, Henry Lavell, Joseph Hall and John Ryan were tried in the criminal court charged with stealing butter, peas and pork from the public stores. Ryan was sentenced to receive 300 lashes, later forgiven, but Barrett, Lavell and Hall were sentenced to be hanged the same day.

Ryan, 24, whose trade was given as 'silk weaver', had been sentenced in 1784 to seven years' transportation for stealing a woollen coat and a man's hat. Lavell, aged 26, had been sentenced to death for forgery at the Old Bailey in 1782. Barrett, 30, had been convicted for theft, and Hall, 35, for highway robbery and assault. All four had been sent to the *Mercury* transport in March 1784 and had escaped when that ship, bound for America, had been taken over by the convicts on board and run into Torbay in Devon. They were recaptured and sent to the hulk, *Dunkirk*, in March 1787.

Clark At one o'clock their sentence was read, the charge being clearly proven...at five o'clock p.m. the battalion was order[ed] under arms for the sentence of the law to be put into execution and soon after we march[ed] to the place of execution which was a tree between the male and female convict camp. At a quarter after five, the unhappy men were brought to the place where they were to suffer.

Bowes A large party of marines were drawn up opposite the gallows and all the convicts were summoned to see the deserved end of their companions. When they arrived near the tree, Major Ross received a respite for 24 hours for Lavell and Hall, but Barrett, who was a most vile character, was turned off about half after six o'clock p.m. He express[ed] not the least signs of fear till he mounted the ladder, and then he turned very pale and seemed very much shocked.

It was some time before the man (a convict who had undertaken the office of hangman) could be prevailed upon to execute his office, nor would he at last have complied if he had not been severely threatened by the provost-marshal, Mr Brewer, and Major Ross threatened to give orders to the marines to shoot him. Just before Barrett was turned off he confessed the justice of his sentence, and that he had led a very wicked life...He then exhorted all of them to take warning by his unhappy fate and so launched into eternity. The body hung an hour and was then buried in a grave dug very near the gallows. The Reverend Mr Johnson prayed very fervently with the culprit before he was turned off.

Thursday 28th

Clark My God, what a terrible day this has been of rain. I never saw, that I recollect, it rain harder. At three o'clock the battalion was under arms for to put the sentence of the law into execution of Hall and Lavell, who were respited by the governor yesterday until today. At four o'clock I brought them with the guard to the place where they were to suffer, the same where their companion died yesterday.

White   When that awful hour arrived, they were led to the place of execution and just as they were on the point of ascending the ladder the judge-advocate arrived with the governor's pardon.

Clark   The whole of the convicts sent a petition to the governor begging that they might be forgiven, and not to suffer death. They also promised that not one amongst them he would have reason to find fault with. The governor, on which, he pardoned them. All the time it rained [as] if heaven and earth was coming together.

Lavell and Hall were placed on short rations on Fort Denison.

Bowes   This day by invitation I accompanied Mr Holt [possibly John Howlett], Midshipman of the *Sirius*, in the *Sirius's* pinnace to a cove a great distance from Sydney Cove, where we saw great numbers of the natives, both men, women and little children. I got an hatchet of one them. They were very social, assisted in drawing the seine and made a fire at the bottom of the rocks as soon as they saw us coming to cook the fish with. In our return we passed by 18 canoes with men and women in them fishing. Every canoe had a fire in the midst of it made upon a hillock of earth, placed there for that purpose to broil the fish upon.

Worgan   We have made some discoveries this last week. One is that the tree which I have said grows something like the fir answers very well for the making of shingles. Our other acquisition is the lighting on a soil which is seemingly fitted for making bricks, and eight or 10 convicts of the trade are now employed in the business.

The tree used for making shingles for the first buildings was the she-oak or casuarina, known also in colonial times as 'Botany Bay wood'.

Friday 29th

The criminal court sat at 8 a.m. Daniel Gordon, John Williams and George Whitaker were charged with stealing 18 bottles of wine, valued at £2, from Zachariah Clarke, agent for the fleet, who kept a large amount of provisions in store. Whitaker was found not guilty, but Gordon and Williams, both Negroes, were sentenced to be hanged. Two other convicts, William Sherman and James Freeman, were found guilty of 'stealing 15 allowances of flour'. Sherman was sentenced to receive 300 lashes and Freeman's sentence was death, the sentences to be carried out the same afternoon.

Freeman, from Watford in Hertfordshire, had been previously sentenced to death in 1784, at the age of 14, for a robbery which gained him 12 shillings. Sherman and Gordon had been sentenced to transportation for stealing and Williams, aged about 21 and known as 'Black Jack', had been sentenced to death, reprieved to transportation to America for seven years, before being sent to Botany Bay in the *Scarborough*.

Clark The Battalion was order under arms at a quarter before four o'clock and we marched to the place of execution. Soon after, the four unhappy men brought down by the guard and with halters about their neck. When the parson had done with them, Major Ross told them, from the petition of yesterday, that the governor had pardoned Gordon on his condition of being banished, which you may think accepted, and the other black who was concerned with Gordon was also pardoned on the same conditions, and Freeman was also pardoned on condition of his becoming the common hangman, which he accepted. Sherman, who was concerned with Freeman, was also forgiven his corporal punishment, but the whole of the convicts was told that the governor would never pardon or receive any more petitions from them. I think after his goodness they ought to behave very well, but I am almost certain that before I am a fortnight older some of them will be brought to trial for capital offences.

In a report to Lord Sydney, Phillip wrote that Gordon and Williams were 'to be exiled from the settlement and when the season permits I intend they shall be landed near the South Cape, where by forming connections with the natives some benefit may accrue to the public'. South Cape was on the southern coast of Tasmania; for the moment, they were sent in chains to Fort Denison in Sydney Harbour.

∞

Six weeks after the landing in Botany Bay, Hunter expressed an optimistic outlook on the relationship between the Aboriginal people and the settlers:

In the different opportunities I have had of getting a little acquainted with the natives who reside in and about this port, I am, I confess, disposed to think that it will be no very difficult matter, in due time, to conciliate their friendship and confidence;

for although they generally appear armed on our first meeting, which will be allowed to be very natural, yet, whenever we have laid aside our arms and have made signs of friendship, they have always advanced unarmed, with spirit and a degree of confidence scarcely to be expected. From that appearance of a friendly disposition, I am inclined to think that by residing some time amongst, or near them, they will soon discover that we are not their enemies, a light they no doubt considered us in on our first arrival.

But the judge-advocate, David Collins, seemed to sense the fragility of the situation:

It was natural to suppose that the curiosity of these people would be attracted by observing that, instead of quitting, we were occupied in works that indicated an intention of remaining in their country...

To such circumstances as these must be attributed the termination of that good understanding which had hitherto subsisted between us and them, and which Governor Phillip laboured to improve whenever he had an opportunity. But it might have been foreseen that this would unavoidably happen; the convicts were everywhere struggling about, collecting animals and gum to sell to the people of the transports, who at the same time were procuring spears, shields, swords, fishing lines and other articles from the natives, to carry to Europe, the loss of which must have been attended with many inconveniences to the owners, as it was soon evident that they were the only means whereby they obtained or could procure their daily subsistence, and although some of these people had been punished for purchasing articles of the convicts, the practice was carried on secretly, and attended with all the bad effects which were to be expected from it.

Collins was concerned, too, at actions of the French party in Botany Bay which might impact on the British settlers:

We also had the mortification to learn that M. De la Pérouse had been compelled to fire upon the natives at Botany Bay, where they frequently annoyed his people who were employed on shore. This circumstance materially affected us, as those who had rendered this violence necessary could not discriminate between us and them.

We were however perfectly convinced that nothing short of the greatest necessity could have induced M. De la Pérouse to take such a step, as we heard him declare that it was among the particular instructions that he received from his sovereign, to endeavour by every possible means to acquire and cultivate the friendship of the natives of such places as he might discover or visit, and to avoid exercising any act of hostility upon them.

MARCH

Sunday 2nd

Nagle The governor had a lighter built for carrying timber from up or down the river and fetching shells for lime and sand or whatever might be wanting for building. When we were not otherwise employed with the governor, we had to tow the lighter up and down the harbour and load her with timber, beside a boat which was built, pulling 16 oars, with shoulder of mutton sails, to go surveying. Therefore eight of us had three boats to take care of, and employed occasionally in all of them.

We went in this boat and two six-oared cutters with the governor to Broken Bay...which is called 16 miles by water. We pulled 16 oars, beside the coxswain, and room for about 10 sitters with provisions and water, the governor, officers and marines in each boat; having no wind, we had to pull all the way.

Bradley As we passed the sandy bay next the south head of Broken Bay [Palm Beach] we were met by three canoes having one man and five women in them. They came alongside of our boats quite familiarly. The governor pushed over to the north shore in the cutter. The tide set so strong to the southward that it was with difficulty the longboat could get round the south head...

When the cutter first landed, they were met by a great number of the natives, men, women and children. The men were all armed with spears, clubs, stone hatchets and wooden swords. They were all very friendly, and, when the longboat landed, were without arms. We passed the night in this cove, on board the boats everybody.

They were probably moored at Pearl Beach or Umina Beach.

William Bradley's father taught mathematics at the Royal Naval Academy in Portsmouth. Bradley was born there in 1758, joined the navy when he was 13, saw action in the East Indies, was promoted to first lieutenant in 1778 and was appointed first lieutenant of the *Sirius* in 1786, as the First Fleet was being put together for the voyage to New South Wales. He had married Sarah Witchell, daughter of the master of the Portsmouth Naval Academy, before he left for Botany Bay; little is known of his married life.

Bradley's original journal is lost; the journal that survives, acquired by the Mitchell Library in 1924, was copied by Bradley from the original some time after 1801. It contains 31 watercolours, and 22 charts are folded and bound into the book. The illustrations were probably painted at the time the copy was produced, from the original drawings, or possibly in some cases from memory. Bradley was a true seaman: details of the weather for every day of the five and a half years covered by the journal are entered in a separate section at the back of the book.

Monday 3rd

Bradley At daylight, went into the north branch of the harbour, which has a shoal and narrow entrance just within which we stopped. Found the natives familiar…All the women we met within this bay, two only excepted, had lost two joints of the little finger on the left hand, which custom like others we are at a loss to account for. It was supposed by some to be the pledge on the marriage ceremony, or on their having children. I cannot agree in that opinion as one of the exceptions was an old woman who had had children and the other a young woman who had not. The others who had all been subject to this custom were of both descriptions, old and young…

When the tide had slackened we pushed up and found several small inlets between mangroves, on one of which islands [probably near Woy Woy] we stopped and pitched the tents. Had very hard rain all the morning.

At Sydney Cove, Worgan reported: 'A bird has been shot today which answers the description given by Dr Goldsmith of the emu; it resembles the ostrich, its flesh proved very good eating, and four of us dined off from one of the side bones'. White wrote: 'This bird is supposed to be not uncommon in New Holland, as it has been frequently seen by our settlers both at Botany Bay and Port Jackson, but is exceedingly shy and runs faster than a greyhound'. Phillip had a greyhound, which evidently had not been able to run the emu down.

Tuesday 4th

The governor's expedition continued in the north arm of Broken Bay.

> **Bradley** At daylight proceeded up and found it to be an extensive and very shoal piece of water, too much so for the boats to go over the bars without the risk of being left dry on the ebb tide. We found natives all the way up. Not being able to determine the extent of this piece of water [Brisbane Water] we returned to the cove in which we first stopped, where we found a straw hat and some strings of beads which favours the opinion of their not having any fixed residence as nothing of that kind had been given them here and several were both at Port Jackson and at Botany Bay. After staying a short time here we went over to the south side of the bay, into the south-west arm off which is an island [Lion Island]. We moored the boats about three miles up this branch, had heavy rain, thunder and lightning all night.

Wednesday 5th

The expedition was also described by the governor:

> **Phillip** Where we attempted to land there was not sufficient water for the boat to approach the rocks on which were standing an old man and a youth. They had seen us labour hard to get under the land, and after pointing out the deepest water for the boats, brought us fire, and going with two of the officers to a cave at some distance, the old man made use of every means in his power to make them go in with him, but which they declined.

They feared a trap, but as Phillip wrote:

> This was rather unfortunate, for it rained hard and the cave was the next day found to be sufficiently large to have contained us all, and which he certainly took great pains to make them understand. When this old man saw us prepare for sleeping on the ground, and clearing away the bushes, he assisted, and was the next morning rewarded for his friendly behaviour.

Phillip thought the south side of Broken Bay 'the finest piece of water he had ever seen, and which therefore he thought worthy to be honoured with the name of Pittwater'. William Pitt was the prime minister of Britain.

Thursday 6th

Bradley One of the women made a fishing hook while we were by her, from the inside of what is commonly called the pearl oyster shell, by rubbing it down on the rocks until thin enough and then cut it circular with another, shape the hook with a sharp point rather bent in and not bearded or barbed.

Phillip One of their modes of fishing was now observed...when a fish which has taken the bait is supposed to be too strong to be handled with the line, the canoe is paddled to shore and while one man gently draws the fish along, another stands prepared to strike it with a spear; in this attempt they seldom fail.

Friday 7th

Bradley Went again into the south-west arm to look into that opening to the north-west; found but few of the natives in it. We landed on an island about two miles up this branch [probably Dangar Island] on which we secured everything for the night. Got a great quantity of mullet in the seine, for which called it Mullet Island.

Saturday 8th

Phillip When we returned...to the spot where the old man had been so friendly he met us with a dance and a song of joy. His son was with him. A hatchet and several presents were made them, and as I intended to return to Port Jackson the next day every possible means were taken to secure his friendship; but when it was dark he stole a spade, and was caught in the fact. I thought it necessary to show that I was displeased with him, and therefore, when he came to me, pushed him away and gave him two or three slight slaps on the shoulder with the open hand, at the same time pointing to the spade.

This destroyed our friendship in a moment, and seizing a spear he came close up to me, poised it, and appeared determined to strike; but whether from seeing that his threats were not regarded— for I chose rather to risk the spear than fire on him—or from anything the other natives said who surrounded him, after a few moments he dropped his spear and left us. This circumstance is mentioned to show that they do not want personal courage, for several officers and men were then near me.

Easty   This night about half past eight o'clock I was confined by Sergeant Hume for bringing a female convict into camp.

Private John Easty kept a diary from November 1786 until May 1793, when he arrived back in England in the *Atlantic*. It is written in neat handwriting in a small notebook which is ruled vertically, as if it was intended to be an account book. Easty wrote in a large, quite stylish hand; his spelling was erratic but his journal, unlike Scott's, is almost free of punctuation. Like Scott's journal, it was given to the Public Library of New South Wales by Sir William Dixson and was published during the 1960s with funding from the William Dixson Foundation.

Sunday 9th

Bradley   At daylight, the old man and his companions came to us just the same as if nothing had happened and without arms. About six o'clock we left Broken Bay and got into Spring Cove in Port Jackson at 11.

Monday 10th

Bradley Were informed by the man employed to get greens for the sick that the French ships were sailed from Botany Bay.

Nothing more was heard of La Pérouse's ships until 1826, when Peter Dillon, an English 'captain-adventurer', found evidence that they had been wrecked on Vanikoro, one of the Santa Cruz Islands, north of Vanuatu.

Bowes   Five of the convict men died last week; there are [a] great number ill on shore now, chiefly of dysenteries.

Clark   Sat as a member of a court-martial for bringing each a convict woman into their tents in the camp and are sentenced to receive each 150 lashes. The governor returned late last night and all the party in good health, which I am very glad of.

One of those court-martialled was John Easty. This is the last entry from Ralph Clark's papers until 15 February 1790; the notebook for that period has not been found.

Wednesday 12th

Easty   This night at five o'clock Easty and Clayton received 150 lashes each.

Thursday 13th

Bradley   The governor met the officers on the subject of grants of land. They were informed that it was not in his authority to do it; pieces of ground for gardens or for feeding their stock he allowed for present use, but not as grants of land.

In other British colonies, grants of land had been provided to officers who wished to remain and settle. No arrangements of this type had been made in New South Wales, perhaps because it was assumed that officers would see their service there simply as a term to be served and would not want to settle in a convict colony so far from England.

Saturday 15th

Bowes   One of the convict men was wounded on the collarbone with a spear which one of the natives throwed at him as he was cutting rushes in a cove some distance from the governor's farm, in company with four other convicts. He said the natives wanted their tools but on refusing to give them they hove their spears at them and afterwards pelted them with stones.

Tuesday 18th

Easty   This day Joseph Hunt, a marine, tried by a court-martial for striking another marine. The court sat four times, when Major Ross would not accept [the verdict] of the court-martial, upon which the court confined themselves—Captain Lieutenant Tench, First Lieutenant Kellow, First Lieutenant Poulden, First Lieutenant Davey, First Lieutenant Timins—and said they would go back to England.

Hunt had struck a fellow marine, William Dempsey, with a stick, apparently because he had seen Dempsey speaking to a convict woman who had come out in Hunt's ship, the *Charlotte*. Hunt did not deny the charge, but threw himself on the mercy of the court and asked three members of the court, Tench, Poulden and Timins, to speak of his good character. This they did, and then took the unusual step of giving the prisoner his choice of alternative sentences: 'either to ask public pardon, before the battalion, of William Dempsey...or to receive 100 lashes on his bare back'.

Later the same day, the commanding officer of the marines and lieutenant-governor of the colony, Major Robert Ross, asked the court to pass a sentence which did not give the prisoner an alternative. They refused Ross's request, and Ross then ordered them to pass 'a sentence without the choice of two sentences'. When they again refused, Ross suspended them from duty and placed them under arrest.

Wednesday 19th

Tench, Kellow, Poulden and Timins wrote to Phillip:

> We conceive the treatment we have received so violent, and our present disgraceful situation so notorious, that we cannot without injustice to our feelings consent to have the arrest we now suffer under taken off until a public reparation should have been made for the indignity we have been used with.

Collins The *Supply* returned from Norfolk island having been absent four weeks and six days. We learned that she made the island on the 29th of last month, but for the five succeeding days was not able to effect a landing, being prevented by a surf which they found breaking with violence on a reef of rocks that lay across the principal bay.

Worgan wrote that on their way to Norfolk Island, 'They fell in with an isle which had never been before discovered. Lieutenant Ball named it (in honour of Lord Howe) Lord Howe's Island. On landing they found a great many turtle, 18 or 20 of which they brought away with them'.

Easty   This day the marines turned out and said they could not work any longer without being paid for it.

Easty's laconic report of a meeting reveals a rising tide of discontent amongst the marines. The officers had already refused to supervise the work of the convicts, but through necessity, because if they did not do it it would not get done, the marines had become heavily involved in the construction of their own barracks. This extra work was being done without the extra pay that soldiers usually received for work outside their normal duties.

Thursday 20th

Ross wrote to Phillip   Finding that the court-martial seemed determined to wrest all power from the commanding officer by passing such a sentence on the prisoner they tried as to leave it solely in his power to be punished or not, as he chose...I had no alternative left but the very mortifying and disagreeable one of suspending the president and members that composed the court-martial from all duty, by putting them under an arrest till such time as the opinion of more competent judges than either them or myself might be had thereupon.

Phillip, aware that the arrest of one-third of the marine officers would probably lead to chaos, replied the same day, taking up Ross's suggestion and challenging him to have it decided informally by the other officers:

The opinion of most competent judges, if you mean the opinion of the officers who compose the detachment, may be had without any official application to me for that purpose, if you and the officers under arrest are satisfied to leave it to their decision, and I shall be very happy if it can be immediately settled by this means.

Friday 21st

Ross wrote to Phillip, ignoring his challenge and again asking him to order a court-martial of the four officers, in order to 'restore harmony and support that military discipline and good order which is absolutely necessary to maintain in the present critical situation of the detachment'.

Saturday 22nd

Phillip issued a general order pointing out that there were not enough officers in the colony to carry out a court-martial and conduct the necessary duties of the camp. The papers of the case were sent to the judge-advocate so that a court-martial could be held when there were enough officers available. In the meanwhile, he ordered: 'The officers now under arrest to return to their duty'.

Sunday 23rd

Bradley   A shark was caught this day 13 feet long and six and a half round. After his jaws were taken out they passed over the largest man in the ship without touching; the liver gave us 26 gallons of oil; he had four hooks cut from within him besides that which caught him.

According to Tench, the liver yielded 24 gallons of oil.

Tuesday 25th

Worgan   All the culinary plants that have come up degenerate exceedingly. Peas, beans, cabbage plants etc do not thrive and many of them have withered. Yams, potatoes, pumpkins, turnips, Indian corn [maize], look somewhat promising. The governor has appropriated an island in the harbour [Garden Island] to the use of the *Sirius*, on which we have landed our livestock, enclosed a part of it for a garden and put a good many different seeds in.

❧

Collins   Great inconvenience was found from the necessity that subsisted of suffering the stock of individuals to run loose amongst the tents and huts; much damage in particular was sustained by hogs, who frequently forced their way into them while the owners were at labour and destroyed and damaged whatever they met with. At first these losses were usually made good from the store, as it was unreasonable to expect labour where the labourer did not receive the proper sustenance; but this being soon found to open a door to much imposition and to give rise to many fabricated tales of injuries that never existed, an order was given that any hog caught trespassing was to be killed by the person who actually received any damage from it.

Collins also noted that there were:

> upwards of 200 patients under the surgeon's care, in consequence of the heavy rains that had fallen. A building for the reception of the sick was now absolutely necessary, and one, 84 feet by 23, was put in hand, to be divided into a dispensary, (all the hospital-stores being at that time under tents) a ward for the troops, and another for the convicts. It was to be built of wood and the roof to be covered in with shingles, made from a species of fir that is found here.
>
> The heavy rains also pointed out the necessity of sheltering the detachment, and until barracks could be built, most of them covered their tents with thatch, or erected for themselves temporary day huts. The barracks were begun early in March; but much difficulty was found in providing proper materials, the timber being in general shaky and rotten. They were to consist of four buildings, each building to be 67 feet by 22, and to contain one company. They were placed at a convenient distance asunder for the purpose of air and cleanliness, and with a space in the centre for a parade...
>
> The long-boats of the ships in the cove were employed in bringing up cabbage tree from the lower part of the harbour, where it grew in great abundance, and was found, when cut into proper lengths, very fit for the purpose of erecting temporary huts, the posts and plates of which being made of the pine of this country, and the sides and ends filled with lengths of the cabbage-tree, plastered over with clay, formed a very good hovel. The roofs were generally thatched with the grass of the gumrush; some were covered with clay, but several of these failed, the weight of the clay and heavy rain soon destroying them.

Newton Fowell, in a letter to his father, added to Collins' description of building techniques:

> The convicts were constantly employed clearing ground, building storehouses for the reception of provisions etc which were built by putting trees about two feet in the ground so as to touch each other and thatched over with rushes. There are likewise a number of hovels built of cabbage tree for the officers and the

battalion; they are chiefly thatched with rushes but some are covered with wooden tiles.

Worgan wrote: 'The cabbage eats something like a nut. The wood of these trees, which is very soft, is of great use to us, for, cut into proper lengths and split in half, they serve for walling the huts.' The cabbage palm or fan palm (*Livistona australis*) is still common in coastal New South Wales; it can be seen in Sydney's Botanic Gardens, at Kurnell on Botany Bay, and in the Royal National Park south of Sydney.

Nagle and Hunter recorded the fishing methods of the settlers and the Aboriginal people.

Nagle When we were not employed with the governor, he would send us a-fishing with a seine or hooks and lines for the use of government, which would be shared out. After the governor and officers, the fish would be served out to soldiers and prisoners in

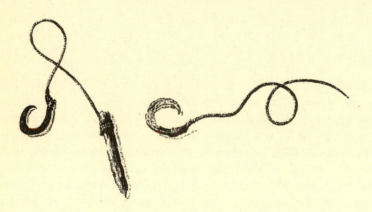

Fish hooks of New South Wales, *from White's* Journal of a Voyage to New South Wales. *The hook on the left is described as 'formed of a hard, black wood-like substance, neatly executed and finished with a small knob to assist in fastening it to the line'. The other is 'of mother of pearl, formed by an internal volute of some spiral shell, assisted by grinding it a little on one side only'. The line is made of 'a grassy substance, dark in colour and nearly as fine as raw silk'.*

rotation. Our customary method was to leave Sydney Cove about four o'clock in the afternoon and go down the harbour and fish all night from one cove to another. We have made 23 hauls of the seine in one night and not catch as many as would fill a bucket, and other times in one or two hauls falling in with schools that would be sufficient to fill our sternsheets.

We then would make a fire upon the beach, cook our supper and take our grog, lay down in the sand before the fire, wet or dry, and go to sleep till morning, though we would be often disturbed by the natives heaving their spears at us at a distance, and being in the night it would be by random. In the morning we would return, take the fish to the governor's house, where they would be shared out as far as they would go.

Hunter The women are chiefly employed in the canoes, with lines and hooks; the lines appear to be manufactured from the bark of various trees which we found here, of a tough stringy nature, and which, after being beaten between two stones for some time, becomes very much like and of the same colour as a quantity of oakum, made from old rope. This they spin and twist into two strands; in fact, I never saw a line with more than two. Their hooks are commonly made from the inside, or mother of pearl, of different shells; the talons of birds, such as those of hawks, they sometimes make this use of, but the former are considered as best.

Collins continued to analyse their relationship with the settlers:

In the course of this month several convicts came in from the woods, one in particular dangerously wounded with a spear, the others very much beaten and bruised by the natives...

There was, however, too much reason to believe that our people had been the aggressors, as the governor on his return from his excursion to Broken Bay, on landing at Camp Cove, found the natives there who had before frequently come up to him with confidence, unusually shy and seemingly afraid of him and his party; and one, who after much invitation did venture to approach, pointed to some marks upon his shoulders, making signs they were caused by blows given with a stick. This, and their running away, whereas they had always before remained on the beach until the people landed from the boats, were strong indications that the man had been beaten by some of our stragglers.

APRIL

Tuesday 1st

Bowes Went into the woods with the steward of the *Golden Grove* and our own steward to collect balsam and other things. The steward of the *Grove* killed a very large snake among some rushes in a swampy place. It was nearly as big as my arm, upwards of eight feet long, a very wide mouth with two rows of very sharp pointed teeth in the upper jaw and two in the under one. The teeth were half an inch long. It was of a very dark colour approaching to black, with large bright yellow spots regularly dispersed over the whole body.

The diamond python is common in eastern and northern Australia and is still seen in areas surrounding Sydney.

Wednesday 16th

Phillip, with a party including Surgeon John White, had crossed to Manly the previous day, at the start of another expedition. White wrote:

> We pursued our route westward, proceeding many miles inland, without being able to trace by a single vestige that the natives had been recently in those parts. We saw, however, some proofs of their ingenuity, in various figures cut on the smooth surface of some large stones. They consisted chiefly of representations of themselves in different attitudes, of their canoes, of several sorts of fish and animals and, considering the rudeness of the instruments with which the figures must have been executed, they seemed to exhibit tolerably strong likenesses.

Thursday 17th

The expedition continued heading west. In a letter to Lord Sydney, Phillip wrote:

> The country we passed through when we left the low grounds was the most rocky and barren I ever saw; the ascending and descending of the mountains being practicable only in particular places, but covered with flowering shrubs; and when about fifteen miles from the sea-coast [probably in the vicinity of Pennant Hills] we had a very fine view of the mountains inland...and

from the rising of these mountains I did not doubt but that a large river would be found.

Tuesday 22nd

White described another expedition led by the governor:

> Landed at the head of the harbour [probably Homebush Bay] with an intention of penetrating into the country westward, as far as seven days' provisions would admit of, every individual carrying his own allowance of bread, beef, rum, and water...In this manner we proceeded for a mile or two through a part well covered with enormous trees, free from underwood. We then reached a thicket of brushwood, which we found so impervious as to oblige us to return nearly to the place from whence we had set out in the morning. Here we encamped near some stagnant water for the night, during which it thundered, lightened and rained. About 11 o'clock the governor was suddenly attacked with a most violent complaint in his side and loins, brought on by cold and fatigue, not having perfectly gotten the better of the last expedition.

Wednesday 23rd

White   The next morning being fine, his Excellency, who was rather better, though still in pain, would not relinquish the object of his pursuit and therefore we proceeded and soon got round the wood or thicket which had harassed us so much the day before.

They continued to head westward, blazing trees with a hatchet so they could find their way back. That night, White wrote, 'We made a kettle of excellent soup out of a white cockatoo and two crows which I had shot as we came along.' On 26 April, 'We came to a pleasant hill, the top of which was tolerably clear of trees and perfectly free from underwood. His Excellency gave it the name of Belle Vue.' It is now known as Prospect Hill.

—⁂—

Born in County Fermanagh, Ireland, in about 1756, John White was in his early 30s when the First Fleet arrived in Botany Bay. He had qualified as a surgeon's mate in 1778, was promoted to surgeon in 1780 and served in the West Indies and India before his appointment as surgeon-general of the expedition to New South Wales at a salary of

£182 10s a year. He had three assistants in the colony—Denis Considen, Thomas Arndell and William Balmain.

White could be outspoken and quick-tempered, but he was forthright, dedicated to his work and observant of the new world around him. A friend, the English naturalist Thomas Wilson, suggested that he record his observations and offered to prepare the material he sent back to England for publication. The first edition of John White's *Journal of a Voyage to New South Wales* was published in mid-1790. About two-thirds of its 300 pages are taken up with description of the events in the colony until November 1788; most of the remainder deals with 'natural history', that is, the plants and animals of the area.

It was a large, weighty book, with 65 plates drawn from preserved specimens sent back to England to be copied by recognised engravers and artists and, in some copies of the book, hand-coloured. The original edition suffered from Wilson's lack of experience in publishing and is somewhat haphazardly presented, but it attracted some 700 advance subscriptions, was translated into German, Swedish and French and was a considerable success.

Wednesday 30th

Collins   Notwithstanding it was the anxious care of every one who could prevent it, that the venereal disease might not be introduced into the settlement, it was not only found to exist amongst the convicts, but the very sufferers themselves were known to conceal their having it. To stop this evil it was ordered by the governor that any man or woman having and concealing this disorder should receive corporal punishment and be put upon a short allowance of provisions for six months.

∽

Hunter In the months of March and April, we found the natives to decrease in their numbers considerably, but we have no reason to suppose that they retire back into the interior parts of the country, for in all the excursions which have been made inland, very few have been seen...they seem to have no fixed place of residence, but take their rest wherever night overtakes them; they generally shelter themselves in such cavities or hollows in the rocks upon the seashore as may be capable of defending them from the rain and in order to make their apartment as comfortable as possible, they commonly make a good fire in it before they lie down to rest, by which means the rock all round them is so heated as to retain its warmth like an oven for a considerable time, and upon a little grass, which is previously pulled and dried, they lie down and huddle together...

As most of the large trees are hollow, by being rotten in the heart, the opossum, kangaroo rat, squirrel, and various other animals which inhabit the woods, when they are pursued, commonly run into the hollow of a tree. In order, therefore, to make sure of them, which they seldom fail in when they find them in the tree, one man climbs even the tallest tree with much ease, by means of notches at convenient distances that are made with a stone hatchet. When he is arrived at the top, or where there may be an outlet for the animal, he sits there with a club or stick in his hand, while another person below applies a fire to the lower opening and fills the hollow of the tree with smoke; this obliges the animal to attempt to make its escape, either upwards or downwards, but whichever way it goes, it is almost certain of death, for they very seldom escape. In this manner they employ themselves, and get a livelihood in the woods.

They also, when in considerable numbers, set the country on fire for several miles extent; this, we have generally understood, is for the purpose of disturbing such animals as may be within reach of the conflagration, and thereby they have an opportunity of killing many. We have also had much reason to believe that those fires were intended to clear that part of the country through which they have frequent occasion to travel of the brush or underwood from which they, being naked, suffer very great inconvenience.

MAY

Thursday 1st

White The *Supply* sailed for Lord Howe's Island to fetch turtle.

Friday 2nd

Easty This morning John Bennett, a convict, received sentence of death for robbing the *Charlotte's* tent of bread and sugar and was taken from the courthouse to the place of execution and was hanged immediately.

John Bennett was 19 years old. He had stolen three pounds of biscuits, four pounds of sugar, a bread-bag and a piece of canvas from the *Charlotte's* tent ashore and was suspected of stealing four shirts and a pair of trousers.

Sunday 4th

Fowell Went among some of the natives. They seemed very friendly; all of them have long beards which is very troublesome to them. One of the party shaved one of them with a pen-knife which must have been very painful to him yet he was very glad to get rid of it.

As the *Charlotte*, the *Lady Penrhyn* and the *Scarborough* prepared to leave the colony, Bowes, who sailed in the *Lady Penrhyn*, wrote: 'Many gentlemen paid us the compliment of coming down to us in boats to take their final leave, which we did with some reluctance, notwithstanding our wishes to get to sea in hopes of falling in with some island which would afford us fresh provisions, which this place would not do.' John Marshall, master of the *Scarborough*, left a Newfoundland dog in the colony in the care of Zachariah Clark.

Monday 5th

In a letter to his mother, Daniel Southwell, master's mate in *Sirius*, commented on the recent good catches of fish:

> This diet is now very usual with us, and being partial to it I do not yet grow tired, though many do. Indeed, I impute the full establishment of my true health in part to it. You positively did not see me so stout and robust at any time while last at home.

Saturday 10th

Bradley The fish caught for several days past has been very trifling which we suppose to be occasioned by the cold weather.

Sunday 11th

Bradley A boat down the harbour met with several of the natives who appeared to be very hungry. They had not any fish with them, and eat the salt meat which our people gave them.

The Commissary, Andrew Miller, signed 'An account of the livestock in the settlement at Port Jackson, May 11th, 1788', which showed that there were seven horses, two bulls and five cows, 29 sheep, 19 goats, 74 pigs, 18 turkeys, 29 geese, 35 ducks, 122 fowls, 87 chickens and five rabbits.

Tuesday 13th

Worgan I walked out today as far as the brick-grounds. It is a pleasant road through the wood about a mile or two from the village, for from the number of little huts and cots that appear now, just above ground, it has a villatick appearance. I see they have made between 20 and 30,000 bricks and they were employed in digging out a kiln for the burning of them.

I afterwards walked to the public farm, where I find they have turned up eight or 10 acres of land, and they talk of putting some corn in the ground soon. The sheep die very fast from some cause. The cows and bulls thrive I think, as do the horses. The hogs don't thrive. The poultry do not increase very fast.

The 'brick-grounds' were just north of the present site of Central Station, an area later known as Brickfield Hill. The public farm was at Farm Cove.

Wednesday 14th

Worgan I have had a most delightful excursion today with Captain Hunter and Lieutenant Bradley. We went in a boat about 12 miles up the harbour. For three or four miles the harbour forms a narrow arm which at high water has the appearance of a river. The sides of this arm are formed by gentle slopes, which are green to the water's edge. The trees are small and grow almost in regular rows so that, together with the evenness of the land for a considerable extent, it resembles a beautiful park. We landed quite up at the head of this branch, where a fresh water river runs into it, but which, at this time was dry in many places.

We walked about two miles up the country in the direction of this river; the ground ran in easy ascents and descents, the soil was extremely rich and produced luxuriant grass...Having extended our excursion as far as we wished, we returned to the place where we landed and after regaling ourselves with a cold kangaroo pie and a plum pudding, a bottle of wine etc, all which comforts we brought from the ship with us, we returned on board.

⸺

Born in London in May, 1757, Dr George Worgan was 30 years old when the First Fleet arrived. He entered the navy in 1775, was qualified as a surgeon's mate in 1778 and was gazetted as a naval surgeon in 1780. In 1786, he joined the *Sirius* as surgeon. His father was a well-known organist and Worgan took a piano with him to the new settlement; on 7 August 1787, at Rio de Janeiro during the voyage out, Bowes reported 'an invitation to dine with him in the *Sirius* and hear his piano forte'.

Worgan's papers, now held in the Mitchell Library, are in the form of a letter to his brother, Richard, in England, which is dated 12 June 1788 and includes a diary describing many of the events of the early days of the settlement.

Thursday 15th

Collins There having been found among the convicts a person qualified to conduct the business of a bricklayer, a gang of labourers was put under his direction and most of the huts which grew up in different parts of the cleared ground were erected by them. Another gang of labourers was put under the direction of a stonemason, and on the 15th the first stone of a building, intended for the residence of the governor until the government house could be erected, was laid on the east side of the cove.

Worgan An inscription engraved on copper, to the following purport is to be placed among the foundation stones, viz. the date of the governor's arrival in this cove and the date of the laying of the foundation stone of his house.

The inscribed copper plate was unearthed, in good order, during excavations in Bridge Street in 1899 and is now held at the Museum of Sydney, on the site of the first Government House.

The bricklayer referred to by Collins was James Bloodworth, sentenced in 1785 to seven years' transportation for an unnamed crime. Bloodworth was involved in the design and construction of most of the settlement's early buildings. Collins also wrote:

Carpenters were now employed in covering in that necessary building, the hospital. The shingles for the purpose being all prepared, these were fastened to the roof (which was very strong) by pegs made by the female convicts. The timber that had been cut down proved in general very unfit for the purpose of building, the trees being for the most part decayed, and when cut down were immediately warped and split by the heat of the sun.

Sunday 18th

Bradley A party visited some of the coves down the harbour where some of the natives were seen. They were all friendly. They seemed to be very badly off for food, not having any fish. At another cove where we landed an old woman with a child remained with the men who met us. They had two fires under a very large hollow rock. We did not find any fish with these people. They were most of them chewing a root much like fern.

Monday 19th

Worgan It has this day been publicly announced that some of the transports will sail for England in six weeks, so a-scribbling we will go. I shall put a letter on board each ship for you. Pray don't neglect to forward those that I intend to inclose in yours, and pray, Mr Dick, have you had an opportunity yet of sending me a packet of news? Who is the King? the Queen? the ministers? What's the whim? Our whim will soon be to go naked, for you know 'When we are at Rome etc.'. As for my part, I shall be obliged soon to make a virtue of necessity, for I have torn almost all my clothes to pieces by going into the woods, and though we do not want for tailors, we do woollen drapers.

Our excursions put me in mind of your going a-steeple hunting. We sometimes put a bit of salt beef, or pork, brisket, a bottle of O-be-joyful in a snapsack, throw it over our backs, take a hatchet, a brace of pistols and a musket and away we go, scouring the woods. Sometimes east, west, north, south. If night overtakes us, we light up a rousing fire, cut boughs and make up a wigwam, open our wallets and eat as hearty of our fare as you of your dainties, then lie down on a bed which, though not of roses, yet we sleep as sound as you do on down. I enjoy these little rambles, and I think you would. However, I think it is hardly worth your while to come and try them.

Wednesday 21st

White   William Ayres, a convict, who was in a state of convalescence, and to whom I had given permission to go a little way into the country for the purpose of gathering a few herbs wherewith to make tea, was after night brought to the hospital with one of the spears used by the natives sticking in his loins. It had been darted at him as he was stooping and while his back was turned to the assailant. The weapon was barbed and stuck so very fast that it would admit of no motion. After dilating the wound to a considerable length and depth, with some difficulty I extracted the spear, which had penetrated the flesh nearly three inches.

After the operation he informed us that he received his wound from three of the natives, who came behind him at a time when he suspected no person to be near him except Peter Burn, whom he had met a little before, employed on the same business as himself. He added that after they had wounded him they beat him in a cruel manner and, stripping the clothes from his back, carried them off, making signs to him (as he interpreted them) to return to the camp.

He further related that after they had left him he saw Burn in the possession of another party of the natives, who were dragging him along with his head bleeding, and seemingly in great distress, while he himself was so exhausted with loss of blood that, instead of being able to assist his companion, he was happy to escape with his life.

Burn's clothing was found a few days later but his body was not recovered.

Sunday 24th

Worgan   I accompanied Captain Hunter and Lieutenant Bradley today, upon an excursion to the point of land that forms the south head of the opening of Port Jackson. They went for the purpose of ascertaining the latitude of it...We saw two natives at a distance in the woods, but they would not be sociable. We likewise saw under us, for we were standing upon a tremendous precipice from which you looked down into the sea (but not without being giddy) five or six canoes, in which were eight or 10 of the damsels of this country, jabbering and fishing. We hollowed to them, and they to us. I tied my handkerchief to a piece of wood and threw it down into the water, which presently one of them paddled after, and, taking it up between her thumb and finger, and after turning it round two or three times, gave it a toss, with the utmost indifference, into the dirtiest corner of the canoe, chattering something at the same time.

There is something singular in the conduct of these Evites, for if ever they deign to come near you to take a present, they appear as coy, shy and timorous as a maid on her wedding night (or least as I have been told maids are) but when they are, as they think, out of your reach, they hollow and chatter to you, frisk, flirt and play a hundred wanton pranks, equally as significant as the solicitations of a Covent Garden strumpet. I cannot say all the ladies are so shy and timorous on your approaching them, for some show no signs of fear but will laugh and frisk about you like a spaniel, and put on the airs of a tantalising coquet.

Indeed, if it were not for the nauseous, greasy, grimy appearance of these naked damsels, one might be said to be in a state of tantalism whenever they vouchsafe to permit us to come near them; but what with stinking fish-oil with which they seem to besmear their bodies, and this mixed with the soot which is collected on their skins from continually setting over the fires, and then, in addition to these sweet odours, the constant appearance of the excrementitious matter of the nose, which is collected on the upper pouting lips in such clusters of dry bubbles and is kept up by fresh drippings; I say from all these personal graces and embellishments every inclination for an affair of gallantry as well as every idea of fond endearing intercourse, which the nakedness of these damsels might excite one to, is banished and I can assure you there is in some of them a proportion, a softness, a roundness and plumpness in their limbs and bodies, were they but cleanly, that would excite tender and amorous sensations, even in the frigid breast of a philosopher.

Sunday 25th

White The *Supply* arrived from Lord Howe's Island without a single turtle, the object for which she was sent; a dreadful disappointment to those who were languishing under the scurvy, many of whom are since dead, and there is great reason to fear that several others will soon share the same fate. This disorder has now risen to a most alarming height, without any possibility of checking it until some vegetables can be raised, which, from the season of the year, cannot take place for many months, and even then I am apprehensive that there will not be a sufficiency produced, such are the labour and difficulty which attend the clearing of the ground.

It will scarcely be credited when I declare that I have known 12 men employed for five days in grubbing up one tree, and when this has been effected the timber (as already observed) has been only fit for firewood, so that in consequence of the great labour in clearing of the ground and the weak state of the people, to which may be added the scarcity of tools, most of those we had being either worn out by the hardness of the timber or lost in the woods among the grass through the carelessness of the convicts, the prospect before us is not of the most pleasing kind.

Monday 26th

Collins   A soldier and a sailor were tried by the criminal court of judicature for assaulting and dangerously wounding John McNeal, a seaman...They were found guilty of the assault and as pecuniary damages were out of the question were each sentenced to receive 500 lashes.

White wrote that they 'could not undergo the whole of that punishment, as, like most of the persons in the colony, they were much afflicted with the scurvy'. Henry Waterhouse, a midshipman in the *Sirius*, said in a letter that 'one...at the first flogging received 400 and the other 100, when the surgeon ordered them on board till their backs were well, then to receive the remainder of their punishment'.

Tuesday 27th

Southwell   We find many salutary herbs that make wholesome drink and [are] of great use to our sick. Balm is here in plenty and several vegetables have been lately found that are of the same kind, though not so good, as at home. Here is spinach, parsley, a sort of broad beans, several wholesome unknown vegetables...a sort of green berries that are pronounced a most excellent antiscorbutic are gathered in abundance and a specie of sorrel etc, all of a peculiar fine acid.

Friday 30th

Fowell In the afternoon two convicts who were sent to cut rushes were found murdered by the natives who had thrown several spears in them. One of them had a large piece of skull cut out of his forehead, supposed to have been done with an axe which they carried with them to build a hut.

William Okey and Samuel Davis were both aged about 19. White reported:

> Okey was transfixed through the breast with one of their spears, which with great difficulty and force was pulled out. He had two other spears sticking in him to a depth which must have proved mortal. His skull was divided and comminuted so much that his brains easily found a passage through. His eyes were out, but these might have been picked away by birds.
>
> Davis was a youth and had only some trifling marks of violence about him. This lad could not have been many hours dead, for he was not stiff nor very cold, nor was he perfectly so when brought to the hospital. From these circumstances we have been led to think that while they were dispatching Okey he had crept to the trees among which he was found, and that fear, united with the cold and wet, in a great degree contributed to his death.

Collins As it was improbable that these murders should be committed without provocation, inquiry was made, and it appeared that these unfortunate men had, a few days previous to their being found, taken away and detained a canoe belonging to the natives, for which act of violence and injustice they paid with their lives.

Saturday 31st

White wrote that Phillip led a party to the 'place where the murder had been committed, in hopes, by some means or other, to be able to find out either the actual perpetrators or those concerned'. When nothing was found there, they walked to Botany Bay, 'as the governor was resolved on whomsoever he found any of the tools or clothing to show them his displeasure, and by every means in his power endeavour to convince them of his motives for such a procedure'.

JUNE

Sunday 1st

White   In the morning the grass was quite white with a hoar frost, so as to crackle under our feet. After breakfast we visited the grave of the French abbé who died whilst the Count de Pérouse was here...Between this and the harbour's mouth we found 49 canoes hauled upon the beach, but not a native to be seen. After we had passed them, we fell in with an Indian path, and, as it took a turn towards the camp, we followed it about two miles, when, on a sudden, in a valley or little bay to the northward of Botany Bay [probably Little Bay or Long Bay] we were surprised at hearing the sound of voices, which we instantly found to proceed from a great number of the natives, sitting behind a rock, who appeared to be equally astonished with ourselves, as from the silence we observed they had not perceived us till we were within 20 yards of them.

Every one of them, as they got up, armed himself with a long spear, the short stick before described, used in throwing it, a shield made of bark and either a large club, pointed at one end, or a stone hatchet. At first they seemed rather hostilely inclined and made signs with apparent tokens of anger for us to return; but when they saw the governor advance towards them unarmed and with his hands opened wide (a signal we had observed among them of amity and peace) they, with great confidence, came up to him and received from him some trifles which he had in his pocket, such as fish-hooks, beads, and a looking-glass.

As there appeared not to be less than 300 of them in this bay, all armed, the soldiers were ordered to fix their bayonets, and to observe a close, well-connected order of march as they descended the hill. These people (as already mentioned) seem to dislike red coats and those who carry arms, but on the present occasion they shewed very little fear or distrust; on the contrary, they in a few minutes mixed with us and conducted us to a very fine stream of water, out of which some of them drank to show that it was good...

This was the greatest number of the natives we had ever seen together since our coming among them. What could be the cause of their assembling in such numbers gave rise to a variety of conjectures. Some thought they were going to war among themselves, as they had with them a temporary store of half-stinking fish and fern root, the latter of which they use for bread. This we remarked as several of them were eating it at the time we were among them. Others conjectured that some of them had been concerned in the murder of our men (notwithstanding we did not meet with the smallest trace to countenance such an opinion) and that, fearing we should revenge it, they had formed this convention in order to defend themselves against us. Others imagined that the assemblage might be occasioned by a burial, a marriage, or some religious meeting.

Bradley   Orders were this day given that no party under six armed men were to go into the woods, on account of the natives being so numerous.

Wednesday 4th

The colony celebrated the King's birthday.

Easty   The *Sirius* and *Supply* fired a royal salute at sun rising, at 12 o'clock and at sunset. At 12 o'clock the battalion of marines marched over the water with their colours and fired three volleys and returned again immediately; the governor gave the marines a pint of porter each man and the convicts half a pint of rum each man; the officers all dined with the governor that day.

Worgan noted that Phillip:

> had previously given a general invitation to the officers to dine with him, and about two o'clock we sat down to a very good entertainment, considering how far we are from Leadenhall Market. It consisted of mutton, pork, ducks, fowls, fish, kangaroo, salads, pies and preserved fruits. The potables consisted of port, Lisbon, Madeira, Teneriffe and good old English porter. These went merrily round in bumpers...
>
> About five o'clock we broke up and walked out to visit the bonfires, the fuel of one of which a number of convicts had been two days collecting. And to one who had never seen any bigger than Tower Hill bonfire on these occasions it was really a noble sight. It was piled up for several yards high round a large tree. Here the convicts assembled, singing and huzzaing. On the governor's approach they all drew up on the opposite side and gave three huzzas. After this salutation a party of them joined in singing 'God Save the King'. The governor stayed about 20 minutes, and then, with many of the officers, returned home, where there was a cold repast for anybody disposed to take supper.

White wrote:

> The day was passed in cheerfulness and good humour, but it was a little damped by our perceiving that the governor was in great pain from a return of his complaint. Though his countenance too plainly indicated the torture which he suffered, he took every method in his power to conceal it, lest it should break in upon the festivity and harmony of the day…and, as it was a day of general rejoicing and festivity, he likewise made it a day of forgiveness, remitting the remainder of the punishment to which the sailors of the *Sirius* were subject, and pardoning Lavell, Sidaway, Hall, and Gordon, who had been confined on a little sterile island, or rather rock, situated in the harbour, until a place of banishment could be found.

White also reported:

> his Excellency said that he had intended to have named the town, and laid the first stone, on this auspicious day, but the unexpected difficulties which he had met with in clearing the ground and from a want of artificers had rendered it impossible; he therefore put it off till a future day. Its name, however, we understand, is to be Albion.

Fowell put it more simply: 'Being the King's birthday we fired three royal salutes and a dinner was given by the governor to all the officers. He then named the town Albion.' Phillip must have changed his mind; there is no further mention of the proposal to give the town the ancient Celtic name for Britain.

Thursday 5th

White   The next morning we were astonished at the number of thefts which had been committed during the general festivity by the villainous part of the convicts, on one another and on some of the officers whose servants did not keep a strict lookout after their marquees.

Scott   Four cows, one bull with one bull calf was drove or strayed away from the governor's farm.

Wednesday 11th

Bradley   Several parties were sent in quest of the bull and cows, which belonged to the settlement, they having been missing some days.

Monday 23rd

White wrote that Samuel Peyton, a convict, was sentenced to be hanged 'for feloniously entering the marquee of Lieutenant Furzer on the night of the 4th of June and stealing from thence some shirts, stockings and combs'.

Tuesday 24th

Tench recorded a letter which Samuel Peyton had written to his mother by a fellow convict:

> I will not distress your tender maternal feelings by any long comment on the cause of my present misfortune. Let it therefore suffice to say that, impelled by that strong propensity to evil, which neither the virtuous precepts nor example of the best of parents could eradicate, I have at length fallen an unhappy, though just, victim to my own follies. Too late I regret my inattention to your admonitions, and feel myself sensibly affected by the remembrance of the many anxious moments you have passed on my account...
>
> Sincerely penitent for my sins, sensible of the justice of my conviction and sentence, and firmly relying on the merits of a blessed redeemer, I am at perfect peace with all mankind and trust I shall yet experience that peace which this world cannot give. Commend my soul to the divine mercy. I bid you an eternal farewell. Your unhappy dying son, Samuel Peyton.

Wednesday 25th

Peyton and another convict, Edward Cormick, also convicted of theft, were hanged.

White They were now turned off, and in the agonising moments of the separation of the soul from the body seemed to embrace each other. The execution of these unhappy youths, the eldest of whom was not 24 years of age, which seemed to make a greater impression on the convicts than any circumstance had done since their landing, will induce them, it is to be hoped, to change their conduct and to adopt a better mode of life than, I am sorry to say, they have hitherto pursued.

Bradley Several canoes came down the harbour and passed within the ship. Some of the men came alongside. We gave them some fish and several other things. They were much pleased and gave us some oysters in return. These people seemed to suffer much from the cold.

Sunday 29th

Worgan No tidings of our cows and bulls yet…Their loss, if it proves one, will be rather a misfortune for our colony and as an additional calamity the sheep, both of the public and private stocks, die very fast.

Monday 30th

White prepared a 'Return of the sick etc at June 30, 1788', which included 30 marines, six of their wives and children and 66 convicts. His return also showed that 53 people had died since leaving England, 45 from among the convicts and eight from the marines' camp.

Watkin Tench. *Artist unknown.*
Mitchell Library, State Library of
New South Wales

Watkin Tench's deadline was approaching. His *Narrative* was to be sent to England on the transports which were due to sail in two weeks.

Born about 1758, Tench had joined the marines in 1776. He came from Chester, Cheshire, where his father Fisher Tench and his mother, Margarita, kept 'an academy for dancing and a most respectable boarding school...thus young Watkin was reared in an atmosphere of cultivation and refinement which has left its mark on his writing'.

Tench wrote two accounts of his time in New South Wales. *A Narrative of the Expedition to Botany Bay* was published in 1789; *A Complete Account of the Settlement at Port Jackson* covers the period to the end of 1791. The *Narrative* went into a third edition within a year of publication and was translated into French, German, Dutch and Swedish.

Tench's manuscript has not survived, but it is clear that he kept a diary from which some of his final manuscript was transcribed direct. The concluding chapters of his first publication, the *Narrative*, summarise the situation of the colony at the end of June 1788, when the transports were about sail for England.

Of the Aboriginal people, Tench wrote:

> There is no part of the behaviour of these people that has puzzled us more than that which relates to their women. Comparatively speaking we have seen but few of them and those have been sometimes kept back with every symptom of jealous sensibility, and sometimes offered with every appearance of courteous familiarity. Cautious, however, of alarming the feelings of the men on so tender a point, we have constantly made a rule of treating the females with that distance and reserve which we judged most likely to remove any impression they might have received of our intending aught which could give offence on so delicate a subject. And so successful have our endeavours been that a quarrel on this head has in no instance that I know of happened. The tone of voice of the women, which is pleasingly soft and feminine, forms a striking contrast to the rough guttural pronunciation of the men. Of the other charms of the ladies I shall be silent...
>
> Soon after our arrival at Port Jackson, I was walking out near a place where I observed a party of Indians busily employed in looking at some sheep in an enclosure and repeatedly crying out, 'Kangaroo, kangaroo'. As this seemed to afford them pleasure, I was willing to increase it by pointing out the horses and cows, which were at no great distance. But unluckily, at the moment, some female convicts, employed near the place, made their

appearance and all my endeavours to divert their attention from the ladies became fruitless. They attempted not, however, to offer them the least degree of violence or injury, but stood at the distance of several paces, expressing very significantly the manner they were attracted...

That greater progress in attaching them to us has not been made I have only to regret, but that all ranks of men have tried to effect it by every reasonable effort from which success might have been expected, I can testify; nor can I omit saying that in the higher stations this has been eminently conspicuous. The public orders of Governor Phillip have invariably tended to promote such a behaviour on our side as was most likely to produce this much wished-for event.

With the transports preparing to leave, others were also summarising their experiences and observations for the mail home.

White We have been here nearly six months and four officers only as yet got huts: when the rest will be provided with them seems uncertain, but this I well know, that living in tents, as the rainy season has commenced, is truly uncomfortable and likely to give a severe trial to the strongest and most robust constitution...

I have already said that the stone of this country is well calculated for building, could any kind of cement be found to keep them together. As for limestone, we have not yet discovered any in the country, and the shells collected for that purpose have been but inconsiderable. From Captain Cook's account, one would be led to suppose that oyster and cockle shells might be procured in such quantities as to make a sufficiency of lime for the purpose of constructing at least a few public buildings, but this is by no means the case. That great navigator, notwithstanding his usual accuracy and candour, was certainly too lavish of his praises on Botany Bay.

Collins Exemplary punishments seemed about this period to be growing daily more necessary. Stock was often killed, huts and tents broke open and provisions constantly stolen about the latter end of the week, for among the convicts there were many who knew not how to husband their provisions through the seven days they were intended to serve them, but were known to have consumed the whole at the end of the third or fourth day...The obvious consequence of this want of economy was that he who had three days to live and nothing to live on before the store would be again open to supply his wants, must steal from those who had been more prov-ident…it soon appeared that there were some among them so inured to the habits of vice, and so callous to remonstrance, that they were only restrained until a favourable opportunity presented itself.

───※───

Bradley and Hunter described some of the sources of local food.

Bradley Saw several of the natives on the high land. They were gathering a kind of fruit which they soaked in water and sucked. On our return to the cove where we landed, we found a native in a tree gathering a fruit of the size of a small pine and of a beautiful pale yellow. He got it by fixing a four-pronged spear over the stalk and twisting them off. It had a sweet taste. We found two children, a boy and a girl, near the tree in which the man was. The children did not appear frightened when we took hold of them. The girl's fin-gers were complete as were the boy's teeth. When the man had got a good quantity of this spongy fruit, he, with the children, walked along the beach and sat down by the side of a pool of fresh water, to which place we followed him. They eat or rather sucked the whole of what they had gathered, frequently dipping them in the water.

Hunter We have seen them roast and chew the fern-root. There is a small fruit here, about the size of a cherry; it is yellow when half grown and almost black when ripe; it grows on a tree which is not tall, but very full and bushy at the top; of this fruit we have often seen them eat. It has a good deal the taste of a fig and the pulp, or inside, very much resembles that fruit in appearance; but the sea is their principal resource, and shell and other fish are their chief support.

The information service at Sydney's Botanic Gardens suggest that the fruit referred to by Hunter is one of the local species of fig, or *Ficus*. The pale yellow fruit described by Bradley could possibly have been the flower of one of the banksias.

───※───

Tench, Hunter and White dealt briefly with the question of cannibalism.

Tench From their manner of disposing of those who die…as well as from every other observation, there seems no reason to suppose these people cannibals. Nor do they ever eat animal substances in a raw state, unless pressed by extreme hunger.

Hunter   Whether any of the natives of this country are cannibals is yet a matter on which we cannot speak positively...I was one day present when two native children were interrogated on the subject of the quarrels of their countrymen; they were particularly asked what the different chiefs did with those they killed; they mentioned some who burnt and buried the slain, but they also particularly named one who ate those he killed.

White was less equivocal   The natives of this country, though their mode of subsisting seems to be so very scanty and precarious, are, I am convinced, not cannibals.

Worgan   They are wonderfully expert at the art of mimicry, both in their actions and in repeating many of our phrases; they will say 'Goodbye' after us very distinctly. The sailors teach them to swear. They laugh when they see us laugh and they appear to be of a peaceable disposition and have a generosity about them in offering you a share of their food; if you meet with any of them they will readily offer you fish, fire and water. They seem to be easily offended and quick and fatal in revenging an injury.

JULY

Friday 4th

White wrote to Phillip   Sir, Among the troops, their wives and children, as well as among the convicts who have been ill, the want of necessaries to aid the operation of medicine has been most materially and sensibly felt. My duty leads me to mention this circumstance to your Excellency in order that you may use such means for their procurement as may seem most expedient.

Items needed included 'blankets and sheets for the hospital, none of which are in the colony, although they are essential and absolutely necessary. The want of them makes that observance and attention to cleanliness (a circumstance which among sick persons cannot be too much inculcated or attended to) utterly impossible'.

White said that sugar, barley, rice, oatmeal, currants, soup and tamarinds were needed to supplement the diet of the marines and their wives and children and to compensate for the diet of salt rations; the latter was a particular problem for the children, because, apart from the lack of variety, they found it unpleasant to eat.

Ross also requested a large number of basic items for the marines' inventory, such as greatcoats, cooking utensils, shoes, needles and thread, scissors and materials for making clothes. In a letter to Stephens, Ross said: 'The non-commissioned officers and privates of the detachment [have] been so very much distressed for tobacco that I own it gave me much satisfaction to find I could procure some for them from the master of one of the transports now going home.'

Saturday 5th

With the transports *Alexander, Borrowdale, Prince of Wales* and *Friendship* preparing to sail, officers and officials were writing reports and despatches to their counterparts in England. Phillip wrote to Evan Nepean, who as Under-Secretary of State in the Home Department was responsible for the administration of the settlement:

> Every possible attention will be given to the cultivation of the flax plant when circumstances permit and on our first arrival in this port it was frequently met with, but when I judged the seed to be ripe and ordered it to be collected, very little was found and none in those places where it had been seen in any quantity, which I impute to the natives pulling up the plant when in flower to make their fishing-lines...
>
> Clothing for the natives, if sent out, will I daresay be very acceptable to them when they come amongst us. I should recommend long frocks and jackets only, which will equally serve both men and women. A great part of the clothing I have, sir, already observed was very bad and a great part of it was likewise too small for people of common size. If some coarse blankets were to be sent out they would greatly contribute to preserve the health of the convicts. In addition to the frocks and jackets for the natives, good house carpenters' axes, hats, hooks and lines will be the most beneficial, as well as most acceptable to the natives.

Phillip also wrote to Lord Sydney I beg leave to assure your lordship that with regular supplies of provisions, for which we must depend on the mother country for a time, I see no difficulties but what a little time and perseverance will do away. A small number of families to be sent out would do more in cultivating the land than all the convicts under our present circumstances, for they destroy and rob in spite of every possible precaution, and punishments have no effect. They will be better when they are separated, but I have only two people in the colony capable of taking charge of a farm.

The very heavy rains we have had for some days has put a stop to all labour and the natives find it very difficult to support themselves in this season, as few fish are caught. I hope after the ships have sailed to be able to persuade some of them to live near us and every possible means shall be used to reconcile them to us and to render their situation more comfortable. At present I think it is inferior to that of the beasts of the field, yet they seem intelligent and merit a better character than what will be given them by Monsieur La Pérouse, from what he said to some of our officers.

Tuesday 8th

Bradley   Went down to one of the lower coves and walked over to the sand hills which are given as a mark for a ship coming from the southward to know when they are near to Port Jackson. We found a good path over the neck of land and not half an hour's walk.

This is the first recorded visit to the beach now known as Bondi.

Wednesday 9th

Phillip   An effort was made by a party of natives which seems to indicate that they were still distressed for provisions, or that they very highly resent the encroachments made upon their fishing places. A general order had been issued to those sent out on fishing parties to give a part of what was caught to the natives if they approached, however small the quantity taken might be, and by these means they had always been sent away apparently satisfied. But on this day about 20 of them armed with spears came down to the spot where our men were fishing, and without any previous attempt to obtain their purpose by fair means, violently seized the greatest part of the fish which was in the seine. While this detachment performed this act of depredation, a much greater number stood at a small distance with their spears poised, ready to have thrown them if any resistance had been made. But the coxswain who commanded the fishing party very prudently suffered them to take away what they chose, and they parted on good terms. This is the only instance in which these people have attempted any unprovoked act of violence, and to this they probably were driven by necessity.

Phillip to Sydney The hutting the battalion is still going on, and though from 70 to 100 convicts have been almost constantly employed assisting in this business, it will not, I apprehend, be finished before the end of July, and every day proves the necessity of proper persons being sent out to superintend the convicts. If a small number of carpenters and bricklayers are sent out with proper people who are capable of superintending the convicts, they will soon be rendered serviceable to the state, and without which they will remain for years a burden to government.

Numbers of them have been brought up from their infancy in such indolence that they would starve if left to themselves, and many (their numbers now exceed 50) from old age and disorders which are incurable, and with which they were sent from England, are incapable of any kind of work.

Phillip to Nepean The masters of the transports having left with the agents the bonds and whatever papers they received that related to the convicts, I have no account of the time for which the convicts are sentenced, or the dates of their convictions. Some of them, by their own account, have little more than a year to remain, and, I am told, will apply for permission to return to England, or to go to India, in such ships as may be willing to receive them. If lands are granted them, government will be obliged to support them for two years, and it is more than probable that one half of them, after that time is expired, will still want support. Until I receive instructions on this head, of course none will be permitted to leave the settlement.

Thursday 10th

Ross wrote to Nepean Take my word for it, there is not a man in this place but wishes to return home, and indeed they have no less than cause, for I believe there never was a set of people so much upon the parish as this garrison is, and what little we want, even to a single nail, we must not send to the commissary for it, but must apply to his Excellency, and when we do he always says there is but little come out, and of course it is but little we get, and what we are obliged to take as a mark of favour.

If you want a true description of this country, it is only to be found amongst many of the private letters sent home. However, I will in confidence venture to assure you that this country will never answer to settle in, for although I think corn will grow here, yet I am convinced that if ever it is able to maintain the people here it cannot be in less time than probably a hundred years hence. I therefore think it will be cheaper to feed the convicts on turtle and venison at the London Tavern than be at the expense of sending them here.

Phillip wrote again to Lord Sydney The natives have ever been treated with the greatest humility and attention and every precaution that was possible has been taken to prevent their receiving any insults; and when I have time to mix more with them every means shall be used to reconcile them to live amongst us and to teach them the advantages they will reap from cultivating the land, which will enable them to support themselves at this season of the year, when fish are so scarce that many of them perish of hunger, at least I have seen strong reason to suppose that to be the case. Their number in the neighbourhood of this settlement, that is within 10 miles to the northward and 10 miles to the southward, I reckon at 1500.

Ralph Clark wrote to his friend Lieutenant George Kempster, quartermaster of marines at Plymouth I am sorry to say that Major Ross and the governor are not on the best of terms, nor is the former with several of us; he is without exception the most disagreeable commanding officer I ever knew...almost every officer with myself have wrote to be relieved at the expiration of the three years, for by God I would not stay longer than I could help in this if they would give me a captain's commission. Duty is much harder here, seldom have more than two nights in bed which is much harder duty than any officers have in the British army in time of war. It is not only the camp, but the worst duty is the duty of sitting as members of the criminal court, a very disagreeable duty, which is the court which tries the seamen either belonging to the ships of war or merchant men and the convicts which duty comes very often. I hope that I never will sit again for I would rather be on guard for a month than to sit on trial for these poor wretches...

Nothing goes amiss here; snakes and lizards are become good eating but these I cannot yet bring myself to stomach, but as for crows, parrots, hawks and every kind of bird, let them feed on carrion or anything else, for they are better than salt beef...

I hope your goodness will excuse the irregularness of this letter but as I am getting the roof of my hut plastered, for which I am grasping every fair moment that offers, for it has rained for near this month with hardly a single day's interruption.

Saturday 12th

Newton Fowell wrote to his father I am very well off for all sorts of clothes except shoes, of which I have only two pair left and what I shall do till you can send some out I don't know. However, I should be very much obliged to you to send me a dozen and a half pair of shoes and some of them of the shooting sort, just such as I left behind me, another sort thick and a few pair thin. I believe my foot has grown much since the last shoes were made me so pray tell Huskin they were rather stinted in the upper leather. The length of my foot at present is 10 inches so he may make them in every way proportionable.

A private letter from Captain James Campbell to Francis Reynolds, the Earl of Ducie, criticising Phillip, is remarkably similar to Major Ross's letter to Nepean, written two days before:

> I do not think (*entre nous*) that your three kingdoms could produce another man, in my opinion, so totally unqualified for the business he has taken in hand, as this man is...there is hardly a day in which the orders of the preceding are not contradicted, men are taken from one piece of work before it is well began and sent to another which is again left in the same state—I must here except such things as are actually carrying on for himself, which are never suffered to be interfered with. Everything that can be got hold of is appropriated to his own use. He is selfish beyond measure, in so much that even the public stores sent out, as we suppose, for the benefit of the colony at large, are, as far as possible by this strange character, looked upon as private property...
> Surely, my lord, administration will never persist in so romantic a scheme as the forcing a settlement in such a country as this at present appears to be. Not one thing can be found that ever promises to be an object of commerce or worthy the attention of a commercial nation...I am myself fully convinced that the nation would save money by feeding their convicts at home upon venison and claret, clothing them in purple and gold, rather than provide for them here the worst fare that can be thought of.

The colony's officials and officers had their salaries paid to their agents in England, who managed their business affairs for them in their absence. Ralph Clark wrote to his agent, B. Hartwell:

> It is the opinion of everybody here that the settlement will be removed to some other place for it is not possible that this place can maintain itself in a century...the whole face of the country is so overgrown with immense large trees, so much so that not a quarter of an acre of clear ground is to be seen, nor is either river or spring to be met with yet or anything in it fit for the subsistence of men, except for its poor wretched inhabitants, who live on limpets and fern roots. The natives are very numerous and are beginning to be very troublesome. Several of the convicts have been killed by them. Not one of them has come into the camps yet.

Monday 14th

Bradley The *Alexander, Prince of Wales, Borrowdale* and *Friendship* transports sailed for England under the direction and command of Lieutenant Shortland, agent for transports. These ships were all in a distressed state when they sailed, both as to sickness, want of provisions and furniture. We made a party to the South Head to see them off the land. They had a fresh gale from the south-west and were soon out of sight, steering to the northward.

Sunday 27th

Bradley Convicts gathering greens for the use of the sick were attacked by the natives. One of them got clear and ran into camp, leaving his companion to do the best he could for himself. He was soon found by a marine who happened to be near, but not before he was wounded by a spear, which passed through one side of his face to his neck.

Monday 28th

Bradley A sailor straggling into the woods met several of the natives who threw stones at him and followed him when he attempted to run away. He with great presence of mind stopped and presented a stick at them in manner of a musket, at which they stopped and by that means he got away clear of them.

Tuesday 29th

White recorded a friendly meeting and observed the natives' fishing methods:

> About ten or twenty yards from the shore, among the long grass, in the shallow water, he struck and took with his fishgig several good fish, an acquisition to which, at this season of the year, it being cold and wet, we were unequal. While he was engaged in watching for them both he and the woman chewed something which they frequently spit into the water and which appeared to us, from his immediately striking a fish, to be a lure. While they were thus employed, one of the gentlemen with me sung some songs and when he had done the females in the canoes either sung one of their own songs, or imitated him, in which they succeeded beyond conception. Anything spoken by us they most accurately recited, and this in a manner of which we fell greatly short in our attempts to repeat their language after them.

∽

Hunter   The natives we have seen accompanied by dogs which appear to be domesticated the same as ours in Europe; they are of a wolf kind and of a reddish colour...of those dogs we have had many which were taken when young, but never could cure them of their natural ferocity; although well fed, they would at all times, but particularly in the dark, fly at young pigs, chickens, or any small animal which they might be able to conquer and immediately kill and generally eat them. I had one which was a little puppy when caught, but notwithstanding I took much pains to correct and cure it of its savageness, I found it took every opportunity which it met with to snap off the head of a fowl or worry a pig, and would do it in defiance of correction. They are a very good-natured animal when domesticated, but I believe it to be impossible to cure that savageness, which all I have seen seem to possess.

John Hunter was born in Edinburgh in 1737, the son of a merchant seaman. He joined the navy at 17 as captain's servant in HMS *Grampus* and served in the West Indies and in North American waters during the War of Independence. He was commissioned rather late in life and

Captain John Hunter, *from* An Historical Journal 1787-
1792. *Engraved from a painting by R. Dighton.*

there may have been some doubts about his seamanship, but he was popular, he was respected for his maturity and judgment, and he was more than just a seaman; he had learnt the classics and music as a young man, he was an excellent draughtsman and an enthusiastic naturalist. Hunter never married, but he kept close ties with family in England.

An Historical Journal, 1787-1792, first published in 1793, was based on his original journal, which is held by the Dixson Library. The original is a large, leather-bound book written in Hunter's neat handwriting.

The published work includes contributions from King, mainly to do with events at Norfolk Island; from Lieutenant Ball, with an account of his voyage back to England in the *Supply*, departing Port Jackson in November 1791; and from Phillip on events in the colony after the publication of *The Voyage of Governor Phillip* in 1789. Like that book it is drawn from his despatches and is referred to as *Phillip* in attributing quotations.

It also includes views of Sydney Cove and Rose Hill said to be based on sketches by Hunter, a number of maps and charts and several illustrations of the Aboriginal people and people of other South Sea islands. However, the best representation of Hunter's talent for drawing is in the sketchbook held in the National Library's Rex Nan Kivell Collection, which contains 95 of his drawings, mainly of plants and animals, 'drawn on the spot in 1788, 89 & 90' and showing sometimes a whimsical charm, unexpected in a bluff naval officer.

AUGUST

Saturday 2nd

The convict Patrick Gray, charged with stealing a pound and a half of pork, admitted the theft and was sentenced to 500 lashes and hard labour in heavy irons for six months.

Thursday 7th

Collins   All public labour was suspended for many days at the beginning of the month of August by heavy rain and the work of much time was also rendered fruitless by its effects; the brick-kiln fell in more than once and bricks to a large amount were destroyed, the roads about the settlement were rendered impassable and some of the huts were so far injured as to require nearly as much labour to repair them as to build them anew.

Tuesday 12th

In a letter to William Collins, Ralph Clark described the celebrations for the birthday of the Prince of Wales   The governor in honour of the day gave a dinner to every gentleman in the settlement and we seemed to enjoy ourselves much more than we did the 4th June, but White and Balmain, in the evening, in the course of conversation, quarrelled about some duty and they went out in the middle of the night to decide it with pistols, without any seconds. The report of the pistols alarmed the guards, for before the patrols could come up with them they had each fired five rounds, without doing any material injury to each other. Balmain received a small flesh wound in the right thigh, a little above the knee. It would not have rested there had not the governor taken the matter in hand and convinced the two sons of Aesculapious that it was much better to draw blood with the point of their lance from the arm of their patients, than to do it with pistol balls from each other.

Saturday 16th

Bradley   A convict who was collecting sweet tea...met 14 natives about a mile from camp. They beat him and made him strip, but were frightened off by two musket shots.

'Sweet tea' was the common plant sarsaparilla (*Smilax glyciphylla*). Collins wrote: 'The leaves of it being boiled, they obtained a beverage not unlike licorice in taste, and which was recommended by some of the medical gentlemen here as a powerful tonic.'

Sunday 17th

Phillip   As it had been supposed that many of the natives had left this part of the coast on account of the great scarcity of fish, the different coves of the harbour were examined in one day. At this time, not more than 67 canoes were counted and about 130 of the people were seen. But it was the season in which they make their new canoes, and large parties were known to be in the woods for that purpose.

According to the NSW Fisheries Research Institute, there is no mass-migration of fish from Sydney Harbour in winter, but fishing in the harbour usually declines during late winter, because the shallow water fish generally caught in nets and by lines move into deeper water in the colder months.

Sunday 24th

Nagle   We were down in Manly Bay...three boats of us, and laying off from the beach, we saw an action between two parties. The one as we supposed was from the interior. They fought on the rising ground nearly in front of us as we lay in our boats. They fought spear in hand with great dexterity for nearly an hour, when the interior party appeared to gain the victory, the others having to retreat with their women and children screeching and hollowing at a dreadful rate till they were out of hearing and we returned to town.

Daniel Southwell, master's mate in the *Sirius*, described the encounter in a letter to his uncle, the Reverend Weeden Butler:

> The people were now more numerous than usual, upwards of 200, as I judge, being in sight...They wanted us much to come on shore, which was impracticable. Indeed, so intent seemed they on persuading us to it that after several waggish intimations from our people that a sight of their ladies would be very agreeable, they caused about 20 of them to pass close by us, to which, indeed, they seemed not at all averse...Some of the young damsels looked well enough, all things considered. They were quite facetious, and so far as our slender knowledge of their dialect extended, kept up a very warm, animated, and amorous discourse. However, they did not forget now and then to give a side glance at their countrymen, with whose grand foible they were no doubt well acquainted, and when they retired seemed to do it rather from a fear of giving them offence than from any inclination of their own.
>
> After this, when all had for some time been quiet and still, sitting quite hush[ed] in the grass, we were not a little surprised to hear a great tumult which proceeded from some who sat farther back among the trees. At first the noise was simply that of men's voices wrangling with the most barbarous dissonance and savage agitation, but now the clashing of spears and the strokes of lances against the target was very distinctly heard. Looking that way, therefore, we saw several of them engaged in warm combat, darting at each other with true savage fierceness. All now ran and seized their weapons, which, by the way, must have been deposited in the grass, as till now they had kept them out of our sight, and a scene of great noise and confusion ensued on all sides.
>
> The women, who hitherto had all huddled together a little way from our boats' station, came running down with every appearance of terror, and calling to us repeatedly. Some stayed behind, anxiously looking out from between the trees as if to observe the event and wait the decision, and the children everywhere were clinging to them and squalling pitiably. What those females meant who thus precipitately came down to us I am at a loss to conclude, but they seemed to supplicate our assistance.

The battle continued long and was now and then interrupted with noisy expostulations, in the midst of which the contending parties would, however, frequently launch a spear at each other with all the rage of madmen. They are dexterous to a degree in the use of the target and during the affray, which lasted an hour, I did not see one of them completely disabled, though frequently forced to quit the field. I mean not by this to say there was really no execution done, but the thickness of the trees greatly impeded our view. Four of our people affirmed that they saw one man carried off the field with a lance fast in his side. It is hard indeed to suppose but that during so long a contest some must be wounded, and in fact we see few of these people anywhere, or of any age, but have many scars and marks of weapons on their bodies.

'Tis odd that the warriors in question would frequently all at once desist from the attack and talk together as though nothing at all had happened, and some others of the multitude would come down and gaze at us just as before. The women were less discomposed, and many of the men, though a part of their corps were still as warmly engaged as ever, came down on the shore to discourse with us in the usual way, and apparently regardless of what was going on among the rest.

Bradley One of the officers was of the opinion that this was a sham fight, from their holding frequent parleys and only one seen to fall.

Southwell thought it may have been a show of strength to impress the settlers or a stratagem to draw them ashore, or simply the way they settled their differences, 'instead of deciding the matter by fisticuffs, as with us boxing Britons'.

Tuesday 26th

Bradley The *Supply* arrived from Norfolk Island…The accounts of the produce of the island are very favourable and flattering to the settlement; the pines are said to be fit for all purpose and of sufficient size to mast a first rate with the stick. There are several other kinds of wood beside the pine with which the island abounds. Mr King, the commandant, is so sanguine as to expect that in the course of three years the island would support itself.

However, it was reported that 'landing is very difficult and frequently dangerous, sometimes altogether impracticable for days and weeks together'. A boat had been lost in coming ashore and James Cunningham, mate of the *Sirius*, two seamen and a convict were drowned.

Saturday 30th

Three cases were heard in the magistrates' court by Collins and Hunter. Nathaniel Mitchell was sentenced to 50 lashes for 'making use of' peas and beans which he was given to sow for Surgeon White. William Davis, John Martin and John Parker each received 25 lashes for lighting a fire in their hut contrary to orders. James Daley, who had kept the colony amused for three weeks by pretending to have found gold, was charged with absconding from the colony and fabricating a false sample. It emerged that the 'gold' he had discovered was made up of scrapings from a guinea and a brass belt buckle. He received 150 lashes and 'the letter R [for rogue] to be cut in canvas and sown upon his jacket'.

SEPTEMBER

Friday 5th

White   About half after six in the evening, we saw an *aurora australis*, a phenomenon uncommon in the southern hemisphere.

Saturday 13th

In the magistrates' court, before Collins and Hunter, evidence was given that on the afternoon of the previous day, two convict women, Lydia Munro and Elizabeth Cole, had been going over the hill on the west side of Sydney Cove 'to have a bathe', when William Boggis and John Owen had followed them and Boggis had demanded to 'have connection' with Munro. When she refused, Boggis threw her down on the ground; she screamed and the Negro convict, Daniel Gordon (who had been banished to Fort Denison in February and released in June) went to her defence, hitting Boggis with a stick.

Boggis, who had been sentenced to 50 lashes on 2 August for gambling, was sentenced to a further 100 lashes; Owen's sentence for aiding and abetting was 50 lashes. The court records are marked 'afterwards forgiven' but no reason is given as to why either man should have been reprieved.

Saturday 27th

In the magistrates' court, four young women were charged with insulting Robert Brown, captain of the storeship *Fishburn*. Phoebe Flarty was about 16 years old, Mary Mitchcraft was 18, Ann Mather was said to be only 15 and Ann Smith, one of four of that name who came with the First Fleet, was also about 18. All had been been convicted in the early months of 1787, not long before the departure of the fleet; it is possible that they had been rounded up in an attempt to take more women to the new settlement. All came on the *Prince of Wales*. In evidence, Captain Brown said that as he walked past them on 23 September, they made fun of him, calling out: 'Who bottles pea soup?' and 'Who puts their men in the coal hole?' History does not relate what these expressions mean; perhaps they were obscure references to sodomy, which might explain why Robert Brown, who was apparently an educated, religious man, was so offended as to take the girls to court. Before Collins and Hunter, Ann Smith denied having said anything and was discharged. The other three were forgiven, on promising they would 'never do the like again'.

28th September

Phillip wrote to Lord Sydney   I am sorry to have been so long without knowing more of these [Aboriginal] people, but I am unwilling to use any force, and hope this summer to persuade a family to live with us, unless they attempt to burn our crops, of which I am apprehensive, for they certainly are not pleased with our remaining amongst them, as they see we deprive them of fish, which is almost their only support; but if they set fire to the corn, necessity will oblige me to drive them to a greater distance, though I can assure your Lordship that I shall never do it but with the greatest reluctance and from absolute necessity.

Phillip also told Lord Sydney that because 'very little of the English wheat had vegetated and a very considerable quantity of barley and many seeds had rotted in the ground...I have thought it necessary to order the *Sirius* to go to the Cape of Good Hope in order to procure grain, and at the same time what quantity of flour and provisions she can receive.'

30th September

The commissary of the settlement, Andrew Miller, compiled 'An account of Provisions remaining in His Majesty's stores at Sydney Cove, New South Wales, 30th September, 1788'.

Flour	414,176	pounds	is 52 weeks' ration.	
Rice	51,330	"	15	"
Beef	127,608	"	43	"
Pork	214,344	"	128	"
Peas	2,305	bushels	58	"
Butter	15,450	pounds	49	"

Collins   His Excellency made known his intention of establishing a settlement on some ground which he had seen at the head of this harbour when he made his excursion to the westward in April last, and which, from its form he had named The Crescent. This measure appeared the more expedient, as the soil in and about the settlement seemed to be very indifferent and unproductive, and by no means so favourable for the growth of grain as that at The Crescent.

David Collins was born in London in 1756, one of eight children, the son of a soldier. After attending grammar school in Devon, where his father was stationed, Collins joined the marines at the age of 14. Like many of the officers of the First Fleet, he served in America during the War of Independence. In 1776, while he was evacuating British troops to Halifax, Nova Scotia, he met and married Maria Proctor, from a prominent Halifax family.

Collins returned to England with Maria in 1777. By 1783, with peace in Europe and America, he was retired and living in the country on half pay. In 1786 he was appointed deputy judge-advocate to the settlement in New South Wales. He arrived in the colony at the age of 31 with no legal training apart from what he had learnt from his studies during the voyage, although two years as adjutant during his American service would have given him a grounding in military legal procedures.

Like Ralph Clark, Collins had to leave his wife behind in England. As his time in New South Wales wore on and was extended, Maria Collins begged him to come home: 'I will cheerfully accompany you to some part of the world where we can live upon your half pay', she wrote in 1791, 'You know we were many years confined to nearly that pittance and you never heard me repine nor ever saw me discontented, nor should you now if you would come and try me.'

Like many of his fellow officers, Collins lived (from time to time, if not permanently) with a convict. Nancy Yeats, also known as Ann Yeats, described as a milliner, had received a death sentence at York in 1785 for stealing a length of cotton. The sentence was commuted to seven years and she was sent to the *Lady Penrhyn* in 1787, aged about 20, for transportation to New South Wales. Her first child with David Collins, a daughter, was born in September 1790.

David Collins was a tall, broad-shouldered man with fair, curly hair. He was described as 'remarkably handsome and his manners extremely prepossessing' with a 'most cheerful disposition'.

OCTOBER

Wednesday 1st

Bradley What has been experienced lately in several instances with the natives has occasioned me to alter those very favourable opinions I had formed of them, and however much I wished to encourage the idea of being friendly disposed, I must acknowledge that [I am] now convinced that they are only so when they suppose we have them in our power or are well prepared by being armed. Lately they have attacked almost every person who has met with them that has not had a musket and have sometimes endeavoured to surprise some who had…That some of them have been killed by musket balls, both at Port Jackson by our people and at Botany Bay by the French, I have not the least doubt…

For a considerable time after our arrival it was supposed that the food of the natives was entirely fish, but the winter convinced us that if they had not some other resource, great numbers of them must perish. As it is, they are very hard put to it when the fish is scarce…having met some of the natives in a most deplorable situation for want of food in the winter months.

Thursday 2nd

White *Sirius* sailed for the Cape of Good Hope for a supply of flour, it being discovered that our stock of this article bore no proportion to the salt beef and pork. The same day the *Golden Grove* sailed for Norfolk Island, with a reinforcement of male and female convicts.

Saturday 4th

White   A convict named Cooper Handley, who went out with an armed party of marines to collect wild vegetables and sweet tea, strayed from them and was afterwards met by the natives, who murdered and mutilated him in a shocking manner. The natives were so near our men that they heard them very distinctly shouting and making a great noise, yet were unable to overtake them in the pursuit. In the evening, a party of soldiers and convicts were sent out to bury the deceased.

Collins   This poor wretch furnished another instance of the consequences that attended a disobedience of orders which had been purposely given to prevent these accidents, and as nothing of the kind was known to happen but where a neglect and contempt of all order was first shown, every misfortune of the kind might be attributed, not to the manners and disposition of the natives, but to the obstinacy and ignorance of our people.

Friday 31st

White   In the evening of this day we had very loud thunder and a shower of hail; many of the hail stones were measured and found to be five-eighths of an inch in diameter.

❧

Collins   A gang of convicts were employed in rolling timber together to form a bridge over the stream at the head of the cove, and such other public works as were in hand went on as usual, those employed on them in general barely exerting themselves beyond what was necessary to avoid immediate punishment for idleness.

The bridge over the 'stream at the head of the cove' was the first bridge over the tank stream, from which Bridge Street takes its name.

The storeships *Fishburn* and *Golden Grove* were preparing to sail for England, carrying with them the last of the dispatches from Governor

Phillip which were used in the compilation of *The Voyage of Governor Phillip to Botany Bay*. Extracts from the book reflect some of Phillip's thoughts and observations at the time:

> The inhabitants of New South Wales...seem to be among themselves perfectly honest and often leave their spears and other implements upon the beach, in full confidence of finding them untouched. But the convicts too frequently carry them off and dispose of them to vessels coming to England, though at the hazard on one side of being prosecuted for theft, and on the other for purchasing stolen goods. Injuries of this nature they generally revenge on such stragglers as they happen to meet, and perhaps have already learnt to distinguish these freebooters by their blue and yellow jackets, as they very early did the soldiers by their red clothes.
>
> Conciliation is the only plan intended to be pursued, but Governor Phillip, when he last wrote, seemed to despair of getting any of them to remain among his people long enough for either to acquire the language of the other, except by constraint. Hitherto he has been unwilling to take this method, but if it can be done in such a manner as not to create any general alarm among them, it will probably turn out to be the kindest piece of violence that could be used. Whenever it shall be practicable, by any means, to explain to them the friendly disposition of Governor Phillip and his people towards them, and to make them understand that the men from whom they receive occasional injuries are already a disgraced class and liable to severe punishment for such proceedings, they will then perhaps acquire sufficient confidence in their new countrymen to mix with them, to enrich themselves with some of their implements, and to learn and adopt some of the most useful and necessary of their arts.

NOVEMBER

Sunday 2nd

Collins The month of November commenced with the establishment of a settlement at the head of the harbour. On the second, his excellency the governor went up to The Crescent with the surveyor-general, two officers and a small party of marines, to choose the spot and to mark out the ground for a redoubt and other necessary buildings, and two days after a party of 10 convicts, being chiefly people who understood the business of cultivation, were sent up to him and a spot upon a rising ground, which his Excellency named Rose Hill, in compliment to G. Rose Esq, one of the Secretaries of the Treasury, was ordered to be cleared for the first habitations. The soil at this spot was of a stiff clayey nature, free from that rock which everywhere covered the surface at Sydney Cove, well clothed with timber and unobstructed by underwood.

Thursday 6th

Private James Baker was spending the night in the convict Mary Phillips's hut when Thomas Bullmore, also a marine private, demanded that she sleep with him. She refused and Bullmore, who had previously been in trouble for fighting with fellow marines, swore at Baker and Phillips and tried to break into the hut. A fight between Bullmore and Baker followed in which Bullmore was hurt before the fight was broken up.

Friday 7th

The next morning, according to one line of evidence, Bullmore, with a second, Richard Asky, went looking for Baker. Apparently against Baker's wishes, they stripped off and fought several rounds, with Luke Haynes seconding Baker. That night, Bullmore reported to the hospital and was admitted by the assistant-surgeon, Dennis Considen.

In the criminal court, John Thomas, charged with the theft of a pair of shoes and a pound of soap, was convicted and sentenced to '500 lashes thus: 400 on his bare back and 100 on his bare backside, in the usual manner'.

Tuesday 11th

Scott Thomas Bullmore died in consequence of a battle fought with James Baker, marine. (But strongly suspected to be ill-used by others.) Baker confined prior to his death and three more confined viz. Asky, Haynes and Dukes, immediately after his decease, for to take their trial.

Collins ordered the criminal court to meet on 17 November to try those involved in the incident.

Friday 14th

A letter from a female convict written on this date is included in the British Museum Papers, published in *Historical Records of NSW Volume 2* in 1893:

> I take the first opportunity that has been given us to acquaint you with our disconsolate situation in this solitary waste of the creation. Our passage, you may have heard by the first ships, was tolerably favourable, but the inconveniences since suffered for want of shelter, bedding, etc. are not to be imagined by any stranger. However, we have now two streets, if four rows of the most miserable huts you can possibly conceive of deserve that name. Windows they have none, as from the governor's house etc. now nearly finished, no glass could be spared, so that lattices of twigs are made by our people to supply their places...
>
> As for the distresses of the women, they are past description, as they are deprived of tea and other things they were indulged in in the voyage by the seamen, and as they are all totally unprovided with clothes those who have young children are quite wretched. Besides this, though a number of marriages have taken place, several women who became pregnant on the voyage and are since left by their partners, who have returned to England, are not likely even here to form any fresh connections...
>
> In short, every one is so taken up with their own misfortunes that they have no pity to bestow upon others. All our letters are examined by an officer, but a friend takes this for me privately.

Saturday 15th

The Reverend Richard Johnson wrote to his friend Henry Fricker With much labour and no small cost we have got into our little cabbage tree cottage. No small curiosity it is I assure you...am happy however that it in some measure answers our purpose, though now and then in excessive rains we are all on a swim within doors. As to the country in general, I confess I have no very great opinion of nor expectation from it. The greatest part of it is poor and barren and rocky, requires a great deal of labour to clear it of trees, roots etc. and to cultivate it, and after all, the corn in general that has been sown hitherto looks very poor and unpromising.

I think I can say none have given it a fairer trial than myself— have been at work in my little farm for a day together, burning wood,

The Reverend Richard Johnson, Australia's
first chaplain. *Artist unknown. National
Library of Australia*

digging, sowing etc. but do not expect to reap anything nearly adequate to my labour. Others seem to be in the same predicament and
all almost, at least with but few exceptions, are heartily sick of the
expedition, and wish themselves back safe in old England...

I am yet obliged to be a field preacher. No church is yet begun of
and I am afraid scarcely thought of. Other things seem to be of greater
notice and concern and most would rather see a tavern, a may house,
a brothel—anything, sooner than a place for public worship.

Richard Johnson was born in Yorkshire in 1755, and went to grammar
school in Hull then to Magdalene College, Cambridge. He was ordained
in 1784 and in 1786 was appointed chaplain for Botany Bay at
an annual salary of £182 10s. His wife, born Mary Burton, was a
Londoner, probably a couple of years older than her husband. They
were married in 1786.

The Johnsons came out in the *Golden Grove* with Samuel Barnes
employed as a servant and chaplain's clerk. They probably lived
aboard the ship until the middle of 1788, when they moved into

the 'little cabbage tree cottage' on the east side of Sydney Cove. In *Richard Johnson, Chaplain to the Colony of New South Wales*, Neil Macintosh wrote:

> This building was to be their home for nearly three years, and it was presumably in this cottage that Mary Johnson gave birth in October 1788 to a stillborn male child. It must have been a difficult experience for Mary as the chaplain was the only officer who brought his wife with him in the First Fleet and the sadness of the event would have been compounded by the loneliness of being the only 'lady' in the colony.

Johnson brought more than 4000 books with him, mainly for use at religious services and for distribution to the convicts. They included 100 Bibles, 500 books of psalms, 200 catechism books as well as 50 copies of Synge's *Religion Made Easy*, 12 copies of Wilson's *Instructions for the Indians*, 50 copies of Woodward's *Caution to Swearers*, and 100 copies of *Exhortations to Chastity*.

Original documents written by Richard Johnson have been found, including two notebooks, letters, a plan of the colony's first church, and a sermon. Most of these relate to the mid-1790s but several entries from the earlier years were printed at the end of the sermon given on his death. The first of these appears on 28 December 1788.

Sunday 16th

White gave a statement on the death of Bullmore   On the 11th of November, by order of Major Ross, I examined into the cause of death of Thomas Bullmore. On opening the cranium, found a quantity of extravasated blood under the skull… (perhaps occasioned by a fall) which in my opinion was the most probable cause of his death. I further examined and looked into the cavities of the breast and abdomen, where the viscera appeared in regular order and without any internal mark of injury. On removing the integuments over the sternum or breast, there appeared a small or inconsiderable contusion, and he had on his face and body other marks of violence.

Monday 17th

In the criminal court, James Baker, Luke Haynes, Richard Asky and Richard Dukes were charged that they 'upon one Thomas Bullmore, feloniously, wilfully and of their malice aforethought, did make an assault and...with both their hands and feet, the said Thomas Bullmore to and against the ground did cast and throw, and the same Thomas Bullmore they with their hands and feet aforesaid, in and upon the head, stomach, back and sides did strike and beat, giving to the said Thomas Bullmore one mortal bruise'.

They were found guilty of manslaughter, and sentenced to 200 lashes. The sentence appears lenient in view of the evidence, perhaps because the members of the court had information which was not given in evidence, as implied by Scott's entry of 11 November.

The Reverend Richard Johnson wrote to Mr J. Stonard Most have wrote to request they might be called home. This however I have not yet done and purpose to give it a little further trial, but give you it as my humble opinion government would act very wisely to send out another fleet to take us all back to England, or to some other place more likely to answer than this poor wretched country, where scarcely anything is to be seen but rocks, or eaten but rats.

Tuesday 18th

White wrote to his editor, Thomas Wilson As the following journal was undertaken at your request, and its principal object to afford you some amusement during your hours of relaxation, I shall esteem myself happy if it answers that purpose. I hope that the specimens of natural history may tend to the promotion of your favourite science, and that on this account it will not be unacceptable to you. By the next conveyance I trust I shall be able to make some additions that will not be unworthy the attention of the naturalists.

The manuscript and 'specimens of natural history' went to England by either the *Golden Grove* or the *Fishburn*. White continued to write with a view to further publication, but the second manuscript has not been found.

Wednesday 19th

Robert Brown, captain of *Fishburn* At two a.m. weighed with a light breeze in company [with] the *Golden Grove*. At four, abreast the north and south forelands at the entrance of the harbour...from which I take my departure.

With the storeships and transports gone and the *Sirius* on the way to the Cape of Good Hope, the *Supply* was the only ship in the harbour and the population of the settlement was fewer than 1100.

Monday 24th

Scott   I set a hen on 17 eggs. She layed one while sitting which made 18. Brought forth 16 chickens.

Tuesday 25th

James Davis, a seaman from the *Sirius*, appeared in the magistrates' court before Collins and Alt, accused of insolence to Robinson Reid, the carpenter of the *Supply*. He was found guilty and sentenced to 400 lashes, '50 on this day, and 50 on every Saturday following until he has received the above mentioned number of 400 lashes'.

DECEMBER

Wednesday 3rd

James Daley, the convict who had been punished in August for fabricating a false sample of gold, was hanged for theft. Collins wrote:

> Before he was turned off, he confessed that he had committed several thefts, to which he had been induced by bad connections, and pointed out two women who had received part of the property for the acquisition of which he was then about to pay so dear a price. These women were immediately apprehended and one of them made a public example of, to deter others from offending in the like manner. The convicts being all assembled for muster, she was directed to stand forward, and, her head having been previously deprived of its natural covering, she was clothed with a canvas frock, on which was painted, in large characters, R. S. G. (receiver of stolen goods) and threatened with punishment if ever she was seen without it.

Thursday 11th

A convict, Charles Wilson, aged about 27, was found dead near the place where he worked. His body was decomposed, the face was black and the eyes were full of maggots.

Sunday 14th

Collins reported the post-mortem on Wilson's body It appeared from the evidence of Mr Balmain, one of the assistant-surgeons, who attended to open him and of the people who lived with the deceased, that he died through want of nourishment and through weakness occasioned by the heat of the sun. It appeared that he had not for more than a week past eaten his allowance of provisions, the whole being found in his box. It was proved by those who knew him that he was accustomed to deny himself even what was absolutely necessary to his existence, abstaining from his provisions and selling them for money, which he was reserving, and had somewhere concealed, in order to purchase his passage to England when his time should expire.

Thursday 18th

Tench Unabated animosity continued to prevail between the natives and us...Early on the morning of the 18th of December word was brought that they were assembled in force near the brick-kilns, which stand but a mile from the town of Sydney. The terror of those who brought the first intelligence magnified the number to 2000, a second messenger diminished it to 400. A detachment under the command of one officer was ordered to march immediately and reconnoitre there. The officer soon returned and reported that about 50 Indians had appeared at the brick-kilns, but upon the convicts, who were at work there, pointing their spades and shovels at them in the manner of guns, they had fled into the woods.

Thursday 25th

Collins Christmas Day was observed with proper ceremony. Mr Johnson preached a sermon adapted to the occasion and the major part of the officers of the settlement were afterward entertained at dinner by the governor.

Sunday 28th

The Reverend Richard Johnson   Rose about four o'clock. At five took boat; went to Rose Hill; arrived about eight o'clock; between nine and 10 began public service. Preached from second chapter Ephesians 17. After sermon I distributed some books among the convicts; to several that could not read I gave spelling books, recommending them to learn to read, assuring them that nothing I could do to further this desirable end should ever be wanting on my part. May the Lord bless this desirable plan, dispose them to be instructed, and by coming to read the scriptures may they be convinced of the sinfulness and folly of their past conduct. Returned about three o'clock and arrived at Sydney about eight. Bless God, O my soul, for this day's mercies and protection.

Tuesday 30th

Collins   It being remarked with concern that the natives were becoming every day more troublesome and hostile, several people having been wounded and others who were necessarily employed in the woods driven in and much alarmed by them, the governor determined on endeavouring to seize and bring into the settlement one or two of those people, whose language it was become absolutely necessary to acquire, that they might learn to distinguish friends from enemies.

Tench   The governor...sent two boats under the command of Lieutenant Ball of the *Supply* and Lieutenant George Johnston of the marines down the harbour with directions to those officers to seize and carry off some of the natives. The boats proceeded to Manly Cove, where several Indians were seen standing on the beach, who were enticed by courteous behaviour and a few presents to enter into conversation. A proper opportunity being presented, our people rushed in among them and seized two men. The rest fled, but the cries of the captives soon brought them back, with many others, to their rescue, and so desperate were their struggles that in spite of every effort on our side only one of them was secured. The other effected his escape. The boats put off without delay and an attack from the shore instantly commenced; they threw spears, stones, firebrands and whatever else presented itself at the boats, nor did they retreat, agreeable to their former custom, until many muskets were fired over them.

The prisoner was now fastened by ropes to the thwarts of the boat and when he saw himself irretrievably disparted from his country-men, set up the most piercing and lamentable cries of distress. His grief, however, soon diminished, he accepted and eat of some broiled fish which was given to him, and sullenly submitted to his destiny.

When the news of his arrival at Sydney was announced, I went with every other person to see him. He appeared to be about 30 years old, not tall, but robustly made and of a countenance which, under happier circumstances, I thought would display manliness and sensibility. His agitation was excessive and the clamorous crowds who flocked around him did not contribute to lessen it. Curiosity and observation seemed, nevertheless, not to have wholly deserted him; he shewed the effect of novelty upon ignorance; he wondered at all he saw; though broken and interrupted with dismay, his voice was soft and musical when its natural tone could be heard, and he read-ily pronounced with tolerable accuracy the names of things which were taught him. To our ladies he quickly became extraordinarily courteous, a sure sign that his terror was wearing off.

Every blandishment was used to soothe him, and it had its effect. As he was entering the governor's house, someone touched a small bell which hung over the door; he started with horror and aston-ishment but in a moment after was reconciled to the noise and laughed at the cause of his perturbation. When pictures were shown to him, he knew directly those which represented the human figure. Among others, a very large handsome print of her royal highness the Duchess of Cumberland being produced, he called out 'woman', a name by which we had just before taught him to call the female convicts...

His curiosity here being satiated, we took him to a large brick house, which was building for the governor's residence; being about to enter, he cast up his eyes, and seeing some people leaning out of a window on the first storey, he exclaimed aloud and testified the most extravagant surprise. Nothing here was observed to fix his attention so strongly as some tame fowls, who were feeding near him; our dogs also he particularly noticed, but seemed more fear-ful than fond of them.

He dined at a side-table at the governor's and eat heartily of fish and ducks, which he first cooled. Bread and salt meat he smelled at, but would not taste; all our liquors he treated in the same manner and could drink nothing but water. On being shown that he was not to wipe his hands on the chair which he sat upon, he used a towel which was gave to him with great cleanliness and decency.

In the afternoon his hair was closely cut, his head combed and his beard shaved, but he would not submit to these operations until he had seen them performed on another person, when he readily acquiesced. His hair, as might be supposed, was filled with vermin, whose destruction seemed to afford him great triumph; nay, either revenge or pleasure prompted him to eat them, but on our expressing disgust and abhorrence he left it off.

To this succeeded his immersion in a tub of water and soap, where he was completely washed and scrubbed from head to foot, after which a shirt, a jacket, and a pair of trousers, were put upon him. Some part of this ablution I had the honour to perform, in order that I might ascertain the real colour of the skin of these people. My observation then was (and it has since been confirmed in a thousand other instances) that they are as black as the lighter cast of the African Negroes. Many unsuccessful attempts were made to learn his name; the governor therefore called him 'Manly', from the cove in which he was captured...

To prevent his escape, a handcuff with a rope attached to it was fastened around his left wrist, which at first highly delighted him; he called it *bengadee* (or ornament), but his delight changed to rage and hatred when he discovered its use. His supper he cooked himself; some fish were given to him for this purpose, which, without any previous preparation whatever, he threw carelessly on the fire, and when they became warm took them up and first rubbed off the scales, peeled the outside with his teeth, and eat it; afterwards he gutted them, and laying them again on the fire, completed the dressing and eat them.

A convict was selected to sleep with him and to attend him wherever he might go. When he went with his keeper into his apartment he appeared very restless and uneasy while a light was kept in, but on its extinction, he immediately lay down and composed himself.

❧

Phillip's most important tasks were to reconcile the settlers to the new land and to reconcile the Aboriginal people to the settlers.

In July, Major Ross, commanding officer of the marines and lieutenant-governor of the colony, wrote to Evan Nepean, Under-Secretary of the Home Department:

> Take my word for it, there is not a man in this place but wishes to return home...I will in confidence venture to assure you that this country will never answer to settle in, for although I think corn will grow here, yet I am convinced that if ever it is able to maintain the people here it cannot be in less time than probably a hundred years hence.

In November, the Reverend Richard Johnson wrote to a friend that in his opinion 'government would act very wisely to send out another fleet to take us all back to England, or to some other place more likely to answer than this poor wretched country, where scarcely anything is to be seen but rocks, or eaten but rats.'

Other writers were more optimistic (or less outspoken), but the settlers were not yet at home in the new country.

During the first year, Phillip had probably not been able to spend as much time as he would have liked with the Aboriginal people. In July, he wrote to Lord Sydney: 'When I have time to mix more with them every means shall be used to reconcile them to live amongst us and to teach them the advantages they will reap from cultivating the land'. The capture of 'Manly' was supposed to be the first step in this process.

1789
A Man or Two in Our Possession

27 March   Six marines hanged for stealing provisions from the public store.

15 April   Smallpox discovered among the Aboriginal people.

21 April   The *Sirius* damaged by a storm off the southern coast of Tasmania.

8 May   The *Sirius* arrived in Port Jackson with relief supplies.

18 May   Arabanoo died of smallpox.

2 June   George Farquhar's play *The Recruiting Officer* performed by the convicts.

6 June   Phillip led an expedition to Broken Bay to trace the Hawkesbury River.

26 June   Tench led an expedition west from Rose Hill and discovered the Nepean River.

8 August   The night-watch was formed in response to an increasing number of thefts.

1 November   With provisions running short, the men's ration was reduced by one-third.

21 November   James Ruse, whose term had expired, was settled on two acres at Rose Hill.

25 November   Bennelong and Colbee captured.

12 December   Colbee escaped from the settlement

23 December   HMS *Guardian*, carrying relief supplies from England, struck an iceberg.

JANUARY

Thursday 1st

Tench Today being New Year's Day, most of the officers were invited to the governor's table. Manly dined heartily on fish and roasted pork. He was seated on a chest near a window, out of which, when he had done eating, he would have thrown his plate, had he not been prevented. During dinner-time, a band of music played in an adjoining apartment, and after the cloth was removed one of the company sang in a very soft and superior style, but the powers of melody were lost on Manly, which disappointed our expectations, as he had before shown pleasure and readiness in imitating our tunes. Stretched out on his chest and putting his hat under his head, he fell asleep.

To convince his countrymen that he had received no injury from us, the governor took him in a boat down the harbour, that they might see and converse with him. When the boat arrived and lay at a little distance from the beach, several Indians who had retired at her approach, on seeing Manly, returned; he was greatly affected, and shed tears. At length they began to converse. Our ignorance of the language prevented us from knowing much of what passed; it was, however, easily understood that his friends asked him why he did not jump overboard and rejoin them. He only sighed, and pointed to the fetter on his leg, by which he was bound.

In going down the harbour he had described the names by which they distinguish its numerous creeks and headlands; he was now often heard to repeat that of *weerong* (Sydney), which was doubtless to inform his countrymen of the place of his captivity, and perhaps invite them to rescue him. By this time his gloom was chased away, and he parted from his friends without testifying reluctance. His vivacity and good humour continued all the evening and produced so good an effect on his appetite that he eat for supper two kangaroo rats, each of the size of a moderate rabbit, and in addition not less than three pounds of fish.

Monday 5th

Scott An animal came at night and destroyed 11 chickens in the hen house. Two lost before and one drowned, which makes 14—two now remain.

Tuesday 6th

Scott   Set a trap for the animal. (Caught a rat).

❧

There was an increasing amount of crime in the early part of 1789. On Saturday 3 January, in a case over the theft of a white shirt, Rebecca Holmes was sentenced to receive 50 lashes, '20 on the east side, 20 on the west side and 10 at the farm', and Mary Marshall was sentenced 'to be stripped and tied to the same cart with Rebecca Holmes'.

On 5 January, William Fraser, who worked as a blacksmith, admitted saying to Sergeant Martin Connor, 'You can kiss my arse.' He was sentenced to 100 lashes but was forgiven all but 25 by the governor. On the 9th, George Legge received a sentence of 100 lashes for stealing two chickens.

On Saturday, 10 January, Easty wrote: 'This day Thomas Sanderson, a convict, was tried by a criminal court for robbing the storehouse and absconding from the quarters and was outlawed on Christmas eve and received sentence of death and was executed this evening.' Collins recorded another conviction on the same day: 'Another convict, named Ruglass, was tried for stabbing Ann Fowles, a woman with whom he cohabited, and sentenced to receive 700 lashes, half of which were inflicted on him while the other unhappy wretch [Sanderson] was suffering the execution of his sentence.'

On 12 January, John Russell, a candle-maker and at about 65 years of age one of the oldest people in the colony, was sentenced to receive 300 lashes for assaulting two women.

Four days later, Thomas Tennant was sentenced to 200 lashes for selling a shirt and Tamasin Allen (described at the Old Bailey in 1786 as 'a lustyish woman with black hair') received 50 lashes for buying it. The convicts were not allowed to buy or sell anything, for fear that it would lead to further crime. Phillip wrote: 'Those who sell their own provisions must support themselves by stealing from others', and presumably the same applied to other articles.

On 20 January, Samuel Barsby and William Bond received sentences of 300 lashes and 150 lashes respectively, for being drunk. The next day John Ruffler was ordered 300 lashes for stealing two quarts of horse beans from the governor's farm. Thomas Prior was sentenced to 300 lashes on the 23rd for buying a a shirt, trousers and shoes, and on the 26th John Robins was ordered 75 lashes for 'drunkenness on the Sabbath day'.

There are no surviving contemporary depictions of flogging at the settlement. Later drawings generally show the person being flogged with his hands above his head, tied to a wooden tripod about seven feet high. The early floggings at Sydney Cove were described as being 'at the cart's tail'; the victim was probably tied to a cartwheel or to the raised back of a cart. The lash was a cat-o'-nine-tails, with nine knotted leather strands at the end of a short whip; after the first few strokes the knots began to bite into the flesh.

FEBRUARY

Monday 2nd

Easty This night at 10 o'clock Captain John Shea of marines departed this life after a long illness, of consumption, and was buried the next day in military form, very neat and handsome.

Wednesday 4th

William Bryant, a Cornishman 'bred from his youth to the business of a fisherman in the western part of England', and put in charge of the fishing boats in Sydney Cove, was found guilty in the magistrates' court of selling, on his own account, the fish he was employed to catch for the colony. Collins wrote that Bryant was given every encouragement 'to keep him above temptation; an hut was built for him and his family, he was always presented with a certain part of the fish which he caught and he wanted for nothing that was necessary'.

He was sentenced to 100 lashes and was 'deprived of the direction of the fish and the boat, to continue in the boat and to be turned out of the hut he is now in'.

Sunday 8th

Easty This day young [Alexander] John Ross was appointed Second-Lieutenant of marines.

Easty's brief entries on 2 and 8 February mask six days of intrigue. On Shea's death, Phillip suggested to Ross that George Johnston, the senior lieutenant in the detachment, should be promoted in his place, but Ross, without telling Phillip, offered the position to David Collins, on the condition that Collins would step down as judge-advocate. This was probably done to make life difficult for Phillip, as there was not a suitable replacement for Collins as judge-advocate and if he had accepted, the courts would have been thrown into chaos. However, Collins, out of loyalty to Phillip and because he disliked Ross, rejected the offer and James Meredith was promoted, as in turn were George Johnston and Ralph Clark. Ross's son Alexander, who was on the company's books as a volunteer, was appointed second-lieutenant. Phillip records that when Ross 'came to ask me if giving his son a commission as a second lieutenant would meet with my approbation...I desired he would excuse me from giving any approbation'. Alexander Ross was nine years old.

Monday 9th

Phillip wrote to Lieutenant King at Norfolk Island The situation of this colony is such that it is necessary to observe the most rigid economy. With respect to provisions, there are only now for 12 months in the stores, and you know how very uncertain supplies from England must be...With respect to clothing, the like economy is necessary, for you cannot receive any further supplies until clothing is sent from England. No shoes will, in future, be issued to the convicts here, except as an encouragement to those who particularly distinguish themselves, and to the overseers.

Another concern was venereal disease which, Phillip told King,

has gained such a footing in this settlement that I now doubt if it will ever be done away. The precautions I ordered to be taken in England have been rendered ineffectual by the infamous conduct of some of the magistrates [in England] in sending on board the transports those who had been turned out of the hospitals as incurable.

Tuesday 17th

The *Supply* sailed for Norfolk Island. Tench wrote that Phillip went down the harbour in her, taking Manly with him,

who was observed to go on board with distrust and reluctance. When he found she was under sail, every effort was tried without success to exhilarate him. At length, an opportunity being presented, he plunged overboard and struck out for the nearest shore. Believing that those who were left behind would fire at him, he attempted to dive, at which he was known to be very expert, but this was attended with a difficulty which he had not foreseen; his clothes proved so buoyant that he was unable to get more than his head under water.

A boat was immediately despatched after him and picked him up, though not without struggles and resistance on his side. When brought on board, he appeared neither afraid or ashamed of what he had done, but sat apart, melancholy and dispirited, and continued so until he saw the governor and his other friends descend into a boat and heard himself called upon to accompany them; he sprang forward and his cheerfulness and alacrity of temper immediately returned and lasted during the remainder of the day. The dread of being carried away, on an element of whose boundary he could form no conception, joined to the uncertainty of our intention towards him, unquestionably caused him to act as he did.

Collins The cove was now, for the first time, left without a ship, a circumstance not only striking by its novelty, but which forcibly drew our attention to the peculiarity of our situation. The *Sirius* was gone to a distant country for supplies, the arrival of which were assuredly precarious. The *Supply* had left us to look after a dangerous reef, which service in an unknown sea might draw upon herself the calamity which she was seeking to instruct others to avoid.

Wednesday 18th

The *Sirius* had arrived in Cape Town early in January, and Hunter was 'anxious to get some account of the transports which under the command of Lieutenant Shortland, the agent, had left Port Jackson on the 14th of July 1788'. On the 18th he wrote: 'To my no small satisfaction (for I was preparing to sail the next day) Mr Shortland arrived in the *Alexander* transport. I was going off from the shore when I discovered the ship coming round Green Point; I rowed directly on board and his people were so happy to see their old friends in Table Bay that they cheered us as we came alongside.'

The Voyage of Governor Phillip to Botany Bay includes an account by Lieutenant John Shortland, captain of the *Alexander*, of their journey to Batavia (now known as Jakarta). They had left Port Jackson in company with the *Prince of Wales*, the *Borrowdale* and the *Friendship*. Due to the lack of supplies in the colony, none of the ships were well-provisioned. They lost sight of the *Borrowdale* and the *Prince of Wales* within a few days and continued in company with *Friendship*. Within a few weeks, Shortland wrote, 'the scurvy began to make its appearance...on the 13th of August five seamen of the *Alexander* were already on the sick list, complaining of pains in the legs and breast, with their gums so swelled and their teeth so loose that that they could not without difficulty eat even flour or rice'. By mid-October:

> The *Alexander* had lost eight of her complement and was reduced to two men in a watch, only four seamen and two boys being at all fit for duty...the *Friendship* had only five men not disabled, and was by no means well provided with provisions. In this melancholy state of both ships, the western monsoon being expected soon to set in, it was indispensably necessary to give up one for the sake of preserving the other.
>
> Upon this subject the masters consulted, and after some time came to an agreement. As the *Friendship* was the smaller vessel and would be cleared more easily than the *Alexander*, having fewer stores on board, Mr Walton, her master, consented that she should be evacuated and sunk, on condition that he should be allowed half freight of the *Alexander*. In four days the *Friendship* and her crew and stores transferred to the *Alexander*, after which she was bored and turned adrift. The ship's company thus made out from both vessels was of no great strength, not amounting to half the proper complement of the *Alexander*, nor was it more than, allowing for the further ravages of disease, was absolutely necessary to work that ship to Batavia.

On 17 November they were off Batavia:

> A gun was fired and a signal made for assistance. At two in the afternoon on the 18th, as no assistance arrived, the still greater effort of weighing anchor was tried and the task performed with the utmost difficulty, after which, standing in with the sea breeze, the ship came again to anchor at five, in nine fathoms. The boat was now hoisted out and sent to beg assistance from the Dutch Commodore, the crew of the *Alexander* being so much reduced as to be unable to furl their own sails. A party was immediately sent to assist, and six of the Dutch seamen remained on board all night, lest any blowing weather should come on. Never, perhaps, did any ship arrive in port more helpless, without being shattered by weather, from the mere effects of a dreadful and invincible disorder.

The epidemic of petty crime continued during February. There were charges of drunkenness, creating a disturbance, insolence, 'using infamous expressions', absence from work, abusing a guard, idleness and disobedience. Sentences for these misdemeanors were generally light—about 25 lashes—but Thomas Church, charged with stealing peas and flour, was sentenced to 300 lashes and John Trace, whose crime was not giving evidence against Thomas Church, received 100 lashes.

Tench wrote of Manly   The gentleness and humanity of his disposition frequently displayed themselves; when our children, stimulated by wanton curiosity, used to flock around him, he never failed to fondle them, and if he were eating at the time constantly offered them the choicest part of his fare…His reserve, from want of confidence in us, continued gradually to wear away; he told us his name, and Manly gave place to Arabanoo. Bread he began to relish and tea he drank with avidity; strong liquors he would never taste, turning from them with disgust and abhorrence. Our dogs and cats had ceased to be objects of fear and were become his greatest pets and constant companions at table. One of our chief amusements, after the cloth was removed, was to make him repeat the names of things in his language, which he never hesitated to do with the utmost alacrity, correcting our pronunciation when erroneous.

Collins   At Rose Hill…two emus or cassowaries, who must have been feeding in the neighbourhood, ran through the little camp and were so intermingled with the people, who ran out of their tents at so strange an appearance, that it became dangerous to fire at them and they got clear off, though literally surrounded by a multitude of people and under the very muzzles of some of their muskets.

MARCH

Friday 6th

Collins   A convict belonging to the brickmaker's gang had strayed into the woods for the purpose of collecting sweet tea…it was supposed that the convict in his search after this article had fallen in with a party of natives, who had killed him. A few days after this accident, a party of the convicts, 16 in number, chiefly belonging to the brick-maker's gang, quitted the place of their employment and providing themselves with stakes, set off toward Botany Bay, with a determination to revenge upon whatever natives they should meet the treatment which one of their brethren had received at the close of the last month.

Near Botany Bay they fell in with the natives, but in a larger body than they expected or desired...they were driven in by the natives, who killed one man and wounded six others. Immediately on this being known in the settlement, an armed party was sent out with an officer, who found the body of the man that had been killed, stripped and lying in the path to Botany Bay. They also found a boy, who had likewise been stripped and left for dead by the natives. He was very much wounded and his left ear nearly cut off.

Saturday 7th

Tench The governor was justly incensed at what had happened and instituted the most rigorous scrutiny into the cause which had produced it. At first the convicts were unanimous in affirming that they were quietly picking sweet tea when they were without provocation assaulted by the natives, with whom they had no wish to quarrel. Some of them, however, more irresolute than the rest, at last disclosed the purpose for which the expedition had been undertaken, and the whole were ordered to be severely flogged. Arabanoo was present at the infliction of the punishment and was made to comprehend the cause and the necessity of it, but he displayed on the occasion symptoms of disgust and terror only.

Wednesday 18th

Private John Easty and Sergeant James Scott recorded the misdeeds and dishonour of their fellow marines. Easty wrote: 'A key was found broke in one of the locks at the public store house, for which Joseph Hunt, a marine, was confined.' Scott said he 'was confined on suspicion of robbing the public store'.

Thursday 19th

Scott Luke Haynes, private marine, with Richard Asky, was confined on the above suspicion (I being sergeant of the quarter guard this day). On the confinement of Haynes and Asky, Hunt informed me that he would discover everything he knew about the business, on which I acquainted Major Ross.

Friday 20th

Scott Joseph Hunt discovered on James Baker, Thomas Jones, James Brown and Richard Dukes, all to be concerned in robbing the store. On this, the three former was confined, Dukes, the latter, being at Rose Hill at this time.

Wednesday 25th

Scott The seven aforesaid marine prisoners was brought to trial. Joseph Hunt, marine, was admitted an evidence for the crown against the other six.

The stolen goods included 100 gallons of liquor, five hundredweight of flour, 16 pounds of butter, a bag of bread, and eight pounds of leaf tobacco.

Collins described the workings of the scam, and how it was unravelled:

> Having formed their party, seven in number, and sworn each other to secrecy and fidelity, they procured and altered keys to fit the different locks on the three doors of the provision store and it was agreed that whenever any one of the seven should be posted there as sentinel during the night, two or more of the gang, as they found it convenient, were to come during the hours in which they knew their associate would have the store under his charge, when by means of their keys and sheltered in the security which he afforded them...they should open a passage into the store, where they should remain shut up until they had procured as much liquor or provisions as they could take off. If the patrols visited the store while they chanced to be within its walls, the door was found locked and secure, the sentinel alert and vigilant on his post, and the store apparently safe.
>
> Fortunately for the settlement, on the night preceding the discovery one of the party intended to have availed himself of his situation as sentinel and to enter the store alone, purposing to plunder without the participation of his associates. But while he was standing with the key in the lock, he heard the patrol advancing.

The key had done its office, but as he knew that the lock would be examined by the corporal, in his fright and haste to turn it back again he mistook the way, and finding that he could not get the key out of the lock, he broke it and was compelled to leave the wards in it; the other part of the key he threw away...

It being supposed that the wards of the key might lead to a discovery of the perpetrator of this atrocious act, they were sent to a convict blacksmith [William Fraser], an ingenious workman through whose hands most of the work passed that was done in his line, who immediately knew them to belong to a soldier of the name of Hunt...who had some time back brought the key to this blacksmith to be altered. On this information Hunt was taken up, but offering to give some material information, he was admitted an evidence on the part of the Crown.

Nagle was on the way back from Cape Town in *Sirius* at the time of the hanging, but described the events in his journal. He explained that they 'had a key made by one of the blacksmiths, a convict, by the means of making stiff clay mortar and taking the key out of the door when opportunity served and having the mould of it'.

Friday 27th

Easty This day at 10 o'clock Luke Haynes, James Baker, James Brown, Richard Asky, Richard Dukes and Thomas Jones was executed between the two storehouses, when they all said that Joseph Hunt was the occasion of all their deaths as he was the first that began the said robbery, but he received a free pardon. There was hardly a marine present but what shed tears, officers and men.

∽

The constant record of both men and women being sentenced to the lash for a variety of offences continued. On 3 March, Collins sentenced Jane Fitzgerald to 25 lashes for disobedience. On the 5th Elizabeth Callyhorn was sentenced to 50 lashes for drunkenness, and two other women received 25 lashes for providing the liquor; on the same day Tamasin Allen and Mary Turner were sentenced to 50 lashes each for stealing six cabbages. On the 9th, Anthony Rope was sentenced to 25 lashes 'for neglecting to work where ordered', and four days later the judge-advocate ordered William Bond 25 lashes for 'neglecting his business as a baker at the hospital'. On Sunday the 15th, at Rose Hill,

George Bannister was sentenced to 50 lashes for stealing three pounds of flour, Peter Opley received 25 lashes for stealing bread, and Thomas Ebden was sentenced to 150 lashes for losing his trousers, shirts and shoes at cards. On the 16th Stephen Le Grove received 50 lashes for being absent from work; on the 18th Mary Marshall and Catherine Smith were sentenced to 50 lashes and 25 lashes for being in possession of soldiers' property; on the 30th Ann Martin was sentenced to 30 lashes for creating a disturbance, and John Hall received 50 lashes for selling shoes to a seaman.

APRIL

Wednesday 1st

Collins The governor thinking it probable that foreign ships might again visit this coast, and perhaps run into this harbour for the purpose of procuring refreshments, directed Mr Blackburn to survey a large bay on the north shore, contiguous to this cove, and a sufficient depth of water being found, his Excellency inserted in the port orders that all foreign ships coming into this harbour should anchor in this bay, which he named Neutral Bay.

Wednesday 15th

Scott I went with a party to cut grass tree for Lieutenant Johnston. Found three natives under a rock, viz. a man and two boys (of which one boy was dead). The governor being acquainted with it, ordered the man and boy to the hospital under care of the surgeon, they having the smallpox.

Tench Intelligence was brought that an Indian family lay sick in a neighbouring cove; the governor, attended by Arabanoo and a surgeon, went in a boat immediately to the spot. Here they found an old man stretched before a few lighted sticks, and a boy of nine or 10 years old pouring water on his head from a shell which he held in his hand; near them lay a female child dead and a little farther off, its unfortunate mother. The body of the woman shewed that famine, superadded to disease, had occasioned her death; eruptions covered the poor boy from head to foot and the old man was so reduced that he was with difficulty got into the boat. Their situation rendered them incapable of escape and they quietly submitted to be led away...

An uninhabited house, near the hospital, was allotted for their reception and a cradle prepared for each of them. By the encouragement of Arabanoo, who assured them of protection, and the soothing behaviour of our medical gentlemen, they became at once reconciled to us, and looked happy and grateful at the change of their situation. Sickness and hunger had, however, so much exhausted the old man that little hope was entertained of his recovery...

Bado, bado (water), was his cry, when brought to him he drank largely at intervals of it. He was equally importunate for fire, being seized with shivering fits, and one was kindled. Fish were produced to tempt him to eat, but he turned away his head with signs of loathing. Nanbaree (the boy), on the contrary, no sooner saw them than he leaped from his cradle and eagerly seizing them, began to cook them. A warm bath being prepared, they were immersed in it, and after being thoroughly cleansed they had clean shirts put on them and were again laid in bed.

The old man lived but a few hours. He bore the pangs of dissolution with patient composure, and though he was sensible to the last moment, expired almost without a groan. Nanbaree appeared quite unmoved at the event and surveyed the corpse of his father without emotion, simply exclaiming *boee* (dead). This surprised us, as the tenderness and anxiety of the old man about the boy had been very moving. Although barely able to raise his head, while so much strength was left to him he kept looking into his child's cradle, he patted him gently on the bosom and, with dying eyes, seemed to recommend him to our humanity and protection. Nanbaree was adopted by Mr White, surgeon-general of the settlement, and became henceforth one of his family...

Arabanoo's behaviour, during the whole of the transactions of this day, was so strongly marked by affection to his countryman, and by confidence in us, that the governor resolved to free him from all farther restraint and at once to trust to his generosity and the impression which our treatment of him might have made for his future residence among us; the fetter was accordingly taken off his leg...

How a disease, to which our former observations had led us to suppose them strangers, could at once have introduced itself, and have spread so widely, seemed inexplicable...Is it a disease indigenous to the country? Did the French ships under Monsieur de Pérouse introduce it? Let it be remembered that they had now been departed more than a year and we had never heard of its existence on board of them. Had it travelled across the continent from its western shore, where Dampier and other European voyagers had formerly landed? Was it introduced by Mr Cook? Did we give it birth here? No person among us had been afflicted with the disorder since we had quitted the Cape of Good Hope, 17 months before. It is true that our surgeons had brought out variolous matter in bottles, but to infer that it was produced from this cause were a supposition so wild as to be unworthy of consideration.

The 'variolous matter' was material from the pustules of patients with a mild form of smallpox, which was used to immunise people and was supposed to reduce the impact of the disease. This method was not replaced by vaccination with cowpox, which gives protection against the disease, until 1798. The variolous matter brought with the First Fleet would presumably have been collected in England at least two years before the outbreak among the Aboriginal people, and there is considerable doubt whether it would have retained its ability to cause infection for that length of time.

> **Collins** From the native who resided with us we understood that many families had been swept off by this scourge, and that others, to avoid it, had fled into the interior parts of the country. Whether it had ever appeared among them before could not be discovered, either from him or from the children; but it was certain that they gave it a name (*galgalla*), a circumstance that seemed to indicate a preacquaintance with it.

King, when he returned to Sydney in 1789, probably expressed the local viewpoint when he referred to it as 'this dreadful disorder, which, there is no doubt, is a distemper natural to the country'. In 1796, in summing up the events in the colony before the publication of his *Account*, Collins wrote: 'Notwithstanding the town of Sydney was at this time filled with children, many of whom visited the natives that were ill of this disorder, not one of them caught it, though a North American Indian, a sailor [Joseph Jeffries] belonging to captain Ball's vessel, the *Supply*, sickened of it and died.'

It is almost self-evident that smallpox must have been introduced by the settlers from England; the view formed by the colonists that it already existed among the Aboriginal people may be little more than wishful thinking. But it is remarkable that not one of the white settlers was affected by the disease. Unfortunately, Surgeon White's opinion on the matter is not known, as his manuscript had been sent to the publisher before the epidemic struck.

One possibility not canvassed by Tench is that the disease was spread through the Aboriginal population from northern Australia. Smallpox was prevalent in the East Indies in the eighteenth century, and it could have been introduced by Macassan fishermen who came down in fleets carrying several hundred men and frequently camped on shore.

Tuesday 21st

The *Sirius* was south of Tasmania, on the way home from Cape Town, with supplies for the settlement. When he left Port Jackson in October, Hunter, against Phillip's advice, had sailed east to take advantage of the powerful westerly winds and the ship had made good time, but on the return voyage, 'Three days had now elapsed', Hunter wrote, 'without a sight of the sun during the day, or a star during the night, from which we could exactly determine our latitude.'

Nagle   The captain thinking to give a wide berth to the five sunken rocks, we got nearer the land, and a gale coming on from the southward, till we were under a reefed forecourse in the night and so dark you could scarcely know the next man to you, the sea dying over us and the pumps going, though she did not leak and the hatches battened down, but the lookout forward cried out 'Land ahead'. We then had to wear ship and stand to the westward. In about an hour there was land ahead again. We then had just room to wear again. Though dark it was, we could then see the surf beating over the rocks, and appeared higher than our mastheads. We found now that we were embayed, and a heavy gale, and a heavy sea rolling in upon us, and nothing but high clifts of rock under our lee.

The captain ordered close reef topsails to be set and loosed the mainsail and set it. He said she must carry it or capsize, or carry away the masts, or go on the rocks. The men at the lee pumps were standing to their knees in water and every man in his station. If she had not had a spar deck upon her she could not [have] carried the sail without filling her gun deck, the sea flying over us under such a press of sail, standing on, expecting every moment the masts to go over the side, and I don't suppose there was a living soul on board that expected to see daylight.

Hunter As we knew not what bay or part of the coast we were upon, nor what dangerous ledges of rocks might be detached some distance from the shore and in our way, we had every moment reason to fear that the next might, by the ship striking, launch the whole of us into eternity. Our situation was such that not a man could have escaped to have told where the rest suffered. However, whatever might have been the private feelings of each individual, I never saw orders executed with more alacrity in any situation; every officer and man took his station for the lookout and, the ship being wore to the eastward, notwithstanding the strength of the gale, the close reefed fore and main top-sails were set over the reefed courses.

Fortunately at this instant the wind favoured us near two points, and the ship lay better up upon this tack than her course upon the other had promised; but still the weather was so thick, the sea so high, the gale so strong and so dead upon the shore, that little hope could be entertained of our weathering the land. We stood on to the eastward, and the ship, to my astonishment, as well as to that of every person on board, bore such a press of sail wonderfully...

I do not recollect to have heard of a more wonderful escape. Every thing which depended upon us, I believe, was done, but it would be the highest presumption and ingratitude to divine providence, were we to attribute our preservation wholly to our best endeavours; His interference in our favour was so very conspicuously manifested in various instances, in the course of that night, as I believe not to leave a shadow of doubt, even in the minds of the most profligate on board, of His immediate assistance.

Collins reported that the *Sirius* 'received considerable damage; the head of the ship, the figure of the Duke of Berwick, was torn from the cutwater and she was afterwards found to have been very much weakened'.

Saturday 25th

At the trial in March of the six men from Captain Campbell's company who were hanged for robbing the storehouse, a convict named Mary Turner had been suspected of giving false evidence and it was ordered that she should be detained. Campbell saw her at large in the town and sent Henry Brewer, the provost-marshal, to judge-advocate Collins to enquire why she was not being held in custody. Although Collins felt that she had lied at the trial, he thought it would be hard to make a convincing case and he was reluctant to proceed against her.

He replied to Campbell on the same day: 'I do not think, on mature consideration, that there would be sufficient proof to affect her either as an accessory at the late business or for perjury at the trial.' He invited Campbell to prosecute her if he wished.

Campbell took offence at this suggestion and wrote to Collins, telling him that he would refuse to sit as a member of the criminal court in future and advising Collins to 'keep copies of such letters as you may choose to write upon the occasion, as I assure you I shall of mine'.

Monday 27th

Campbell wrote to Ross, enclosing copies of his correspondence with Collins. Ross then called a meeting of the marines' officers. In a letter to Lord Sydney, Phillip wrote:

> The tenor of Major Ross's discourse appeared calculated to induce them to join Captain Campbell in declining the duty of the criminal courts, saying that he had told the governor that both he and the officers at large considered that service as what they had volunteered, not as a duty, that the governor's conduct in calling on Captain Campbell or on officers for that service was oppressive, and that he thought it hard officers should be obliged to sit as members of the criminal court, and oppressive to the highest degree.

✑

Collins The convicts, among other public works, were now employed in forming a convenient road on the west side from the hospital and landing-place to the storehouses, and in constructing a stable at Farm Cove, with some convenient out-houses for stock.

During April, Tench reported: 'Two more natives, one of them a young man and the other his sister, a girl of 14 years old, were brought in by the governor's boat in a most deplorable state of wretchedness from the smallpox.' (Hunter put the girl's age at 'about 10' and thought the man was her father.) The man died within a few days, but Tench wrote: 'The girl recovered and was received as an inmate with great kindness in the family of Mrs Johnson, the clergyman's wife. Her name was Booron, but from our mistake of pronunciation she acquired that of Abaroo, by which she was generally known.'

MAY

Wednesday 6th

Phillip asked Ross to obtain the opinion of each officer individually as to whether they considered themselves bound to sit on criminal courts. Ross reported Tench's reply: 'I had no knowledge of the Act of Parliament previous to my arrival in this country; from the moment I read it I looked on it as Captain Tench's duty to sit on criminal courts whenever ordered, and still look on it as such.' George Johnston, Creswell, Furzer, Poulden, John Johnstone, Shairp, Davey, Clark, Dawes, Long and Faddy all replied in similar fashion, as Phillip knew they would.

(Phillip had defused the issue for the moment. He wrote to Lord Sydney on 5 June, setting out the situation in full, but it was not until July 1791 that he received a reply from Sydney's successor. Lord Grenville advised that the attorney-general had expressed the view that officers serving in New South Wales were bound to perform the duty of a member of the criminal court when summoned and that they would be guilty of a misdemeanour if they refused. Lord Grenville added: 'The proceedings of Major Ross according to your representation appear to have been in many instances but ill-calculated to promote that good understanding so essentially necessary for securing the prosperity of the colony'.)

Friday 8th

Hunter A light air by northward in the night carried us by daylight in sight of the entrance of Port Jackson, and in the evening…we entered between the heads of the harbour and worked up to Sydney Cove, where we anchored before dark after an absence of 219 days, 51 of which we lay in Table Bay, Cape of Good Hope, so that, although during this voyage we had fairly gone round the world, we had only been 168 days in describing that circle.

Hunter had discovered that the use of the constant westerly winds—the roaring forties—on both legs of the voyage brought the colony much closer to its source of supply.

Collins The *Sirius* brought 127,000 [pounds] weight of flour for the settlement and a twelvemonth's provision for her ship's company;

but this supply was not very flattering, as the short space of four months at a full ration would exhaust it. It was, however, very welcome, and her return seemed to have gladdened every heart.

The *Sirius* had been built in 1780 for the East India Company. Her length was 142 feet, beam 32 feet. She carried 20 guns. King wrote:

> She was built in the river for an east country ship and in loading her, she took fire and was burnt down to her wales. The government wanting a roomy vessel to carry stores abroad in 1781, purchased her bottom, which was rebuilt with such stuff as, during the war, could be found. She went two voyages as the *Berwick* storeship and without any repairs she was reported, when the present expedition was thought of, as fit for the voyage to New Holland, when she was named the *Sirius*. Experience, however, evinced that she was altogether adequate to the service for which she was destined, and carried her crew safe through one of the most tremendous gales, on a lee shore, that the oldest seaman remembered.

Sirius is the brightest star in the sky and therefore well-known to sailors.

Bradley returned in the *Sirius* From the great number of dead natives found in every part of the harbour it appears that the smallpox had made dreadful havoc among them. We did not see a canoe or a native the whole way coming up the harbour and were told that scarce any had been seen lately, except laying dead in and about their miserable habitations, whence it appears that they are deserted by their companions as soon as the disorder comes out on them, and those who are attacked with this disorder left to shift for themselves. We judge this from their having been found not buried in every part of the harbour.

Hunter As soon as the ship was secured I went on shore to wait on the governor, whom I found in good health. He was sitting by the fire, drinking tea with a few friends, among whom I observed a native man of this country, who was decently clothed, and seemed to be as much at his ease at the tea table as any person there. He managed his cup and saucer as if he had been long accustomed to such entertainment.

Saturday 9th

Hunter The governor and his family did me the honour to dine on board, when I was also favoured with the company of Arabanoo, whom I thought a very good-natured, tractable fellow. He was about 30 years of age and tolerably well-looked.

Monday 18th

Scott wrote that Arabanoo 'died of the smallpox and was buried in the governor's garden'.

Fowell Arabanoo was at this time quite reconciled to this way of living...While he lay ill, he suffered himself to be bled and took all medicines that were offered him with a great deal of confidence. He was much regretted by everyone, as it was supposed he would have been of infinite service in reconciling the natives to us. He was a very good mimic and was very much attached to several particular people. When he was first taken, he had a voracious appetite, but as he found he got his meals regularly, that wore off. He was very fond of bread and vegetables.

Tench The character of Arabanoo, as far as we had developed it, was distinguished by a portion of gravity and steadiness...his countenance was thoughtful, but not animated; his fidelity and gratitude, particularly to his friend the governor, were constant and undeviating and deserve to be recorded. Although of a gentle and placable temper, we early discovered that he was impatient of indignity and allowed of no superiority on our part. He knew that he was in our power, but the independence of his mind never forsook him. If the slightest insult were offered to him, he would return it with interest...

By his death, the scheme which had invited his capture was utterly defeated. Of five natives who had been brought among us, three had perished from a cause which, though unavoidable, it was impossible to explain to a people who would condescend to enter into no intercourse with us. The same suspicious dread of our approach and the same scenes of vengeance acted on unfortunate stragglers continued to prevail.

Hunter   When we returned from our voyage, I went up to see what progress was made at...Rose Hill. It certainly very much exceeded my expectations; the quantity of ground prepared for receiving grain at the proper time was considerable, a number of huts were built, the gardens were in tolerable appearance and there was altogether every prospect, in due time, of a very extensive farm, and we knew that if there were people enough to labour it might be carried at least 20 miles to the westward and every foot of the ground apparently as good as that on which they were now at work; but we found here that although the land was tolerable, there would be great, and I think an insurmountable difficulty, in attempting an extensive farm, chiefly for want of water.

Collins   Of the native boy and girl who had been brought up in the last month, on their recovery from the smallpox, the latter was taken to live with the clergyman's wife and the boy with Mr White, the surgeon, to whom, for his attention during the cure, he seemed to be much attached.

JUNE

Tuesday 2nd

Bradley   Twenty canoes passed Sydney Cove going down the harbour; this was the first time any number of them had been seen together since the smallpox having been among them.

Tench   The anniversary of his Majesty's birthday was celebrated, as heretofore, at the government house, with loyal festivity. In the evening, the play of *The Recruiting Officer* was performed by a party of convicts, and honoured by the presence of his Excellency and the officers of the garrison...

Some of the actors acquitted themselves with great spirit and received the praises of the audience. A prologue and an epilogue, written by one of the performers, were also spoken on the occasion which, although not worth inserting here, contained some tolerable allusions to the situation of the parties and the novelty of a stage-representation in New South Wales.

Saturday 6th

Phillip went back to Broken Bay. Collins, who went on the expedition, said it was 'in the hope of being able, from the head of that harbour, to reach the mountains inland'. Others in the party were Hunter, Captain John Johnstone, White, Worgan, Newton Fowell and a large troop of marines. They crossed the harbour to Manly and walked to Broken Bay, sending the boats on to meet them at Pittwater.

Hunter   We left Port Jackson at six o'clock in the morning, just as the day was dawning and we arrived at the south branch of Broken Bay at three in the afternoon...In the course of the little excursions of one boat's crew this afternoon, a native woman was discovered concealing herself from our sight in the long grass, which was at this time very wet and I should have thought very uncomfortable to a poor naked creature. She had before the arrival of our boats at this beach been with some of her friends employed in fishing for their daily food, but were upon their approach alarmed, and they all made their escape except this poor young creature who had just recovered from the smallpox, was very weak, and unable from a swelling in one of her knees to get off to any distance...

She appeared to be about 17 or 18 years of age, had covered her naked body over with the wet grass, having no other means of hiding herself. She was very much frightened on our approaching her and shed many tears with piteous lamentations. We understood none of her expressions but felt much concern at the distress she seemed to suffer. We endeavoured all in our power to make her easy, and with the assistance of a few expressions which had been collected from poor Arabanoo whilst he was alive, we soothed her distress a little, and the people belonging to the boats were immediately ordered to bring some fire up, which we placed before her, pulled some grass, dried it by the fire and spread it round her to keep her warm, then shot some birds, such as hawks, crows, gulls and skinned them and laid them on the fire to broil, together with some fish of which she eat.

We then gave her water, of which she seemed to be much in want, for when the word *baado* was mentioned, which is their expression for water, she put her tongue out to show us how very dry her mouth was, and indeed from its colour and appearance, she had a considerable degree of fever on her. Before we retired to rest for the night, we saw her again, and got some firewood laid within her reach, with which she might in the course of the night recruit her fire. We also cut an extraordinary quantity of grass, dried it, covered her well and left her to her repose, which I conjecture from her situation was not very comfortable or refreshing.

Sunday 7th

Hunter We employed this day in going up the south branch, which the governor has named Pittwater. So much of the day was spent in this examination that when we returned down near to where we had passed the last night, it was thought too late to proceed farther. We therefore encamped on the same spot. Our tents etc were no sooner up than we went to visit our young female friend, whom we now found in a little bark hut upon the beach. This hut was the place in which she and her friends were enjoying themselves when the arrival of our boats alarmed them.

She was not now alone as before. She had with her a female child about two years old and as tiny a little creature of that age as I ever saw, but upon our approach, the night being cold and rainy and the child terrified exceedingly, she was laying with her elbows and knees on the ground covering the child from our sight with her body, probably to shelter it from the wet, but I rather think on account of its terrors.

On our speaking to her, she raised herself up and sit on the ground with her knees up to her chin and her heels under her, and was at that moment I think the most miserable spectacle in the human shape I ever beheld. The little infant could not be prevailed on to look up, it lay with its face upon the ground and its hand over its eyes. We supplied her as before with birds, fish and fuel to keep her fire in with. We pulled a quantity of grass to make her a comfortable bed and covered her little miserable hut so as to keep out the weather. She was now so reconciled to our frequent visits, seeing we had nothing in view but her comfort in them, that when she wanted *baado*, or *magra*, which signifies fish, she would ask for them, and when she did it was always supplied her.

Monday 8th

Hunter In the morning we visited her again. The child had now got so much the better of its fears that it would allow us to take hold of its hand. I perceived that, young as it was, it had lost the two first joints of the little finger of the left hand, the reason or meaning of

Illustration from the title page of Hunter's Historical Journal, *engraved in England from a sketch by Hunter. The officers on the expedition were Phillip, Collins, Hunter, Captain John Johnstone, Surgeons White and Worgan and Newton Fowell; it is not possible to identify them with any certainty.*

which we have not yet been able to learn. We left all the fish we had remaining and gave her a quantity of firewood and water within her reach, and took our leave. We embarked in the boats and sailed across the bay to the north branch.

The governor's party spent the Tuesday, Wednesday and Thursday exploring the various arms of Broken Bay, looking for the entrance to the river. On Friday the 12th, starting from a camp on Dangar Island (which they called Mullet Island) they worked their way westward and, Hunter wrote, 'were led into a branch which had not before now been discovered. We proceeded up this for a considerable distance, found good depth of water and every other other appearance of its being the opening of an extensive river. We continued to row up the whole of this day'.

Saturday 13th

Hunter We continued going up till the evening, when it was found impossible at this time to make any farther discovery, our provision

125

being nearly expended. We filled our water cask where we gave up further pursuit, and there although the tide was high the water was perfectly fresh. The general depth of this river was from three to seven fathoms and its breadth was from 100 to 300 fathoms.

They had discovered the main course of the river which Phillip named the Hawkesbury, after Sir Charles Jenkinson, Baron Hawkesbury, President of the Council of Trade in William Pitt's government.

Sunday 14th

Hunter   We returned down the river, and as the wind blew fresh and fair for us, we sailed down and in the afternoon arrived in the south branch or Pittwater, fixed our tents for the evening and caught some fish in order to lengthen out our provision. Our female friend had left this place.

Friday 19th

Collins   The *Sirius* had, in the gale of wind which she met with off Tasman's Head, sustained much more damage and was upon inspection found to have been weakened much more than was at first conjectured. This was the more unfortunate as, from the nature of our situation, many important services were yet to be rendered by her to the colony. It became, therefore, a matter of public concern to have her damages repaired.

Nagle   We took the ship down to Elbow Cove [Mosman Bay] about two miles from Sydney Cove on the north side, to refit the ship for sea service. We cut down timber and made a frame alongside the rocks and filled it up with rocks, then levelled with earth. The ship could lay alongside the wharf in five fathom water.

Collins   She could have been refitted with much ease at Sydney, but there was no doubt that the work necessary to be done to her would meet with fewer interruptions if the people who were engaged in it were removed from the connections which seamen generally form where there are women of a certain character and description.

Thursday 25th

In the magistrates' court before Collins and Hunter, Ann Fowles was charged (as Elizabeth Fowles) with 'stealing two pairs of shoes, two check shirts, one blue cross band silk handkerchief and some provisions'. She was found guilty and sentenced 'to be publicly flogged with 50 lashes for three successive Thursdays; to have her head shaved and to wear a canvas cap with the word *thief* on it'.

Friday 26th

Tench At this period I was unluckily invested with the command of the outpost at Rose Hill, which prevented me from being in the list of the discoverers of the Hawkesbury. Stimulated, however, by a desire of acquiring further knowledge of the country, on the 26th instant, accompanied by Mr Arndell, assistant surgeon of the settlement, Mr Lowes, surgeon's mate of the *Sirius*, two marines and a convict, I left the redoubt at daybreak, pointing our march to a hill, distant five miles in a westerly or inland direction...We continued to march all day through a country untrodden before by a European foot. Save that a melancholy crow now and then flew croaking overhead or a kangaroo was seen to bound at a distance, the picture of solitude was complete and undisturbed. At four o'clock in the afternoon we halted near a small pond of water where we took up our residence for the night, lighted a fire, and prepared to cook our supper; that was, to broil over a couple of ramrods a few slices of salt pork and a crow which we had shot.

Saturday 27th

Tench At daylight we renewed our peregrination and in an hour after we found ourselves on the banks of a river, nearly as broad as the Thames at Putney and apparently of great depth, the current running very slowly in a northerly direction. [Phillip later named this river after Evan Nepean.] Vast flocks of wild ducks were swimming in the stream, but after being once fired at, they grew so shy that we could not get near them a second time. Nothing is more certain than that the sound of a gun had never before been heard within many miles of this spot. We proceeded upwards, by a slow pace, through reeds, thickets and a thousand other obstacles which impeded our progress, over coarse sandy ground, which had been recently inundated, though full 40 feet above the present level of the river.

Traces of the natives appeared at every step, sometimes in their hunting huts, which consist of nothing more than a large piece of bark, bent in the middle and open at both ends, exactly resembling two cards set up to form an acute angle; sometimes in marks on trees which they had climbed, or in squirrel traps or, which surprised us more, from being new, in decoys for the purpose of ensnaring birds. These are formed of underwood and reeds, long and narrow, shaped like a mound raised over a grave, with a small aperture at one end for admission of the prey and a grate made of sticks at the other; the bird enters at the aperture, seeing before him the light of the grate between the bars of which he vainly endeavours to thrust himself, until taken. Most of these decoys were full of feathers, chiefly those of quails, which showed their utility. We also met with two old damaged canoes hauled up on the beach, which differed in no wise from those found on the sea coast.

Monday 29th

Phillip returned to Broken Bay. Hunter wrote:

> The same gentlemen who were on the former expedition were also on this, with the addition of five marines. On the whole our numbers amounted to about 40. The two boats were well armed and capable of making a powerful resistance, in case as we advanced up the river we should find the interior parts of the country well inhabited and the people of a hostile disposition.

The party again crossed to the north arm of the harbour and walked to Pittwater.

Tuesday 30th

Hunter We embarked in the boats, and as it was intended to reach as high up the river this day as possible, we passed Mullet Island and proceeded into the river. Before night we had advanced as far up as a point on which we rested a night last time we were here, and which was within three or four miles as high as we had advanced into this river. Here we rested for the night.

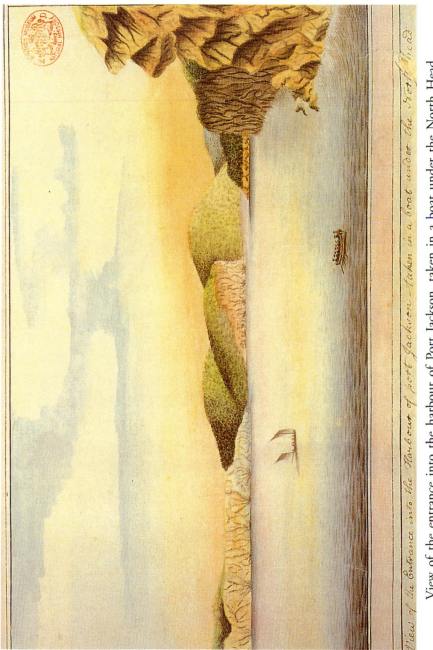

View of the entrance into the harbour of Port Jackson, taken in a boat under the North Head.
The boats are probably the yawl and longboat belonging to the Sirius. Port Jackson Painter, 1788.
Natural History Museum, London.

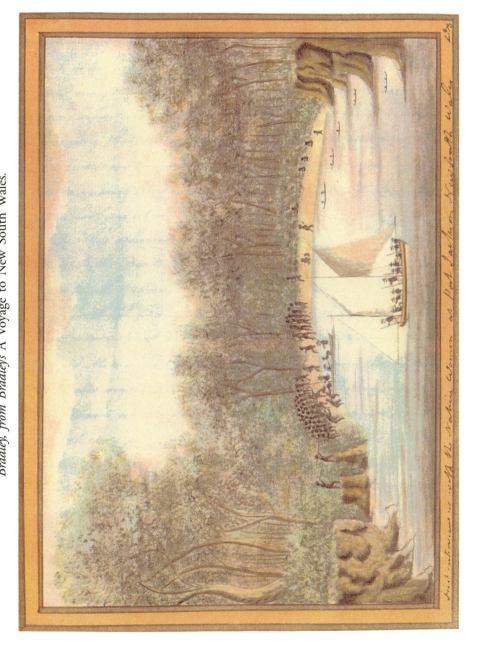

First interview with the Native women at Port Jackson, New South Wales (January 29 1788). The pinnace stands offshore while those in the longboat meet the Aboriginal women for the first time. Hunter wrote: 'They laughed immoderately, although trembling at the same time, through an idea of danger'. Watercolour by William Bradley, from Bradley's A Voyage to New South Wales.

A New South Wales native striking fish by moonlight while his wife paddles him along with a fire in the canoe ready to broil the fish as caught. *Port Jackson Painter, Natural History Museum, London.*

Cameragal, the chief of the most powerful tribe … He holds two fighting spears and a fizgig in one hand and two throwing sticks in the other. *Port Jackson Painter, Natural History Museum, London.*

George Raper's drawing and description of various implements and weapons. The 'throwing stick with which they dig for fern root' was a spear-thrower, known as a wigoon. Number '2' may have been used as a throwing stick, thrown end over end at small animals. Natural History Museum, London.

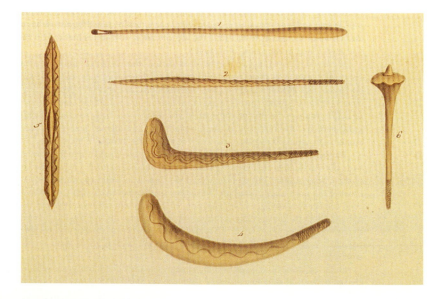

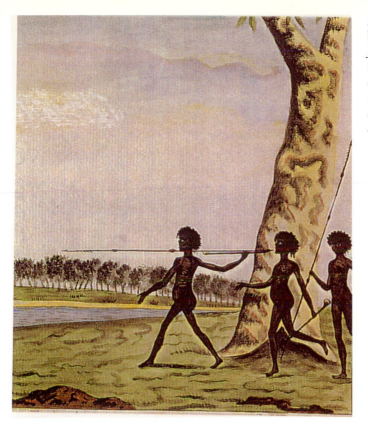

Detail from An attack by Natives, *by the Port Jackson Painter, showing the use of the* womera, *or throwing stick as it was called by the settlers. Natural History Museum, London.*

Detail from a watercolour by the Port Jackson Painter. White described the hatchet as made of 'very hard black pebble stone, rubbed down at one end to an edge; the handle is a stick of elastic wood, split, which being bent round the middle of the stone, and the extremities brought together, is strongly bound with slips of bark and holds the head very firmly.' The club, White wrote, 'is a stick of the natural growth … the root of which is cut round into a large knob; the end is made rough with notches, that it may be held more firmly in the hand'. Natural History Museum, London.

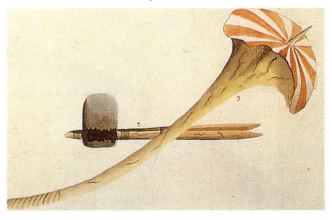

Sydney Cove, Port Jackson, 1788, *from Bradley's Voyage, showing the settlement's earliest buildings. This view also appears as an etching in Hunter's Historical Journal, dated 20th August, 1788; it may have been a copy done by Bradley and given to Hunter. The ships shown are not the Sirius or the Supply; the Golden Grove and the Fishburn were the only ships from the First Fleet remaining in Port Jackson in August 1788.*

His Majesty's Ship *Sirius* in Sydney Cove, 1789, *George Raper. It appears that she is moored just outside the cove. The building on the point is the observatory.* Sirius *came out with a 25-foot launch, a 27-foot yawl, a 16-foot cutter, two smaller cutters and 'a supply of boats disassembled, carried in cases'. The small boats may be, left to right, one of the smaller cutters, the yawl and the launch. Natural History Museum, London.*

19ᵗʰ March, 1790. View of the west side of Sydney Bay, Norfolk Island, showing the method by which the crew and provisions etc etc were saved from the wreck, George Raper. Collins wrote: 'Mr Keltie the master, Mr Brooks the boatswain and Mr Donovan, a midshipman of the Sirius ... ventured off to the end of the ship in one of the island boats through a very dangerous surf and brought on shore the end of a hawser, to which was slung the grating that saved the lives of the officers and people'. Natural History Museum, London.

7th September, 1790. Detail from a painting entitled, The governor making the best of his way to the boat after being wounded, with the spear sticking in his shoulder. *Port Jackson Painter, Natural History Museum, London.*

View of the east side of Sydney Cove, drawn by George Raper from the Sirius at anchor, probably early in 1790. The judge-advocate's house is the gabled building behind and just to the left of the flag; the next building to the left is the commissary's office. Two sawpits stand to the left of the boathouse. The largest of the three boats may be the boat described by Nagle in 1788 as 'pulling 16 oars, with shoulder of mutton sails, to go surveying', which was built at Sydney Cove. Natural History Museum, London.

A View of Governor Phillip's House ... *Port Jackson Painter, undated. The spire on the roof is a lightning conductor. Other details include the kitchen, joined to the main building by a covered walk, the original canvas house with its blue panels and, immediately to the right, the well mentioned by Collins and a privy. Natural History Museum, London.*

Go-mah. (Murry)

Gomah Murry, *Hunter's drawing of a king parrot, from his sketchbook. Hunter's illustrations were attractively presented, if not always strictly accurate as to colouring or proportion. National Library of Australia.*

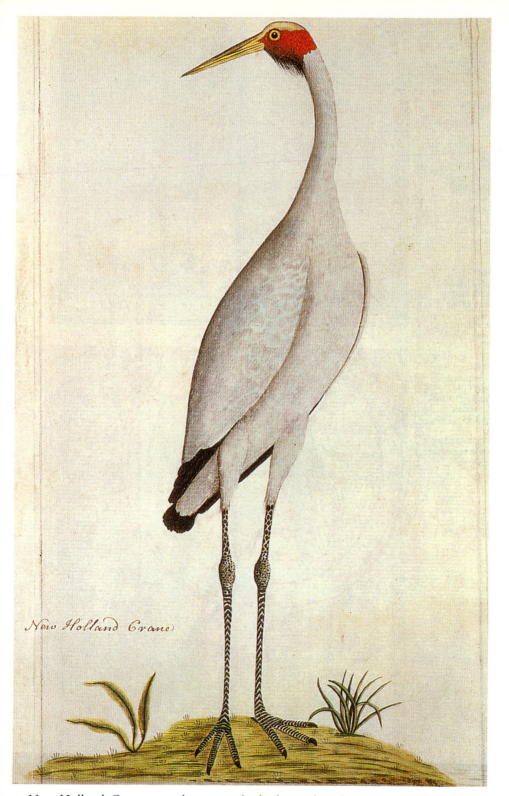

New Holland Crane, *now known as the brolga and no longer seen in the Sydney region. Port Jackson Painter, Natural History Museum, London.*

Method of climbing trees, *Port Jackson Painter.* Phillip wrote: 'In this manner do these people climb trees whose circumference is ten or fifteen feet or upwards, after an opossum or a squirrel, though they rise to a height of 60 or 80 feet before there is a single branch.' *Natural History Museum, London.*

A woman of New South Wales curing the headache; the blood which she takes from her own gums she supposes comes along the string from the part affected by the patient. This operation they call beeannee. *Port Jackson Painter, Natural History Museum, London.*

Detail from View of the Governor's House at Sydney, Port Jackson, 1791, *by William Bradley. The painting gives a rare view of convicts at work, pulling a cart across the jetty in front of Government House. Other activity includes a sentry on duty at the storehouse and, on the right, two Aboriginal children and an adult dancing for a pair of settlers. The drab colours reflect the drought conditions prevailing that summer. National Library of Australia.*

JULY

They explored various branches of the Hawkesbury as they worked their way westward, and on 4 July entered what is now known as the Grose River, west of Richmond.

Hunter We advanced up this branch about 13 or 14 miles before we put ashore for the night…in the woods, we frequently saw fires, and sometimes heard the natives. In the afternoon we saw a considerable number of people in the wood, with many fires in different places. We called to them in their own manner by frequently repeating the word *cowee*, which signifies 'come here'.

At last two men came to the waterside with much apparent familiarity and confidence. I thought from this circumstance that they had certainly seen us before, either at Botany Bay, Port Jackson or Broken Bay. They received a hatchet and a wild duck which had been just before shot from the boat and in return they threw into the boat a small coil of line, made of the hair of some animal, and also offered a spear, which was refused. The only argument against their having seen us before is that they are the first we have met with who appeared desirous of making a return for any presents they received…

The natives here appear to live chiefly on the roots which they dig from the ground, for these low banks appear to have been ploughed up as if a vast herd of swine had been living on them. We put ashore and examined those places which had been dug and found the wild yam in considerable quantity, but in general very small, not larger than a walnut. They appear to be in greatest plenty upon the banks of the river: farther back they are scarce. We frequently, in some of the reaches which we passed through this day, saw very near us the hills which we suppose we see from Port Jackson, and were called by the governor the Blue Mountains.

Sunday 12th

The governor's party had spent several days on their way back downstream towards Broken Bay. On this day, Hunter wrote: 'We struck our tents and sailed for Pittwater, where about noon we encamped upon a point pretty high up.' Phillip was still hoping to find Aboriginal people who they could bring to live in the settlement. Bradley was not in the governor's party, but he records that they 'met with a man, woman and child, the woman was the same they met with before in the south arm of Pittwater just recovering from the smallpox; she was now quite recovered of the disease but one of her legs was contracted. This family would have been taken by force but the wind not being fair the officer in the boat did not think it a proper opportunity.'

Monday 13th

Hunter By four o'clock in the afternoon arrived at the north part of Port Jackson; but we might as well have been 50 leagues off, for here we could have no communication either with the *Sirius* or the settlement, and no boat had been ordered to meet us. We went immediately to work and made a large fire, by which we lay all night, which happened to be very cold.

Tuesday 14th

Hunter The next day we crossed the hills, and came to the mouth of the northwest harbour [Middle Harbour] but could not find the means of crossing it...We found this morning a canoe on the beach with which we had no doubt of getting two men across the water, who could in a short time walk over to the cove where the *Sirius* lay [in Mosman Bay], but this prospect was disappointed by the first man who entered the canoe having overset her, and she immediately sunk, and he was obliged to swim ashore. After this we went to work and made a catamaran of the lightest wood we could find, but when finished and launched, it would not, although pretty large, bear the weight of one man.

It was now proposed to walk round the head of the north-west harbour, which would have been a good long journey for at least two days, and our provision was nearly expended. To this proposal I was under the necessity of objecting for want of shoes, the last march having torn all but the soles from my feet, and they were tied on with spun-yarn...when two of the people who were with us proposed swimming over the water [probably from Clontarf to The Spit] and to cross through the wood to the *Sirius*. The distance across was not more than two cables' length, or 400 yards. They immediately stripped and each had a dram. They tied up in a handkerchief a shirt, pair of trousers and pair of shoes each, which was rested upon their shoulders. Thus equipped they took the water, and landed on the other side in seven minutes, but one, having taken the cramp, was obliged to disengage himself from his bundle, which was of course lost. They set off through the wood and in an hour and a half arrived on board, the one with his shirt and trousers, the other perfectly naked. Upon their information, a boat was sent down and took us up after a pretty fatiguing walk.

Monday 20th

Petty crime and crushing punishment continued on a regular basis. In the magistrates' court, Thomas Kidner and Thomas Bryant were sentenced to 150 lashes for buying 'necessaries' from a marine. James Bird received 100 lashes for selling the fish he was employed to catch for the hospital. John Ryan was charged with being 'found on the other side of the hospital, contrary to an order to that purpose', and in defiance of notices placed on trees in the area to the effect that 'any person who was found nearer to the point than where these notices were stuck up would be punished, unless he gave a satisfactory account of his business'. Ryan pleaded that he could not read, but was found guilty and received 50 lashes.

Saturday 25th

Before Hunter and Collins, William Boggis was found guilty of stealing a shirt and sentenced 'to receive 100 lashes on his bare breach at Rose Hill, to work with an iron on his leg, and to wear a label with the word *thief* printed on it and made fast upon his clothing'. Carolina Laycock was involved in the theft and was sentenced 'to be publicly whipped with 50 lashes on her naked back'. John Ferguson was sentenced to 100 lashes for 'writing a scandalous and obscene paper'.

Tuesday 28th

John Cullyhorn, a former seaman aged about 33, had been convicted of stealing and sentenced to death in July 1782, the sentence later commuted to transportation for seven years, which had now expired. A petition was delivered to the judge-advocate signed by Cullyhorn and five other convicts, saying that the time for which they had been sentenced had expired and that they expected to receive rations in future without working.

Collins Notwithstanding little more than two years had elapsed since our departure from England, several convicts about this time signalled that the respective terms for which they had been transported had expired and claimed to be restored to the privileges of free men. Unfortunately, by some unaccountable oversight, the papers necessary to ascertain these particulars had been left by the masters of the transports with their owners in England, instead of being brought out and deposited in the colony...

It must be acknowledged that these people were most peculiarly and unpleasantly situated. Conscious in their own minds that the sentence of the law had been fulfilled upon them, it must have been truly distressing to their feelings to find that they could not be considered in any other light or received into any other situation than that in which alone they had been hitherto known in the settlement...The governor, however, terminated this business for the present by directing the judge-advocate to take the affidavits of such persons as would make oath that they had served the term prescribed by the law, and by recommending them to work for the public until some information was received from government on that head.

Bradley The parson and the native girl [Abaroo] went down the harbour to endeavour to have an interview with the natives. They met with a party of them, some of whom the girl said were her relations. She told them how well she was treated, that she had recovered by the care taken of her and that she was very happy, and used every persuasion to get one or more of them to return with her, but to no purpose.

❦

Collins The observatory which was erected on our first landing being found small and inconvenient, as well for the purpose of observing as for the residence of Lieutenant Dawes and the astronomical instruments, the stone-cutters began preparing stone to construct another, the materials for which were found in abundance upon the spot, the west point of the cove.

William Dawes, second lieutenant of marines, had skills in surveying, engineering and astronomy. He brought with him instruments from the Board of Longitude with which he was to observe a comet, not seen since 1661, which Dr Maskelyne, the Astronomer Royal, believed would be seen again in southern skies in 1789. Southwell wrote of Dawes:

To give you his character in a few words, he is a most amiable man, and though young, truly religious, without any appearance of formal sanctity... He has a great share of general knowledge, studious, yet ever cheerful, and the goodness of his disposition renders him esteemed and respected by all who know him.

AUGUST

Sunday 2nd

Bradley The surgeon-general and the native boy [Nanbaree] went about the harbour for the same purpose; they soon met with a party of the natives who knew the boy, but they could not prevail on any to come with them. The boy was much inclined to join the naked tribe.

Saturday 8th

Tench To repress the inroads of depredation and to secure to honest industry the reward of its labour had become a matter of the most serious consideration; hardly a night passed without the commission of robbery.

Collins The first attempt toward a police [force] in this settlement commenced... A convict of the name of Harris presented to the judge-advocate a proposal for establishing a night-watch, to be selected from among the convicts, with authority to secure all persons of that description who should be found straggling from the huts at improper hours.

It was to have been wished that a watch established for the preservation of public and private property had been formed of free people and that necessity had not compelled us, in selecting the first members of our little police, to appoint them from a body of men in whose eyes, it could not be denied, the property of individuals had never before been sacred. But there was not any choice.

Regulations were drawn up: the watch was 'authorised to patrol at all hours in the night and to visit such places as may be deemed necessary for the discovery of any felony, trespass, or misdemeanor and for the apprehending and securing for examination any person or persons'.

Members of the watch carried a short staff 'to distinguish them in the night and to denote their office in the colony'.

Saturday 15th

Sarah Bellamy, who in 1785 at the age of 15 had been sentenced to transportation for stealing a purse, was brought before Hunter and Collins. From her evidence, and that of Captain Meredith of the marines, James Keltie, master of the *Sirius*, and two members of the newly-formed night-watch, it emerged that on 1 August, Meredith, helped by Keltie, had tried to climb in through the window of Sarah Bellamy's hut. Meredith and Keltie were both drunk. Bellamy and a child who was also in the hut screamed in fear, and the noise attracted the night-watch.

In evidence, Keltie said he 'did not want to sleep with her, he only wished to sleep on the hearth stone if she would let him in'. He said he had tried to persuade Meredith to leave but Meredith had persisted and 'caught hold of her...and pulled her by the hair and beat her'. Sarah Bellamy said that, having given him his hat, which had fallen through the window, she told him she 'hoped he would go away. He had a woman at home of his own and how would he like it if she was to disturb her so?' Meredith allegedly shouted: 'I will have my revenge on you, I would no more mind killing you than I would flying in the air', and ordered her to be taken to the guard-house. She went quietly, telling Meredith that 'he was a gentleman and she but a poor prisoner, therefore she must go wherever he bade her, but she did not know what she had done, that he had come and disturbed her peace'.

Asked if she wished to make an accusation, she replied: 'No', but that she was 'determined not to put up with such unmerited treatment from Captain Meredith or anybody else'. The charge against her was dismissed.

Saturday 22nd

A child named Ann Maria Partridge, the daughter of Lieutenant Henry Ball, commander of the *Supply*, and the convict Sarah Partridge, was baptised. Sarah Partridge, aged about 25, had been charged with theft at the Old Bailey in 1784, with two companions. They had been acting suspiciously and a shop assistant was ordered to follow them. It was noted that they 'were very genteel ladies, they do not look like thieves' but they were followed to a brothel next to the Bear Tavern in Hart

Street, where the stolen goods were found. She was sentenced to death, commuted to transportation to America and sent from Newgate prison to the *Lady Penrhyn* in January 1787. Sarah Partridge does not appear in the colonial records before or after this date and it is likely that Ball kept her on board the *Supply*, victualled from his private stores.

Wednesday 26th

Ross wrote to Phillip, complaining that Phillip, on going to Rose Hill, had left orders with the judge-advocate which Ross, as lieutenant-governor, considered should have been left with him.

Thursday 27th

An acid correspondence between Phillip and Ross was concluded by Phillip:

> I have, sir, only to wish that the peace of the settlement may not be disturbed, and that you will be so good as to be a little more guarded in your expressions, for I am certain you will think on reflection that the answer you gave to the convict who came to tell you his time was expired—'Would to God my time was expired too'—was not calculated to make him satisfied with his situation.

SEPTEMBER

Friday 4th

Collins   In England, some dependence had been placed on fish as a resource for the settlement, but sufficient for general distribution had not hitherto been caught at any one time. On the fourth of this month the people belonging to the *Supply* had a very large haul; their seine was so full that had they hauled it ashore it must have burst; the ropes of it were therefore made fast on shore and the seine was suffered to lie until left dry by the tide. The fish were brought up to the settlement and distributed among the military and convicts.

Thursday 10th

A charge was made against Private Henry Wright that on 23 August he 'with force and arms at a certain place near Long Cove...violently and feloniously did make an assault, and her, the said Elizabeth Chapman, then and there feloniously did ravish, and carnally know'.

Elizabeth Chapman was eight years old. She appeared in the witness box, along with seven others, including her mother, who in evidence said that Wright 'had the character of doing such things with children'. Wright was sentenced to be hanged.

Saturday 12th

Collins The butter which had hitherto been served at six ounces per week to each man in the settlement being expended, the like quantity of sugar was directed to be issued in its stead. This was the first of the provisions brought from England which had wholly failed, and fortunately the failure was in an article which could be the best spared. It never had been very good and was not strictly speaking a necessary of life.

HMS *Guardian* of 44 guns, commanded by Lieutenant Edward Riou, sailed from England with relief supplies for the colony. According to Collins, she and the *Lady Juliana*, which had sailed in July, had on board 'two years provisions, viz. 295,344 pounds of flour, 149,856 pounds of beef and 303,632 pounds of pork for the settlement'. A 'List of goods sent by the *Guardian*' included 900 pairs of men's shoes, 600 pairs of women's shoes, 1500 pounds of soleing leather, 3000 fish hooks, 310 fishing lines, 16 chests of medicines, 15 casks of wine, 15 barrels of gunpowder, 2250 pounds of portable soup, as well as sailcloth, bedding, thread, needles and material for making clothes, medicine and supplies of brown sugar, sago, rice, currants, cinnamon, nutmeg, cloves, barley and tamarinds.

Wednesday 16th

Phillip signed a pardon for the convicted rapist and child molester, Henry Wright. 'Some favourable circumstances have been represented to me in his behalf', he wrote, 'inducing me to extend grace and mercy unto him, and to grant him a pardon for his said crime, on condition of his residing during the term of his natural life on the Island of Norfolk.'

> **Collins** This was an offence that did not seem to require an immediate example; the chastity of the female part of the settlement had never been so rigid as to drive men to so desperate an act, and it was believed that beside the wretch in question there was not in the colony a man of any description who would have attempted it.

No further explanation was given as to why Phillip saw fit to grant a pardon. It may have been because of representations from Wright's fellow marines and perhaps the fragment of a clue exists in a crossed-out entry in Easty's journal of 10 September, the day of Wright's conviction: 'This night I was confined for being drunk upon my post.'

In any case, the governor's mercy was misplaced; at Norfolk Island in July 1791 Ralph Clark recorded that Wright was made to 'run the gauntlet through all the men and women...for attempting to deflower a girl about 10 years of age'.

Wednesday 30th

> **Bradley** Captain Hunter returned from Botany Bay, having surveyed the bay and taken an eye sketch of the branches, all except that to the north-west, which they only traced a few miles. They met but few natives; those were all friendly. In some of the caves, skeletons of some and loose bones of others were found, who had no doubt died of the smallpox by their bodies not having been removed.

Tench, who was with Hunter's party, wrote scathingly of Cook's assessment of the area:

> So complete an opportunity of forming a judgment enables me to speak decisively of a place which has often engaged conversation and excited reflection...We are unanimously of [the] opinion that had not the nautical part of Mr Cook's description, in which we include the latitude and longitude of the bay, been so accurately laid down, there would exist the utmost reason to believe that those who have described the contiguous country had never seen it. On the sides of the harbour, a line of sea coast more than 30 miles long, we did not find 200 acres which could be cultivated.

OCTOBER

Monday 5th

Scott A craft of about 20 tons burden, the first of the sort that has been built here, was launched, called the *Prince of Wales*.

Collins From the quantity of wood used in her construction she appeared to be a mere bed of timber, and when launched was named by the convicts, with an happiness that is sometimes visible in the allusions of the lower order of people, *The Rose Hill Packet*.

Collins added a footnote:

She was afterwards generally known by the name of *The Lump*, a word more strictly applying to her size and construction.

Thursday 8th

From Chatham Barracks, in Kent, Elizabeth Macarthur wrote to her mother of her 'husband's exchange into a Corps destined for New South Wales, from which we have every reasonable expectation of reaping the most material advantages...By the last accounts from Port Jackson— where the new settlement is established—we learn that the wheat which had been sown flourished in a manner nearly incredible and that the settlers are making rapid progress in building, so that by the time our Corps arrives everything will be made comfortable for their reception.'

Collins Our enemies the rats, who worked unseen and attacked us where we were most vulnerable, being again observed in numbers about the provision store, the commissary caused the provisions to be moved out of one store into another, for alas at this period they could be all contained in one. These pernicious vermin were found to be very numerous, and the damage they had done much greater than the state of our stores would admit. Eight casks of flour were at one time found wholly destroyed. From the store, such as escaped the hunger of the different dogs that were turned loose upon them flew to the gardens of individuals, where they rioted upon the Indian corn that was growing and did considerable mischief.

NOVEMBER

Sunday 1st

Collins This month opened with a serious but prudent and necessary alteration in our provisions. The ration which had hitherto been issued was, on the first of the month, reduced to two-thirds of every species, spirits excepted, which continued as usual. This measure was calculated to guard against accidents, and the necessity of it was obvious to everyone, from the great uncertainty as to the time when a supply might arrive from England, and from the losses which had been and still were occasioned by rats in the provision store.

The governor, whose humanity was at all times conspicuous, directed that no alteration should be made in the ration to be issued to the women. They were already upon two-thirds of the man's allowance, and many of them either had children who could very well have eaten their own and part of the mother's ration, or they had children at the breast, and although they did not labour, yet their appetites were never so delicate as to have found the full ration too much, had it been issued to them. The like reduction was enforced afloat as well as on shore, the ships' companies of the *Sirius* and *Supply* being put on two-thirds of the allowance usually issued to the king's ships.

Saturday 7th

Following an order given to the night-watch that anyone other than officers found 'out of their quarters, especially in the female camp' should be taken to the guard-house, Private William Roberts was taken into custody and delivered to the guard by the watchman, the convict Thomas Oldfield, who said that 'he had found him after hours in the women's camp and had therefore made a prisoner of him'.

Sunday 8th

Collins wrote to Phillip On Sunday last I received a message from Major Ross, by the adjutant, informing me 'that one of the convict watchmen having, the night before, taken up and confined in the guardhouse a soldier belonging to the detachment under his command who was not committing any unlawful act, he considered it as an insult offered to the Corps'.

Phillip asked Ross to discuss the incident with him and Ross replied that he would not come until the following day and that he would bring two of his officers with him. Phillip, realising that he would be hard-pressed to find more than two officers to do his bidding, advised Ross that he would place no restrictions on the number of officers attending; he could bring them all if he wished. Ross's bluff had been called again; he backed down and sent a message that he did not wish to pursue the matter. But Phillip had to compromise; an addendum was added to the night-watch regulations to the effect that night-watchmen were 'not in future to stop any soldier unless he is found in a riot or committing any unlawful act'.

Saturday 21st

James Ruse, who described himself as 'bred a husbandman, near Launcester in Cornwall', was settled on two acres at Rose Hill.

> **Tench** James Ruse, convict, was cast for seven years at Bodmin assizes, in August 1782; he lay five years in prison and on board the *Dunkirk* hulk at Plymouth and then was sent to this country. When his term of punishment expired, in August 1789, he claimed his freedom and was permitted by the governor, on promising to settle in the country, to take...an uncleared piece of ground, with an assurance that if he would cultivate it, it should not be taken from him. Some assistance was given him to fell the timber, and he accordingly began.

Collins wrote that Phillip:

> caused two acres of ground to be cleared of the timber which stood on them and a small hut to be built for him. This man had been bred to the business of a farmer and during his residence in this country had shown a strong inclination to be industrious and to return to honest habits and pursuits. Rewarding him, therefore, was but holding out encouragement to such good dispositions.
>
> The governor had, however, another object in view beside a wish to hold him up as a deserving character; he was desirous of trying, by this means, in what time an industrious active man, with certain assistance, would be enabled to support himself in this country as a settler and for that purpose, in addition to what

he caused to be done for him at first, he furnished him with the tools and implements of husbandry necessary for cultivating his ground, with a proportion of grain to sow it, and a small quantity of livestock to begin with.

In the criminal court, Ann Davis was charged with stealing shirts, handkerchiefs, waistcoats, caps and a long list of other clothes and goods from the hut where Mary Marshall and Robert Sidaway lived. The stolen goods were found in Davis's possession and she was found guilty and sentenced to be hanged. When she claimed she was pregnant, Collins organised a jury of 'twelve of the discreetest women among the convicts, all of whom had been mothers of children'. Tench, who was a member of the court, wrote that following the examination the forewoman, 'a grave personage between 60 and 70 years old', announced to the court, 'Gentlemen, she is as much with child as I am'.

Monday 23rd

Ann Davis was hanged. Nagle wrote: 'When brought to the gallows, leading her by two women, she was so much intoxicated in liquor that she could not stand without holding her up. It was dreadful to see her going to eternity out of this word in such a senseless, shocking manner.' She was the first woman to be hanged in the colony.

It was a cloudy day with some rain. The temperature was in the high seventies and the wind mainly from the south. Bradley wrote: 'Governor Phillip, judging it necessary that a native should be taken by force...I was ordered on this service, having the master, two petty officers and a boat's crew with me in one of the governor's boats.'

Newton Fowell   On their landing in the lower part of the harbour two men came on the beach, some fish was shown them and they immediately came to the boat for them, when they were immediately seized and carried off in less than a minute. As soon as the boat left the beach the whole place was covered with them, all armed, but the boat being out of their reach, no mischief was done...Two men were appointed to take care of them and an iron ring with a rope fast to it was made fast round one of each of their legs.

Tench   Nanbaree and Abaroo welcomed them on shore, calling them immediately by their names, Bennelong and Colbee. But they seemed little disposed to receive the congratulations, or repose confidence in the assurances of their friends. The same scenes of awkward wonder and impatient constraint which had attended the introduction of Arabanoo, succeeded. Bennelong we judged to be about 26 years old, of good stature and stoutly made, with a bold intrepid countenance which bespoke defiance and revenge. Colbee was perhaps near 30, of a less sullen aspect than his comrade, considerably shorter, and not so robustly framed, though better fitted for purposes of activity. They had both evidently had the smallpox, indeed Colbee's face was very thickly imprinted with the marks of it. Positive orders were issued by the governor to treat them indulgently and guard them strictly.

✑

Collins   During the month of November a brick house was begun on the east side of the cove for the judge-advocate. The huts which were got up on our first landing were slight and temporary, every shower of rain washed a portion of the clay from between the interstices of the cabbage-tree of which they were constructed, their covering was never tight, their size was necessarily small and inconvenient, and although we had not hitherto been so fortunate as to discover limestone anywhere near the settlement, yet to occupy a brick house put together with mortar formed of the clay of the country and covered with tiles, became, in point of comparative comfort and convenience, an object of some importance.

DECEMBER

Sunday 6th

The Reverend Richard Johnson   Rose at three o'clock. At four took boat for Rose Hill, arrived there about eight, performed divine service in the hospital. Preached from Matthew iii.12. The weather very hot, my spirits much depressed and the more so on seeing such inattention among the people. After service, I visited some of their huts; found great murmuring amongst them. Several sick, owing to the shortness of provisions, the heat of the weather and the hardness of their labour. Oh, that these hardships may bring them to think and repent of their past folly. Returned home to Sydney much fatigued about seven o'clock in the evening.

Friday 11th

The *Guardian*, carrying supplies for the colony, left the Cape of Good Hope on the last leg of her voyage to New South Wales. At the Cape she had taken on board livestock for the settlement and 'a garden which had been prepared under the immediate direction of Sir Joseph Banks and in which there were near 150 of the finest fruit trees, several of them bearing fruit'.

Saturday 12th

Colbee escaped. Hunter wrote:

> When it was pretty dark, their keepers were sitting within the door of their house, eating their supper; Bennelong was within also and employed in the same manner. Colbee was at the door, sitting just on the outside, and had with him something for his supper, which he pretended to be employed about. The end of his rope was in the hand of his keeper. While they in the inside were thus amused, Colbee drew the splice of his rope from the shackle and in a moment was over the paling of the yard and out of sight. An immediate search was made for him, but without effect; we saw him no more, however we heard afterwards that he joined his friends again and will no doubt be careful how he confides hereafter in us. His friends would certainly be something surprised to see him so well clothed, for he carried off his whole wardrobe. I suppose it would cost him some trouble to get the shackle from his leg, which was riveted on.

Tench Had those appointed to watch them been a moment later, his companion would have contrived to accompany him. But Bennelong, though haughty, knew how to temporise. He quickly threw off all reserve and pretended, nay, at particular moments, perhaps felt satisfaction in his new state. Unlike poor Arabanoo, he became at once fond of our viands, and would drink the strongest liquors, not simply without reluctance, but with eager marks of delight and enjoyment. He was the only native we ever knew who immediately shewed a fondness for spirits—Colbee would not at first touch them. Nor was the effect of wine or brandy upon him more perceptible than an equal quantity would have produced upon one of us, although fermented liquor was new to him.

In his eating, he was alike compliant. When a turtle was shown to Arabanoo, he would not allow it to be a fish, and could not be induced to eat of it. Bennelong also denied it to be a fish, but no common councilman in Europe could do more justice than he did to a very fine one that the *Supply* had brought from Lord Howe Island, and which was served up at the governor's table on Christmas Day. His powers of mind were certainly far above mediocrity. He acquired knowledge, both of our manners and language, faster than his predecessor had done. He willingly communicated information, sang, danced and capered, told us all the customs of his country and all the details of his family economy.

Love and war seemed his favourite pursuits, in both of which he had suffered severely. His head was disfigured by several scars; a spear had passed through his arm and another through his leg; half of one of his thumbs was carried away and the mark of a wound appeared on the back of his hand. The cause and attendant circumstances of all these disasters, except one, he related to us. 'But the wound on the back of your hand, Bennelong, how did you get that?' He laughed, and owned that it was received in carrying off a lady of another tribe by force. 'I was dragging her away: she cried aloud, and stuck her teeth in me.' 'And what did you do then?' 'I knocked her down, and beat her till she was insensible, and covered with blood...'

Whenever he recounted his battles...the most violent exclamations of rage and vengeance against his competitors in arms, those of the tribe called Cameragal, in particular, would burst from him. And he never failed at such times to solicit the governor to accompany him, with a body of soldiers, in order that he might exterminate this hated name.

Wednesday 23rd

Philip Schaeffer, a widower with a daughter, Elizabeth, aged about 10, was aboard the *Guardian*, 12 days after she left the Cape of Good Hope bound for Port Jackson. Born in Germany, Schaeffer had served in the Hessian Corps, a German unit which fought on the British side in the American War of Independence. He had then gone to live in England, and in 1789 was appointed one of the superintendents of convicts in New South Wales, at an annual salary of £40. In a letter to Evan Nepean, Schaeffer wrote: 'On the 23rd December 1789 the ship came upon a great island of ice...Captain Riou put two boats out in order to investigate it. These two boats were forced to make haste to return to the ship and be hoisted on board on account of a strong wind. It rained and the weather closed in. An hour later the ship ran on to the same ice and was helpless, lost her rudder and sprang a leak. The master inspected her closely and declared her lost.'

Collins wrote later:

> She received so much injury that Lieutenant Riou was compelled, in order to save her from instantly sinking, to throw overboard the greatest part of her valuable cargo both on the public and private account. The stock was all killed (seven horses, 16 cows, two bulls, a number of sheep, goats and two deer), the garden destroyed, and the ship herself saved only by the interposition of providence and the admirable conduct of the commander.

The value of goods jettisoned was put at £70,000, but still it was assumed that the ship would sink. The lifeboats were lowered and the crew, except for 20 men who volunteered to try to save her, took to the boats in heavy seas. The boatswain of the *Guardian*, John Williams, wrote:

> After the boats left us we had two chances—either to pump or sink. We could just get into the sail room. We got up a new forecourse and stuck it full of oakum and rags and put in under the ship's bottom, this called 'fothering the ship'. We found some benefit of it, for pumping and bailing we gained on her; that gave us a little hope of saving our lives.

ↄℊ

Collins At Rose Hill, where as yet there was not any night-watch established, petty thefts and depradations were frequently committed, particularly on the wheat as it ripened. The bakehouse also was robbed of a quantity of flour by a person unknown. These offences were generally attributed to the reduction which had taken place in the ration of provisions...

Mr Dodd, the superintendent of that settlement, a few days before Christmas cut and sent down a cabbage which weighed 26 pounds. The other vegetable productions of his garden, which was by no means a rich mould, were plentiful and luxuriant.

The 1789 harvest at Rose Hill produced about 200 bushels of wheat and small amounts of barley, oats, maize and flax. The governor's farm at Sydney (Farm Cove) produced 25 bushels of barley.

ↄℊ

145

In 1789 a London newspaper, the *Morning Herald*, made light of the colony's prospects: 'The settlement we are making at Botany or rather Jackson's Bay reminds us of the origin of the Roman Empire, which sprang out of a nest of robbers...The thief colony may hereafter become a great empire, whose nobles will probably, like those of the nobles of Rome and other empires, boast of their blood.' (Many a true word is spoken in jest.)

The nest of robbers was more secure than it had been a year before. They were becoming familiar with the surrounding countryside and had established a promising farming area at Rose Hill. But hard times lay ahead, and little progress had been made in reconciling the Aboriginal people 'to live amongst us and to teach them the advantages they will reap from cultivating the land'.

The Europeans had learned, perhaps, from Arabanoo, something of the Aboriginal character, and that reconciliation was going to be a complex process. Tench wrote:

> His fidelity and gratitude, particularly to his friend the governor, were constant and undeviating, and deserve to be recorded. Although of a gentle and placable temper, we early discovered that he was impatient of indignity and allowed of no superiority on our part. He knew that he was in our power, but the independence of his mind never forsook him. If the slightest insult were offered to him, he would return it with interest.

The death of Arabanoo had been a setback. Newton Fowell wrote in May: 'He was much regretted by everyone, as it was supposed he would have been of infinite service in reconciling the natives to us.' In November, Hunter wrote: 'The two children mentioned formerly [Nanbaree and Abaroo] and who were very happy amongst us, were yet too young to be of use in reconciling the natives to us.'

The need to communicate was urgent. Bennelong was captured because, Hunter said: 'The governor was desirous of having a man or two in our possession, to whom we might teach enough of our language without the danger of losing any part of their own, to render them useful to their countrymen.'

1790
Shipwreck, Starvation and the Second Fleet

28 February   John Irving became the first convict to be emancipated.

6 March   Two companies of marines and more than 200 convicts sailed for Norfolk Island to reduce pressure on the supplies at Sydney Cove.

19 March   The *Sirius* wrecked on the reef at Norfolk Island.

27 March   Weekly ration reduced to four pounds of flour, two and a half pounds of pork and one and a half pounds of rice. Working hours were reduced.

12 April   William Lane sentenced to 2000 lashes for stealing bread.

15 April   Phillip requested permission to return to England 'for a twelvemonth'.

17 April   The *Supply* sailed for Batavia to obtain provisions.

3 May   Bennelong escaped from the settlement.

3 June   The *Lady Juliana* arrived, carrying provisions and convicts.

20 June   The storeship *Justinian* arrived, 'laden entirely with provisions'.

26 June   The *Surprize* arrived, with convicts and the first detachment of the NSW Corps.

23 July   A return showed 316 convicts in employment at Sydney Cove, with 413 'under medical treatment'.

23 July   A midshipman and two marines were drowned in Sydney Harbour when their boat was destroyed by a whale.

6 August   The number of sick reduced to 220, with 89 deaths recorded since 27 June.

7 September   Governor Phillip was speared at Manly.

8 October   Bennelong returned to the settlement with his 'wife', Barangaroo, and dined at Government House.

9 December   John Macentire, Governor Phillip's gamekeeper, was speared near Botany Bay.

14 December   Watkin Tench led an expedition of revenge for the spearing of Macentire.

27 December   A temperature of 109 degrees Fahrenheit was recorded.

JANUARY

Wednesday 20th

Tench Our impatience of news from Europe strongly marked the commencement of the year. We had now been two years in the country, and 32 months from England, in which long period no supplies, except what had been procured at the Cape of Good Hope by the *Sirius*, had reached us. From intelligence of our friends and connections we had been entirely cut off, no communication whatever having passed with our native country since the 13th of May, 1787, the day of our departure from Portsmouth.

Famine besides was approaching with gigantic strides and gloom and dejection overspread every countenance. Men abandoned themselves to the most desponding reflections and adopted the most extravagant conjectures. Still we were on the tiptoe of expectation; if thunder broke at a distance or a fowling-piece of louder than ordinary report resounded in the woods, 'A gun from a ship,' was echoed on every side, and nothing but hurry and agitation prevailed. For 18 months after we had landed in the country, a party of marines used to go weekly to Botany Bay, to see whether any vessel, ignorant of our removal to Port Jackson, might be arrived there. But a better plan was now devised, on the suggestion of Captain Hunter.

Hunter That every assistance necessary for strangers might be at hand, I offered, with a few men from the *Sirius*, to go down to the South Head of the harbour, there to build a lookout house and erect a flagstaff upon the height which might be seen from the sea, and also communicate information of ships in the offing to the governor at Sydney Cove. The governor approved of my proposal. I went down with six men and was accompanied by Mr White and Mr Worgan, the surgeons of the settlement and *Sirius*. We erected a flagstaff and lived in a tent for 10 days, in which time we completed a tolerably good house.

Tench Here on the summit of the hill every morning from daylight until the sun sunk did we sweep the horizon in hope of seeing a sail. At every fleeting speck which arose from the bosom of the sea, the heart bounded and the telescope was lifted to the eye. If a ship appeared here, we knew she must be bound to us, for on the shores of this vast ocean (the largest in the world) we were the only community which possessed the art of navigation and languished for intercourse with civilised society. To say that we were disappointed and shocked would very inadequately describe our sensations. But the misery and horror of such a situation cannot be imparted, even by those who have suffered under it.

Collins This little establishment was of such importance that our walks were daily directed to a spot whence it could be seen, thus fondly indulging the delusion that the very circumstance of looking out for a sail would bring one into view.

❧

Collins A sufficient quantity of fish having been taken one night in this month to admit the serving of two pounds to each man, woman and child belonging to the detachment, the governor directed that a boat should in future be employed three times in the week to fish for the public, and that the whole quantity caught should be issued at the above rate to every person in turn.

FEBRUARY

Monday 1st

In a letter to Lord Sydney, Phillip described the tense, unsatisfactory state of the marine detachment The strength of the detachment consists of only 18 officers, one of whom is on duty at Norfolk Island, and a second has never done any duty since he was appointed by Major Ross; of the 16 remaining for the duty of this settlement, five have been put under arrest by the commandant and are only doing duty till a general court-martial can be assembled... a sixth officer is suspended in consequence of a representation made by the corps of his unofficerlike behaviour...a seventh is suspended by his commandant for unofficerlike behaviour...and both adjutant and quartermaster of the detachment have been equally under his displeasure...

Your Lordship will excuse my having entered on this detail; it will point out the necessity of some change being made, or an additional force being sent out, and it will prevent my troubling your lordship further on this subject.

Wednesday 3rd

Bradley The governor and Bennelong visited the lookout post. Bennelong, being now well reconciled, generally accompanies the governor in little excursions. He threw a spear on the South Head against a strong wind 98 yards, which was considerably farther than I ever noticed before. In their return to Sydney Cove they saw some women on a point of land near Rose Bay to which they rowed, throwed them a jacket and several other things. Among this party was a woman whom Bennelong was very fond of (Barangaroo) and with whom he had much conversation. He wanted her to come to the boat, telling her that he was fast by the leg and could not get to them.

Saturday 13th

Phillip wrote to Lord Sydney As the land for several miles to the southward and 20 miles to the westward of Rose Hill, that is to the banks of the Nepean, is as fine land for tillage as most in England... I propose that tract of land for those settlers which may be sent out, and though they will be placed at some distance from each other... they will have nothing to apprehend from the natives, who avoid those parts we most frequent and always retire at the sight of two or three people who are armed.

As the labour of clearing the ground of timber will be great, I think each settler should not have less than 20 men on his farm, which I suppose to be from 500 to 1000 acres; it will be necessary to give that number of convicts to those settlers who come out and to support them for two years from the public stores; in that time, if they are any ways industrious—and I do not think they will be able to do it in less time—at the expiration of the two years, they may return half the convicts they have been allowed, and would want no further assistance from government.

Sunday 14th

Bradley The *Sirius* was ordered to be got ready for sea, it being judged that the state of the colony with respect to provisions was such as made it necessary that she should be sent for supplies to relieve it and China was determined on as a proper place for that purpose.

Monday 15th

Ralph Clark's journal resumes   Went up the harbour in my boat
and went into Lane Cove where I was yesterday to see Dourrawan
and Tirriwan, the two natives that I exchanged the hatchet with yesterday for their two spears...I asked them if they would give me the
children for my hat, which they seemed to wish most for, but they
would not on any account part with their children, which I liked
them for.

   The governor has often asked me, as the natives seemed not so
much afraid of me as they are of everybody else, to take one of them
and bring them in. Yesterday and today I might with great ease, and
without running any danger, have taken these two men, but, as I
told Ellis when he asked me if I did not intend to take them, I told
him that it would be very ungenerous to take them, for after they
had placed such confidence in us, that I could not think of doing it.

Clark had apparently settled his differences with the irascible Robert
Ross; the entry for the day concludes: 'Went and drinked tea with
Major Ross and Captain Campbell.'

Wednesday 17th

Clark   About four o'clock this afternoon, Major Ross came over to
the guard room to me, where, after a little conversation on different subjects, he put the following questions to me: viz. 'How I should
like to go to Norfolk Island?' I made him for answer, 'Not at all.'
He then said: 'I am going.' I said: 'It is impossible.' He said that it
was very true and that there was two of the companies to go with
him. 'If so I shall be very happy to go with you or Captain Campbell.'
He said that he was much obliged to me and should be very happy
for me to go with him. He said that he would not take Captain
Campbell's companies with him. He should leave him to take the
command and care of the remainder of the detachment that would
be left behind.

Thursday 18th

Clark   After I was relieved from guard I went down to my island to
look at my garden and found that some boat had landed since I
had been there last and taken away the greatest part of a fine bed

of onions. It is impossible for anybody to attempt to raise any garden stuff for, before it comes to perfection, they will steal it. I thought that having a garden on an island it would be more secure, but I find that they even get at it. My corn comes well as corn can do. I have that they will be so good as to let that remain, but I am much afraid that they will not.

Saturday 20th

Clark   Rainy weather. Begun writing a letter to my beloved to send by the *Sirius* after she has landed us at Norfolk Island, but I hope the arrival of some ships with provisions for us will prevent our going there.

Sunday 21st

Clark   Fine weather. Soon after breakfast I went out in my boat down to my island to see my garden and found that some person had been there again and have taken away all my potatoes. Whoever they are, I wish that they were in hell for their kindness. Returned to dinner at Major Ross's.

Monday 22nd

The *Guardian* arrived back at the Cape of Good Hope. The boatswain, John Williams, wrote: 'Sometimes our upper deck scuppers was under water outside, and the ship laying like a log on the water, and the sea breaking over her as if she was a rock in the sea.' In a subsequent letter to Nepean, Philip Schaeffer said: 'It was very cold and my poor innocent child did not know what to do for fear of death at any moment, and you may guess how I felt to see a child in such a state...we reached the Cape of Good Hope after a voyage of nine weeks of suffering on the sea and the sadness and toil were beyond description.'

One of the five boats which left the *Guardian* was picked up by a French ship and taken into the Cape. The others were lost. The small amount of supplies saved in the *Guardian* was eventually taken on by other ships calling at the Cape en route for Sydney Cove.

Friday 26th

Clark   Went on shore at a fig tree, of which we eat a great many all of us in the boat, they being ripe, but before we got home they all gave us the grips.

Hunter   I received an order to prepare the *Sirius* for sea and to embark the lieutenant-governor, with one company of marines and the officers, baggage, and also 186 convicts; in all 221 persons, with such a proportion of the remaining provisions and other stores as the settlement at that time could furnish, and I was directed to land them upon Norfolk Island. Lieutenant Ball, commander of his Majesty's armed tender *Supply* was ordered under my command, and he also embarked a company of marines and 20 convicts.

Sunday 28th

Clark   After breakfast, I went down to my island to gather my Indian corn, but found the greatest part already gathered...Some boat must have landed yesterday or the day before and taken the corn away. In the place of my having about six bushels of corn, I have not now got above a bushel. They have stole about 1500 cobs of corn.

Clark also recorded the first emancipation of a convict: 'By the General Order of this day I find that the governor has remitted the remainder of the sentence of transportation on John Irving.' Aged about 30, Irving was the first convict to be emancipated. He had been sentenced to transportation in 1784 for stealing a silver cup but, apparently trained as a surgeon, he had proved his worth on the voyage out from England. Clark wrote: 'I am very glad that Irving goes with us for I think [he is] the best surgeon amongst them.'

∽

Daniel Southwell, aged 21 when he sailed from England in the *Sirius* as a midshipman, had passed examinations which qualified him for a lieutenancy and he was promoted when the mate of the *Sirius* was invalided home to England from Rio de Janeiro. Southwell kept an intermittent journal covering the voyage and first two years at the settlement. He also wrote frequently to his mother and an uncle, the Reverend Weeden Butler, whose son was a young seaman on the *Prince of Wales*. The journal and 16 of Southwell's letters are held by the British Museum and were published in 1893 in *Historical Records of New South Wales*.

At the end of February 1790 Southwell was sent by Hunter to do service in the lookout post at South Head, instead of going to Norfolk Island in his ship as he would have expected. He wrote to his uncle:

> As my wish was to see what was to be seen while abroad, and several of the young men had seen Norfolk Island, I waited on Captain Hunter to apply for one who was willing to stay in my room, and observed that 'twas a particular service (for 'tis a hazardous business landing so many people and provisions in a tremendous surf) and that as being a mate (of which there are only three) it was rather a matter of surprise.
>
> He took this (I spoke it with some appearance of dissatisfaction) as I meant he should, viz. that it had rather the appearance of undervaluing my intended services, but he soon relieved me by giving me such reasons for the governor's choice as occasioned me to acknowledge myself honoured by it, and indeed the attention he pays to me while here and approbation of my conduct seem fully to warrant what was said.

MARCH

Monday 1st

Collins A reduction in the allowance of spirits took place. The half pint *per diem* which had hitherto been issued to each man who was entitled to receive it was to be discontinued and only the half of that allowance served. Thus was the gradual decrease in our stores followed by a diminution of our daily comforts and necessaries.

Clark All of us going to Norfolk Island (Major Ross excepted) dined with the governor today... Sold my boat to Davey for 10 guineas, which is four less that what I gave for her and I think she is well sold. In part of payment I am to have a large sow, which is what I want, for I have not got such a thing.

Clark also wrote that an order was given that no one was to 'kill, sell or otherwise dispose of any livestock until further orders'. This was done to preserve supplies, but an exception was made for those about to leave for Norfolk Island, who might not be able to take their live-stock with them.

Collins The mention of future regulations in this order instantly begat an opinion among the convicts that on the departure of the ships all the livestock in the colony would be called in, or that the owners would be deprived of the benefits which might result from the possession of it. Under colour, therefore, of its belonging to those who were exempted in the late order, nearly all the stock in the settlement was in the course of a few nights destroyed, a wound being thereby given to the independence of the colony that could not easily be salved, and whose injurious effects time and much attention alone could remove.

Major Ross listed the dozen marines who wished to stay on in the colony after their three-year tour of duty. Captain Tench wished to serve a further term 'as a soldier', as did Lieutenant Dawes and Sergeant William Baker. Private Isaac Tarr wished to remain as a settler. Lieutenant Shairp and Privates James Kirby and Thomas Tynan said they could not decide whether to remain as settlers or as soldiers until they heard what terms the Government would offer to settlers. Privates John Colethread, Thomas Bramwell, Patrick Connell, James Angell and Thomas Jackson said they wished to remain as settlers, provided due encouragement was given. Some 230 said they wanted to return to England.

Thursday 4th

George Johnston, the son of Captain-Lieutenant George Johnston and Esther Abrahams, was baptised. Abrahams, aged 21, had been transported for stealing 'two cards of lace' and had arrived in the colony with a one-year-old daughter. Johnston, Abrahams and her two children were all about to embark for Norfolk Island.

Clark Sent all my stock on board, consisting of two sows, one cock and six hens. I have left my house in the care of Sergeant Chapman with liberty to live in it until my return, if ever I should want it. At 12 o'clock all of us that are going to Norfolk met at Major Ross's house and went with him to the governor's to take our leave of him, after which I went on board to see my things put to right and order my servant to put what things I may want in the passage to be nearest at hand in my cabin...

The bill which I had from Davey I have left it with Captain Campbell to purchase me some tea and sugar and some soap from the first ships that may arrive. Captain Campbell has been very kind. He asked me if I wanted anything that he had, he would let me have it. I told him I was much obliged to him. He said I know that you have not much tea. I have put up a caddy for you with Major Ross's. He also gave me half a dozen pairs of stocking, which I want very much. The servility and friendship that Captain Campbell has shown to me I am afraid I never will have it in my power to make him a sufficient acknowledgement for. His attention has been more like a father than a friend. His and Major Ross's friendship to me is what I call real and sincere.

Saturday 6th

Clark Fine moderate weather, little wind. About six o'clock got under way, a great swell setting into the harbour. Just as we came abreast of the outer South Head it fell calm and the swell was setting us fast to leeward on the North Head which, had not a puff of wind filled the sails, we should have been drove on shore on the North Head, and everybody on board thought of no other but that we should. If we had, the ship would have been in pieces in a few minutes from the great sea that was breaking on the rocks and the most of us on board would have been lost, but by great good fortune the puff of wind shoved us clear out of the harbour as it did the *Supply*. When we had got out a little from under the land we soon got a fresh breeze from the southward, which is a fair wind. I have been very sick all day, seasick, as was everybody in the ship for a few hours after we got out of the harbour.

Collins Much room was made everywhere by the numbers who had embarked (in all 281 persons); the military quarters had a deserted aspect and the whole settlement appeared as if famine had already thinned it of half its numbers. The little society that was in the place was broken up and every man seemed left to brood in solitary silence over the dreary prospect before him.

Friday 19th

The *Sirius* had arrived at Norfolk Island the previous Saturday, the 13th, and most of the passengers—the convicts and marines—had gone ashore. Clark wrote: 'Got on shore about half after two, not without getting my feet wet. I never landed in such a bad place in my life; at the best of times it is a very bad landing for there is always a great swell round the island.'

The remaining passengers, including Major Ross, went ashore on 14 and 15 March. Clark wrote:

> I think Captain Hunter might have been more civil in sending Major Ross on shore than in the manner he did, for I think that had Major Ross been a convict he could [not] have been treated worse than he was today by Captain Hunter, in the manner he was shoved out of the ship by him, into a boat loaded full with cots, hammocks, hogs, pigs, geese, turkeys, fowls etc, so much that he had not room for his feet.

Hunter was anxious to get everything ashore as soon as possible, for on 15 March he wrote: 'These people were no sooner on shore than the wind shifted to the eastward and the weather became hazy and blew strong, so that I had no prospect of being able to land any part of the provisions.'

By 19 March, the weather had improved. Hunter wrote: 'I steered in for Sydney Bay and as we drew near I observed the *Supply* lying to in the bay, and the signal upon the shore was flying that longboats, or any other boats, might land without any danger from the surf.'

Jacob Nagle, Newton Fowell and William Bradley were also on board the *Sirius*, with King, Major Ross and Ralph Clark watching from the shore.

Nagle Having a fine pleasant day, with a light breeze off shore, all the seamen that could muster hooks and lines was catching groupers, not thinking of any danger. At 12 o'clock, when thinking of going to dinner, Captain Ball of the *Supply* brig hailed us and informed Captain Hunter that we were too close in, the swell of the surf having hold of us, though it did not break. Captain Ball, being at a distance outside of us, perceived it sooner than we did.

Hunter There is a reef of sunken rocks which lies off the west point of the bay and which (as the wind freshened and the sea rose) broke a considerable way out. The *Supply*, having drawn ahead, could not weather this reef. On this she tacked and, as we drew near, I plainly perceived that we settled so fast to leeward that we should not be able to weather it, so, after standing as near as was safe, we put the ship in stays; she came up almost head to wind, but the wind just at that critical moment baffled her, and she fell off again.

Nothing could now be done but to wear her round in as little room as possible, which was done, and the wind hauled upon the other tack, with every sail set as before; but still perceiving that the ship settled into the bay and that she shoaled the water, some hands were placed by one of the bower anchors, in five fathoms water. The helm was again put down and she had now some additional after-sail, which I had no doubt would ensure her coming about. She came up almost head to wind, and there hung some time, but by her sails being all a-back, had fresh stern way; the anchor was there-fore cut away and all the haulyards, sheets and tacks let go, but before the cable could be brought to check her, she struck upon a reef of coral rocks which lies parallel to the shore, and in a few strokes was bulged.

Nagle We opened the main hatch and sounded the well, found four foot [of] water in her hold. We were then about three-quarters of a mile from the shore and as the rocks cut her bottom the bal-last and pig ballast fell out and the heavy surf rolling aboard of us still drove her further in.

Bradley The ship by the heavy surf which broke over her was thrown well in upon the reef; it being impossible to hold an idea of getting her off again, everybody was employed getting provisions as it could be got at on the gun deck and securing it there. Mr Ball came as near the ship in his boat as he could, to ask if the *Supply* could be of any use; Captain Hunter told him 'No', that the *Sirius* was gone and desired him to take care of the *Supply*.

King From noon until four o'clock, every person was employed in getting a hawser from the ship, and fastening it to a tree on the shore. A heart was fixed on the hawser as a traveller and a grating was slung to it, fastened to a small hawser, one end of which was on shore and the other end on board. At five o'clock, the surgeon's mate came on shore by the grating, being hauled through a very great surf: he brought me a note from Captain Hunter, desiring to know if I thought it would be safe for the sailors to abide by the wreck all night.

The wind was now at south and the weather had a very threaten-ing appearance, and as the surf had risen considerably I thought there was the utmost danger of the ship's parting at the flowing tide, the consequence of which must have been the destruction of every person on board. I therefore made a signal for the wreck to be quitted and by the time it grew dark the captain and most of the sailors were on shore, being dragged through a very heavy surf; many of them received violent blows from the rocks over which they were dragged.

Captain Hunter and Mr Waterhouse were got on shore together and just as they got footing on the reef the captain was so much exhausted that he had nearly quitted his hold. The first and second lieutenant, with some of the sailors, remained on board all night.

Fowell As she lay with her broadside on shore she made a very good breakwater and boats came very easy under our lee and loaded with bread and flour which was the principal things to be saved as salt water would entirely ruin them...

It is unnecessary to say that all people met with a loss, though some were much luckier than others in saving most [of] their things. The officers who landed in Cascade Bay lost the greatest part of their clothes and all their stock. My loss was not very much as I saved above half my clothes but they are all very much stained with a blue clay that is found on the reef which the surf must have washed into my chest.

Hunter wrote later Providence was kind to us. We had for several days the weather fine and the surf uncommonly smooth for this place, for although there was a continual surf breaking upon the ship and all the way between her and the shore, yet it was considered here as uncommonly smooth. Each of those fine days we got on shore from 20 to 30 casks of provisions, with various other articles of both public and private property; such articles as would swim were entrusted to the chance of being thrown on shore by the surf... taking the whole together, we saved more provisions than we could have reasonably expected.

Ralph Clark's journal contains a list of the items which he lost in the wreck of the *Sirius*, including a uniform coat worth £2 10s, 13 pairs of breeches, 13 pairs of stockings, 23 shirts, a mattress, a pair of steel mounted pistols worth £4 4s, a tin tea kettle and 'all my books', valued at £10 10s, the total value lost put at £47 18s 8d. Included among the books he lost was probably his diary from March 1788 to February 1790. It is likely that Jacob Nagle also lost his diary in the wreck.

George Raper, born in London in 1769, entered the navy in 1783, joined the *Sirius* in 1786 as able seaman and was made a midshipman in 1787 when he was 18 years old. In *The Art of the First Fleet*, the art historian Bernard Smith says: 'As a midshipman he became Hunter's and Bradley's pupil in nautical matters, which included...surveying, reducing and copying charts and making views.'

From 1789 he began to sign and date his work. Most of his early paintings are of birds and flowers; however he soon started to produce illustrations which form a record of some of the events of the expedition. Raper may have lost some paintings in the wreck of the *Sirius*, but he was apparently able to save his painting case; a number of maps and views of the island, including two paintings of the wreck of the *Sirius*, are dated 1790; he returned to the mainland in February 1791.

Tuesday 23rd

At Sydney Cove, Mary and the Reverend Richard Johnson's daughter was baptised. Johnson wrote later to his friend Henry Fricker: 'As to my family, we are in a thriving way. Mrs J. has had a second child—the first was a boy, but stillborn—the latter is a girl, a sweet babe about five weeks old...Have given it the name of Milbah Maria—Milbah [is] a name amongst the natives.'

Wednesday 24th

The *Supply* left Norfolk Island to return to Sydney Cove. King was on board *Supply*, but Hunter and most of the crew of the *Sirius* remained on the island.

Saturday 27th

Collins   The long-expected signal not having been displayed, it became necessary to put the colony upon a still shorter ration of provisions. It was a painful but a necessary duty. The governor directed that the provisions should in future be served daily, for which purpose the store was to be opened from one to three in the afternoon. The ration for the week was to consist of four pounds of flour, two pounds and a half of pork, and one pound and a half of rice, and these were to be issued to every person in the settlement without distinction; but as the public labour must naturally be affected by this reduction, the working hours were in future to be from sunrise, with a small interval for breakfast, until one o'clock. The afternoons were to be allowed the people to receive their provisions and work in their gardens.

Collins   The weather had been very wet during this month; torrents of rain again laid every place under water; many little habitations which had withstood the inundations of the last month now suffered considerably; several chimneys fell in, but this was owing, perhaps, as much to their being built by job or task-work, (which the workmen hurried over in general to get a day or two to themselves) as to the heavy rains.

APRIL

Friday 2nd

The Reverend Richard Johnson   Set off for Rose Hill this morning about five o'clock; arrived there at nine. Performed divine service. Returned home to Sydney about eight o'clock in the evening. A very unpleasant day altogether. And though I have been to Rose Hill from time to time for now two years, I have no place provided for myself, neither a room, a table, nor a stool, and no place of worship. In short, no attention seems to be paid to these things, though I have so frequently desired it. God help me to bear with such treatment in a becoming manner.

Monday 5th

Tench   News was brought that the flag on the South Head was hoisted. Less emotion was created by the news than might be expected. Everyone coldly said to his neighbour: 'The *Sirius* and *Supply* are returned from Norfolk Island'...The governor, however, determined to go down the harbour, and I begged permission to accompany him. Having turned a point about half way down, we were surprised to see a boat, which was known to belong to the *Supply*, rowing towards us. On nearer approach, I saw Captain Ball make an extraordinary motion with his hand, which too plainly indicated that something disastrous had happened, and I could not help turning to the governor, near whom I sat, and saying, 'Sir, prepare yourself for bad news'.

A few minutes changed doubt into certainty, and to our unspeakable consternation we learned that the *Sirius* had been wrecked on Norfolk Island on the 19th of March. Happily, however, Captain

Hunter and every other person belonging to her were saved. Dismay was painted on every countenance when the tidings were proclaimed at Sydney. The most distracting apprehensions were entertained; all hopes were now concentred in the little *Supply*.

King In the evening, all the military and staff were assembled at the government house, when his Excellency laid before every one present the situation of the colony...

Every person's opinion was asked respecting how robbing gardens could be prevented and what was the best mode that could be adopted for procuring fish to make a saving of the salt provisions, when it was determined to call in all private boats and to employ them fishing for the public; that an officer was to superintend the fishing; that the gamekeepers were to kill kangaroo for the public and that the following ration should commence on the 12th of this month; two pounds and a half of flour, two pounds of pork and two pounds of rice for seven men for one day, at which ration there will be pork until the 26th August, rice until the 13th September and flour until the 19th of December.

The *Supply* is also to be sent to Batavia for provisions and her commander is ordered to take a ship up to bring a further supply. I am to go on board the above vessel and to make the best of my way to England with Governor Phillip's dispatches.

Philip Gidley King, the son of Utricia Gidley and Philip King, a draper from a small market town in Cornwall, was born in April 1758 and was sent to the naval school at Yarmouth at the age of seven. At 12, he joined the navy as captain's servant in HMS *Swallow*, and became a midshipman three years later. He served in the East Indies, saw action in American waters during the War of Independence, and was commissioned as second lieutenant in HMS *Renown* on Christmas Day in 1778. Soon after, he was transferred to HMS *Ariadne*, captained by Arthur Phillip.

Aged 30 when he arrived in Botany Bay, King had 18 years' experience in the navy and was regarded as loyal, diligent and reliable—one of the navy's 'most promising young men'. Later, a fellow-traveller on a second voyage to New South Wales described him as 'a pleasant companion, because full of information, having travelled and read a good deal'.

King had spent only four weeks at Sydney Cove when he was sent as commandant to Norfolk Island on 14 February 1788. He did not return to Port Jackson until 5 April 1790, and 12 days later he sailed for England. However, his journals, now held by the Mitchell Library, provide a detailed record of the arrival of the First Fleet and the first few weeks of the settlement, and a review of the state of the colony two years later, during his brief stay en route for England.

King's journal covered the period from the end of 1786, when he joined *Sirius*, which was being fitted out for the voyage, until April 1790, when he left Norfolk Island. An entry in January 1789 reads, 'The 8th ushered a male child into the world, and as he was the first born on the island, he was baptised by the name of Norfolk.' King was the father. The mother was Ann Inett, aged about 33, who had been sentenced to death in Worcester in 1786 for stealing clothing worth £1 0s 6d. She was reprieved to seven years' transportation, and came out in the *Lady Penrhyn*. She was one of six women, chosen for their good behaviour on the voyage to Botany Bay, who were included in the party that settled Norfolk Island in February 1788. Ann Inett had come back to Sydney Cove with King in the *Supply*, but did not to return to England with him.

Philip Gidley King, *from* The Voyage of
Governor Phillip to Botany Bay. *Artist unknown.*

Friday 9th

The Reverend Richard Johnson wrote to Henry Fricker 'Tis now about two years and three months since we first arrived at this distant country; all this while, we have been as it were buried alive, never having an opportunity of hearing from our friends...We have been anxiously looking out for a fleet for a long time, but hitherto none has appeared, and 'tis now generally conjectured that the fleet expected is either lost or taken by some enemy.

Our hopes now are almost vanished and every one begins to think our situation not a little alarming...

Have a native girl under my care. Have had her now about 11 months...Have taken some pains with Abaroo (about 15 years old) to instruct her in reading and have no reason to complain of her improvement; she can likewise begin to speak a little English and is useful in several things about our little hut. Have taught her the Lord's Prayer etc and as she comes better to understand may endeavour to instruct her respecting a supreme being etc...I long to hear from you—much more to see you, but when or whether ever this will be, God only knows.

A letter written by a convict on this day was later reprinted in the *Gazetteer*:

> To give a just description of the hardships that the meanest of us endure, and the anxieties suffered by the rest, is more than I can pretend to. In all the Crusoe-like adventures I ever read or heard of, I do not recollect anything like it, for though you may be told of the quantity of salt meat that is allowed us, its quality in boiling does not make it above half as much, besides other inconveniences I cannot now mention and which I think make so many of the children very unhealthy. On the same account, I believe few of the sick would recover if it was not for the kindness of the Reverend Mr Johnson, whose assistance out of his own stores makes him the physician both of soul and body.

King described a visit to Rose Hill with Phillip We left Sydney Cove at eight in the morning and arrived at Rose Hill before noon. About two miles below this settlement the harbour becomes quite narrow, being not more than 10 or 12 yards across, and the banks are about six feet high. Here the country has the appearance of a park. In rowing up this branch, we saw a flock of about 30 kangaroos or *paderong*, but they were only visible during their leaps, as the very long grass hid them from our view. We landed about half a mile from the settlement and walked up to it.

This settlement is on an elevated ground, which joins to a fine crescent, as regular as if formed by art; it is probable that this crescent and the regular slopes which surround the settlement have been formed by very heavy rains. The soil is loam, sand, and clay; the trees are not so large here as lower down the harbour, but the large roots lying on the ground render it difficult to clear. A fine stream of fresh water runs into the head of the harbour, which in the winter and when heavy rains fall sometimes rises seven or eight feet and becomes a rapid torrent. A redoubt is constructed here, in which are very good barracks for officers and soldiers; there is likewise a storehouse.

On the opposite side of the brook there is a farmhouse, where a servant of Governor Phillip's [Henry Dodd] resides, who is charged with the superintendence of the convicts and the cultivation of the ground, to which charge he is very equal and is of the greatest service to the governor, as he has no other free person whatever to overlook any piece of work carrying on by the convicts.

Near to this farmhouse there is a very good barn and a granary. The convicts' houses form a line at some distance, in front of the barracks, with very good gardens before and behind each house. Indeed, the whole, joined to the pleasantness of the situation, makes it a beautiful landscape.

Monday 12th

In the criminal court, James Williams and William Lane were charged with stealing 13 pounds of biscuit valued at six shillings and sixpence from the government store. Williams was found 'guilty of stealing under twelve pence' and sentenced to 500 lashes. Lane said that he saw a lock broken open and took the biscuit because he was so hungry. He was found guilty and was sentenced to receive 2000 lashes.

On the same day William Parr was charged with stealing a pumpkin valued at sixpence from another convict; like Lane he admitted to the theft, saying it was caused by hunger. His sentence was 500 lashes.

Wednesday 14th

Phillip delivered orders to Lieutenant Henry Lidgbird Ball, who was to be in command of *Supply* on the journey to Batavia:

> You will immediately on your arrival wait on the governor-general or commander-in-chief of that settlement and request that you may be permitted to purchase such a quantity of flour for the use of this settlement as the vessel under your command can stow...and you are at the same time to request that the governor and council will permit a ship to bring provisions to this colony, the immediate necessity of which (from the storeships not having arrived) you will explain...The species and quantity of provisions wanted is flour 200,000 pounds, beef 80,000 pounds, pork 60,000 pounds and rice 70,000 pounds. You will draw bills on the Lords Commissioners of His Majesty's Treasury for what you purchase for the use of this settlement, and taking care that they are accompanied by proper vouchers that the same was bought at the market price.

Daniel Southwell, doing duty at the lookout at South Head, wrote a letter to his uncle, the Reverend Weeden Butler:

> I early and late look with anxious eyes toward the sea and at times, when the day was fast setting and the shadows of the evening stretched out, have been deceived with some fantastic little cloud, which, as it has condensed or expanded by such a light, for a little time has deceived impatient imagination into a momentary idea that it was a vessel altering her sail or position while steering in for the haven.

In a letter published later in *The Oracle*, an officer who has not been identified wrote:

> I am a stranger to sickness, and find that neither heat, cold, wet or dry affect my constitution in any shape whatever...It is true our present allowance is a short one; two pounds of pork (which was cured four years ago, and shrinks to nothing if boiled), two pounds-and-an-half of flour, a pound of rice and a pint of peas per week is what we live upon...to help us out, we use every means to get fish, and sometimes with good success, which is an incredible relief. On the fishing service, the officers, civil and military, take it in turns every night to go out for the whole night in the fishing-boats, and the military, besides, keep a guard at

Botany Bay and carry on a fishery there, taking it three days and three days, turn and turn about.

Were the ground good, our gardens would be found of infinite use to us in these days of scarcity, but with all our efforts we cannot draw much from them; however, they afford something, and by industry and incessant fatigue mine is one of the best. Were you to see us digging, hoeing, and planting, it would make you smile.

As to parade duties and show, we have long laid them aside, except the mounting a small guard by day and a picket at night. Our soldiers have not a shoe, and mount guard barefoot. Pride, pomp, and circumstance of glorious war are at an end. After having suffered what we do, I shall be grievously hurt, on landing in England, to meet the sneers of a set of holiday troops, whose only employ has been to powder their hair, polish their shoes, and go through the routine of a field-day, though I must own that our air, gait, and raggedness will give them some title to be merry at our expense. So incessantly have we been employed that no military manoeuvre of the least consequence has been practised by us since our embarkation at Plymouth. To cut down trees, turn up ground and build houses have engrossed all our labour and attention.

Thursday 15th

Phillip wrote to Lord Sydney   As the settlement is now fixed, whenever his Majesty's service permits I shall be glad to return to England, where I have reason to suppose my private affairs may make my presence necessary, but which I do not ask in any public letters. Nor should I mention a desire of leaving this country at this moment but that more than a year must pass before it can possibly take place, and I make no doubt but that every inconvenience now felt in this colony will be done away before this letter reaches your lordship. I am sorry to say that nine-tenths of us merit every little inconvenience we now feel.

A pair of pigeons, for Lady Chatham, will, I hope, live to be accepted.

Phillip to Nepean   Mrs Phillip was supposed to be dying when I left England, and whoever the estate goes to some steps should be taken to secure the payment of two annuities for which I gave security and for which it is probable no provision will be made. I should have no objection to return here...but to come to England for a twelve-month is what I wish, for many reasons.

White also wrote a letter for despatch in the *Supply*, to a Mr Skill, a shop-keeper in the Strand:

> In the name of heaven, what has the ministry been about? Surely they have quite forgotten or neglected us, otherwise they would have sent to see what become of us, and to know how we were likely to succeed. However, they must soon know from the heavy bills which will be presented to them, and the misfortunes and losses which have already happened to us, how necessary it becomes to relinquish a scheme that in the nature of things can never answer. It would be wise by the first steps to withdraw the settlement, at least such as are living, or remove them to some other place...
>
> The *Supply* tender sails tomorrow for Batavia in hopes that the Dutch may be able to send in time to save us; should any accident happen to her, Lord have mercy on us! She is a small vessel to perform so long and unexplored a voyage.

Saturday 17th

King I took leave of his Excellency and at noon we sailed with the wind at south-west, carrying with us the fervent prayers of those we left behind for our safety. At one in the p.m. we were abreast of the heads of the entrance of Port Jackson and at sunset it bore west-south-west 15 miles.

Tench We followed her with anxious eyes until she was no longer visible.

King, with instructions to make his way from Batavia to England with Phillip's dispatches, commented on the colony's development during the two years he had been away on Norfolk Island:

> When I left Port Jackson in February 1788, the ground about Sydney Cove was covered with a thick forest, but on my arrival at this time, I found it cleared to a considerable distance, and some good buildings were erected. The governor, the lieutenant-governor, the judge-advocate and the greatest part of the civil and military officers were comfortably lodged. The governor's house is built of stone and has a very good appearance, being

70 feet in front. The lieutenant-governor's house is built of brick, as are also those belonging to the judge and the commissary. The rest of the houses are built with logs and plastered, and all the roofs are either covered with shingles or thatched.

The hospital is a good temporary building, the soldiers were in barracks, and the officers had comfortable huts with gardens adjoining to them, but unfortunately these gardens afford but little, as there is not more than two feet of soil over a bed of rocks and this soil is little better than black sand and to this inconvenience must be added the depredations of rats and thieves.

King wrote of Bennelong:

He is a very intelligent man and much information may, no doubt, be procured from him when he can be well understood... He is a stout, well made man, about five feet six inches high, and, now that the dirt is washed from his skin, we find his colour is a dark black; he is large featured and has a flat nose; his hair is the same as the Asiatics, but very coarse and strong. He is very good-natured, being seldom angry at any jokes that may be passed upon him, and he readily imitates all the actions and gestures of every person in the governor's family. He sits at table with the governor, whom he calls *beanga*, or father, and the governor calls him *doorow*, or son. He is under no restraint, nor is he the least awkward in eating...

He sings, when asked, but in general his songs are in a mournful strain, and he keeps time by swinging his arms. Whenever asked to dance, he does it with great readiness; his motions at first are very slow, and are regulated by a dismal tune, which grows quicker as the dance advances, till at length he throws himself into the most violent posture, shaking his arms and striking the ground with great force, which gives him the appearance of madness. It is very probable that this part of the dance is used as a sort of defiance, as all the natives which were seen when we first arrived at Port Jackson always joined this sort of dance to their vociferations of *woroo, woroo,* [which means] go away.

King added:

A vocabulary of the language, which I procured from Mr Collins and Governor Phillip, both of whom had been very assiduous in procuring words to compose it; and as all the doubtful words are here rejected, it may be depended upon to be correct.

The list included:

aragoon	a war shield
bogay	to dive
boorana	yesterday
binyang	a bird
birrang	the stars
bangaray	the red kangaroo
banarang	blood
carall	the black cockatoo
caragarang	the sea
currayura	the sky
dyennibbe	laughter
eora	men or people
gall gall	smallpox
garaway	the white cockatoo
gweeang	fire
jamel jamel	a hawk
mogo	a stone hatchet
marryang	the emu
morungle	thunder
magra	fish
manga	lightning
murray	large
nowey	a canoe
murray nowey	the *Sirius*
nangara	to sleep
patanga	an oyster
patagarang	the grey kangaroo
panna	rain
tingo	a dog
tonga	to weep
tangora	to dance
waddy	a stick or tree
wolaba	a young kangaroo
yannadah	the moon
yaban	to sing

King's vocabulary gives the meaning of the word *eora* as 'men or people', and lists a similar word, *yora*, as meaning 'a number of people'. A vocabulary with Daniel Southwell's papers included *eorah* as meaning simply 'people'. In Collins's *Account*, the meaning of *eora* is given as 'the name common for the natives'. Recently, *eora* has been used as a collective description for the tribes of the Sydney region. This is probably not the original meaning; it is likely that the Aboriginal people of the Sydney region used the word to describe Aboriginal people generally, not just the people of the Sydney region.

Watkin Tench commented on the difficulty in compiling a vocabulary:

> How easily people unused to speak the same language mistake each other, everyone knows. We had lived almost three years at Port Jackson (for more than half of which period, natives had resided with us) before we knew that the word *beeal* signified 'no', and not 'good', in which latter sense we had always used it without suspecting that we were wrong, and even without being corrected by those with whom we talked daily. The cause of our error was this; the epithet *weeree*, signifying 'bad', we knew...in order to find out their word for 'good', when Arabanoo was first brought among us, we used jokingly to say that anything which he liked was *weeree*, in order to provoke him to tell us that it was 'good'. When we said *weeree*, he answered *beeal*, which we translated and adopted for 'good', whereas he meant no more than simply to deny our inference, and say, 'No, it is not bad.'

∽

Collins On the 7th, about four hundredweight of fish being brought up, it was issued agreeable to the order, and could the like quantity have been brought in daily, some saving might have been made at the store, which would have repaid the labour that was employed to obtain it. But the quantity taken during this month, after the 7th, was not often much more than equal to supplying the people employed in the boats with one pound of fish per man, which was allowed them in addition to their ration.

Neither was much advantage obtained by employing people to shoot for the public. At the end of the month only three small kangaroos had been brought in.

Tench The distress of the lower classes for clothes was almost equal to their other wants. The stores had been long exhausted and winter was at hand. Nothing more ludicrous can be conceived than the expedients of substituting, shifting, and patching which ingenuity devised, to eke out wretchedness and preserve the remains of decency. The superior dexterity of the women was particularly conspicuous. Many a guard have I seen mount in which the number of soldiers without shoes exceeded that which had yet preserved remnants of leather.

Nor was another part of our domestic economy less whimsical. If a lucky man who had knocked down a dinner with his gun or caught a fish by angling from the rocks, invited a neighbour to dine with him, the invitation always ran, 'Bring your own bread'. Even at the governor's table, this custom was constantly observed. Every man when he sat down pulled his bread out of his pocket and laid it by his plate.

Collins The peas were all expended. Was this a ration for a labouring man? The two pounds of pork, when boiled, from the length of time it had been in store, shrunk away to nothing; and when divided among seven people for their day's sustenance, barely afforded three or four morsels to each.

Tench wrote that the usual method of cooking the pork 'was to cut off the daily morsel and toast it on a fork before the fire, catching the drops which fell on a slice of bread, or in a saucer of rice'. He said that 'every grain of rice was a moving body, from the inhabitants lodged within it', but the 'flour was the remnant of what was brought from the Cape by the *Sirius*, and was good; instead of baking it, the soldiers and convicts used to boil it up with greens'.

MAY

Monday 3rd

Tench Our friend Bennelong, during this season of scarcity, was as well taken care of as our desperate circumstances would allow. We knew not how to keep him, and yet were unwilling to part with him. Had he penetrated our state, perhaps he might have given his countrymen such a description of our diminished numbers and diminished strength as would have emboldened them to become more troublesome. Every expedient was used to keep him in ignorance; his allowance was regularly received by the governor's servant, like that of any other person, but the ration of a week was insufficient to have kept him for a day. The deficiency was supplied by fish, whenever it could be procured, and a little Indian corn, which had been reserved, was ground and appropriated to his use. In spite of all these aids, want of food has been known to make him furious, and often melancholy.

There is reason to believe that he had long meditated his escape, which he effected in the night of the 3rd instant. About two o'clock in the morning he pretended illness and, awaking the servant who lay in the room with him, begged to go downstairs. The other attended him without suspicion of his design and Bennelong no sooner found himself in a backyard than he nimbly leaped over a slight paling, and bade us adieu.

Perhaps Bennelong escaped because he wasn't getting enough to eat, perhaps he wanted his freedom, but Southwell observed, in a letter to the Reverend Weeden Butler, that 'Bennelong spoke in raptures of a famed charmer, (Odooroodah) greatly admired by himself and many of his countrymen; indeed it is more than probable that his reasons for leaving us were not uninfluenced by some such inducement'.

Tuesday 25th

Joseph Elliott was found guilty of stealing potatoes from the Reverend Richard Johnson. He pleaded guilty, but said in his defence that he had been hard at work all day and was very hungry. Collins wrote:

> It might have been supposed that the severity of the punishments which had been ordered by the criminal court on offenders convicted of robbing gardens would have deterred others from committing that offence, but while there was a vegetable to steal there were those who would steal it.

The sentence passed on Joseph Elliott was a move away from what Collins called 'the great weight of corporal punishment', but was no less harsh, as Tench pointed out:

> The following sentence of a court of justice, of which I was a member, on a convict detected in a garden stealing potatoes, will illustrate the subject. He was ordered to receive 300 lashes immediately, to be chained for six months to two other criminals, who were thus fettered for former offences, and to have his allowance of flour stopped for six months.

Elliott's flour ration, 'without which', Collins wrote, 'he could not long have existed', was restored on 31 May.

⌒

Collins Our fishing tackle began now, with our other necessaries, to decrease. To remedy this inconvenience, we were driven by necessity to avail ourselves of some knowledge which we had gained from the natives, and one of the convicts (a rope-maker) was employed to spin lines from the bark of a tree which they used for the same purpose.

JUNE

Thursday 3rd

Collins The first and second days of this month were exceedingly unfavourable to our situation; heavy rain and blowing weather obstructed labour and prevented fishing. But it was decreed that on the third we should experience sensations to which we had been strangers ever since our departure from England. About half past three in the afternoon of this day, to the inexpressible satisfaction of every heart in the settlement, the long-looked-for signal for a ship was made at the South Head. Every countenance was instantly cheered, and wore the lively expressions of eagerness, joy and anxiety; the whole settlement was in motion and confusion.

Tench Finding that the governor intended to go immediately in his boat down the harbour, I begged to be of his party. As we proceeded, the object of our hopes soon appeared; a large ship, with English colours flying, working in between the heads which form the entrance of the harbour...We pushed through wind and rain, the anxiety of our sensations every moment redoubling. At last we read the word 'London' on her stern. 'Pull away, my lads! She is from old England! A few strokes more, and we shall be aboard! Hurrah for a bellyfull and news from our friends!' Such were our exhortations to the boat's crew.

A few minutes completed our wishes and we found ourselves on board the *Lady Juliana* transport, with 225 of our countrywomen whom crime or misfortune had condemned to exile. We learned that they had been almost 11 months on their passage, having left Plymouth, into which port they had put in July 1789. We continued to ask a thousand questions on a breath. Stimulated by curiosity, they inquired in turn, but the right of being first answered, we thought, lay on our side. 'Letters! Letters!' was the cry. They were produced, and torn open in trembling agitation. News burst upon us like meridian splendour on a blind man. We were overwhelmed with it; public, private, general, and particular.

Phillip received a letter from the Home Secretary, Lord Grenville
In the course of the autumn I expect that about 1000 more convicts of both sexes will be embarked from the several gaols and despatched to Port Jackson, together with a suitable proportion of clothing and provisions for their use. This measure will render it necessary that you should make arrangements for their accommodation, as well as for their employment on their arrival.

Phillip was also advised by Grenville, that as a result of his despatches reporting the problems experienced with the Marine Corps, the Home Office had decided to replace the marines with a corps of infantry recruited specifically for the colony. The New South Wales Corps, as it was to be known, was to consist of '300 rank and file and a suitable number of officers'; the majors and captains of each company were to recruit their own soldiers and receive a fee of three guineas for each man recruited.

Grenville added that the non-commissioned officers and privates who wished to remain in the colony as settlers would be encouraged by grants of land. Tench summarised the terms:

> To every non-commissioned officer an allotment of 130 acres of land if single and of 150 acres if married. To every private soldier an allotment of 80 acres if single and of 100 acres if married, and also an allotment of 10 acres for every child, whether of a non-commissioned officer or of a private soldier.

Those who wished to remain in the colony and enlist in the new corps were to be encouraged by a bounty of £3 and an assurance that after a further five years' service they would be 'entitled to double the former portion of land, provided they then choose to become settlers in the country'.

No arrangements were made for granting lands to officers who wished to settle.

Friday 11th

Collins   When the women were landed on the 11th, many of them appeared to be loaded with the infirmities incident to old age, and to be very improper subjects for any of the purposes of an infant colony. Instead of being capable of labour, they seemed to require attendance themselves and were never likely to be any other than a burden to the settlement.

Thursday 17th

Phillip wrote to Lord Grenville   In order to know in what time a man might be able to cultivate a sufficient quantity of ground to support himself, I last November ordered a hut to be built in a good situation, an acre of ground to be cleared, and once turned up it was put into the possession of a very industrious convict [James Ruse] who was told if he behaved well he should have 30 acres. This man had said the time for which he had been sentenced was expired, and wished to settle. He has been industrious, has received some little assistance from time to time, and now tells me that if one acre more is cleared for him he shall be able to support himself after next January, which I much doubt, but think he will do tolerably well after he has been supported for 18 months. Others may prove more intelligent, though they cannot well be more industrious.

Sunday 20th

Tench   We were joyfully surprised on the 20th of the month to see another sail enter the harbour. She proved to be the *Justinian* transport, commanded by Captain Maitland, and our rapture was doubled on finding that she was laden entirely with provisions for our use. Full allowance and general congratulation immediately took place. This ship had left Falmouth on the preceding 20th of January and completed her passage in exactly five months.

Collins   We now learned that three transports might be hourly expected, having on board the thousand convicts of whose destination we had received some information by the *Lady Juliana*, together with detachments of the corps raised for the service of this country. The remainder of this corps (which was intended to consist of 300 men) were to come out in the *Gorgon* man of war, of 44 guns. This ship was also to bring out Major Grose, who had been appointed lieutenant-governor of the territory in the room of Major Ross, which officer, together with the marines under his command, were intended to return to England in that ship.

Monday 21st

Collins On the day following her [*Justinian's*] arrival, everything seemed getting into its former train. The full ration was ordered to be issued; instead of daily, it was to be served weekly as formerly, and the drum for labour was to beat as usual in the afternoons at one o'clock. How general was the wish that no future necessity might ever occasion another deduction in the ration, or an alteration in the labour of the people.

Saturday 26th

Collins The *Surprize* transport, Nicholas Anstis master (late chief mate of the *Lady Penrhyn*) anchored in the cove from England, having on board one captain, one lieutenant, one surgeon's mate, one sergeant, one corporal, one drummer and 23 privates of the New South Wales Corps, together with 218 male convicts...

We had the mortification to learn that the prisoners in this ship were very unhealthy, upwards of 100 being now in the sick list on board. They had been very sickly also during the passage and had buried 42 of these unfortunate people. A portable hospital had fortunately been received by the *Justinian* and there now appeared but too great a probability that we should soon have patients enough to fill it, for the signal was flying at the south head for the other transports, and we were led to expect them in as unhealthy a state as that which had just arrived.

Monday 28th

Easty The *Neptune* transport arrived here with 500 convicts and the *Scarborough* with 250 and 105 soldiers of the New South Wales Corps, the convicts all very sickly.

Tuesday 29th

Collins We were not mistaken in our expectations of the state in which they might arrive. By noon the following day 200 sick had been landed from the different transports. The west side afforded a scene truly distressing and miserable; upwards of 30 tents were pitched in front of the hospital, the portable one not being yet put up, all of which, as well as the hospital and the adjacent huts, were filled with people, many of whom were labouring under the complicated diseases of scurvy and the dysentery, and others in the last stage of either of those terrible disorders, or yielding to the attacks of an infectious fever.

The appearance of those who did not require medical assistance was lean and emaciated. Several of these miserable people died in the boats as they were rowing on shore, or on the wharf as they were lifting out of the boats, both the living and the dead exhibiting more horrid spectacles than had ever been witnessed in this country. All this was to be attributed to confinement, and that of the worst species, confinement in a small space and in irons, not put on singly, but many of them chained together.

࿆

Tench These ships…brought out a large body of convicts, whose state and sufferings will be best estimated by the following return.

Names of the ships	Number of people embarked	Number of persons who died on the voyage	Number landed sick at Port Jackson
Neptune	530	163	269
Surprize	252	42	121
Scarborough	256	68	96
	1038	273	486

N.B. Of those landed sick, 124 died in the hospital at Sydney.

The Reverend Richard Johnson described the landing of the Second Fleet in an undated letter to Mr John Thornton:

Have been on board these different ships. Was first on board the *Surprize*. Went down amongst the convicts, where I beheld a sight truly shocking to the feelings of humanity, a great number of them laying, some half and others nearly quite naked, without either bed or bedding, unable to turn or help themselves.

Spoke to them as I passed along, but the smell was so offensive that I could scarcely bear it.

I then went on board the *Scarborough*; proposed to go down amongst them, but was dissuaded from it by the captain. The *Neptune* was still more wretched and intolerable, and therefore never attempted it. Some of these unhappy people died after the ships came into the harbour, before they could be taken on shore; part of these had been thrown into the harbour, and their dead bodies cast upon the shore and were seen laying naked upon the rocks. Took an occasion to represent this to his Excellency, in consequence of which immediate orders were sent on board that those who died on board should be carried to the opposite shore and be buried.

The landing of these people was truly affecting and shocking; great numbers were not able to walk, nor to move hand or foot; such were slung over the ship side in the same manner as they would sling a cask, a box, or anything of that nature. Upon their being brought up to the open air some fainted, some died upon deck and others in the boat before they reached the shore. When come on shore many were not able to walk, to stand, or to stir themselves in the least, hence some were led by others. Some creeped upon their hands and knees, and some were carried upon the backs of others...

The misery I saw amongst them is unexpressible; many were not able to turn, or even to stir themselves, and in this situation were covered over almost with their own nastiness, their heads, bodies, clothes, blanket, all full of filth and lice. Scurvy was not the only nor the worst disease that prevailed amongst them (one man I visited this morning, I think, I may say safely had 10,000 lice upon his body and bed); some were exercised with violent fevers, and others with a no less violent purging and flux.

The complaints they had to make were no less affecting to the ear than their outward condition was to the eye. The usage they met with on board, according to their own story, was truly shocking; sometimes for days, nay, for a considerable time together, they have been to the middle in water chained together, hand and leg, even the sick not exempted—nay, many died with the chains upon them. Promises, entreaties, were all in vain, and it was not till a very few days before they made the harbour that they were released out of irons.

Collins   Parties were immediately sent into the woods to collect the acid berry of the country [possibly *persoonia* or *geebung*] which for its extreme acetosity was deemed by the surgeons a most powerful antiscorbutic. Among other regulations, orders were given for baking a certain quantity of flour into pound loaves, to be distributed daily among the sick, as it was not in their power to prepare it themselves.

An Edinburgh weekly paper, *The Bee*, carried a report from the colony: 'Our new guests expressed great concern at not finding everything here in a very prosperous state. They had been led to believe that matters were in a very fair train, and that plenty of conveniences were ready for their reception at landing; but they found quite the contrary to be the case.'

Scott   The master of the *Lady Juliana* sent a great quantity of goods (his own private property) on shore to be sold, but at an exorbitant price; moist sugar that could be purchased at Rio for a vintem or three halfpence a pound he sold for 18 pence in bills and 16 ready money, soap three shillings ready money, tobacco eight shillings, fourpenny thread two shillings per ounce, ribbon from two to three shillings and ninepence per yard, bread sixpence per pound, six-penny paper at two shillings per quire and everything else in like proportion.

Collins   An instance of sagacity in a dog occurred on the arrival of the *Scarborough*, too remarkable to pass unnoticed; Mr Marshall, the master of the ship on quitting Port Jackson in May 1788, left a New-foundland dog with Mr Clark, the agent...On the return of his old master, Hector swam off to the ship and getting on board recognised him and manifested in every manner suitable to his nature his joy at seeing him; nor could the animal be persuaded to quit him again, accompanying him always when he went on shore and returning with him on board.

JULY

Wednesday 7th

Collins   Every exertion was made to get up the portable hospital, but, although we were informed that it had been put up in London in a very few hours, we did not complete it until the 7th, when it was instantly filled with patients.

Thirty convicts and one sailor were buried during the week.

Friday 9th

Sydney King Inett was baptised. He was the second son of the convict Ann Inett and Lieutenant Philip Gidley King, who was on his way to England, via Batavia.

Saturday 17th

Phillip complained about conditions on the Second Fleet in a despatch to Grenville:

> I will, sir, insert an extract from the surgeon's report, who I directed to examine these people: 'After a careful examination of the convicts, I find upwards of 100 who must ever be a burden to the settlement, not being able to do any kind of labour, from old age and chronical diseases of long standing. Amongst the females there is one who has lost the use of her limbs upwards of three years, and amongst the males two who are perfect idiots.
>
> Such are the people sent from the different gaols and from the hulks, where it is said the healthy and the artificers are retained. The sending out the disordered and helpless clears the gaols and may ease the parishes from which they are sent, but, sir, it is obvious that this settlement, instead of being a colony which is to support itself, will, if the practice is continued, remain for years a burden to the mother country.

Phillip also described his plans for Rose Hill:

> I am laying out a town at Rose Hill in which the principal street will be occupied by the convicts; the huts are building at the distance of 100 feet from each other and each hut is to contain 10 convicts; in these huts they would live more comfortable than they could possibly do if numbers were confined together in large buildings, and having good gardens which they cultivate, and frequently having it in their power to exchange vegetables for little necessaries which the stores do not furnish, makes them begin to feel the benefits they may draw from their industry.

Friday 23rd

Three marines who were fishing in the harbour picked up midshipman John Ferguson at the lookout at South Head and were on their way up the harbour when, according to Scott: 'The punt or small boat which they were in was attacked by a whale that came into the harbour and beat her all to pieces'.

Southwell   This monstrous creature, either through being mischievous or playful, no sooner espied the boat than he pursued and never left her till he had overturned and sent her to the bottom. For more than 10 minutes were these unfortunates a prey to inexpressible anguish and horror. At first, in rising, he half-filled the boat and with their hands against the whale did they bear the boat off. In vain they threw out their hats, the bags for our provisions and the fish they had caught, in hopes to satisfy him or turn his attention. It seemed bent on their destruction, and with one sudden and tremendous gambol consigned three of their number to their hapless fate and an endless eternity.

Scott   Three of the men drowned, viz. Mr Ferguson, midshipman, John Bates and Thomas Harp, marines. John Wilkins, marine, was saved by swimming upwards of a mile. He got safe on the south shore and proceeded to the lookout house with the disagreeable news of such a sad catastrophe...Wilkins says that after the boat was stove that he was on the back of the whale for some time before he attempted to make for the shore.

Phillip prepared a '**Return of male convicts, with their respective employments, on the 23rd of July 1790**'.

At Sydney Cove:

40 Making bricks and tiles.
50 Bringing in bricks etc for the new storehouse.
19 Bricklayers and labourers employed in building a storehouse and huts at Rose Hill.
 8 Carpenters employed at the new store and in building huts at Rose Hill.
 9 Men who can work with the axe and who assist the carpenters.
 2 Sawyers.
 9 Smiths.
10 Watchmen.
40 Receiving stores and provisions from the ships.
12 Employed on the roads, mostly convalescents.
18 Bringing in timber.

  4 Stone masons.

10 Employed in the boats.

  3 Wheelwrights.

  6 Employed in the stores.

38 Employed by the officers of the civil and military departments at their farms. These men will be employed for the public when the relief takes place.

  2 Assistants to the provost-marshal.

  3 Gardeners and labourers employed by the governor.

  3 Coopers.

  6 Shoemakers.

  4 Tailors.

  5 Bakers.

  6 Attending the sick at the hospital.

  3 Barbers.

  3 Gardeners and others employed at the hospital.

  3 Employed by the governor bringing in of wood etc.

316

413 Under medical treatment.

729

At Rose Hill:

  2 Employed at the store.

  3 Servants to the three superintendents.

  1 Employed in taking care of the stock.

  2 Employed at the hospital.

  5 Men who work with the axe in building huts.

  1 Baker.

  1 Cook.

  4 Boys variously employed.

  1 Assistant to the provost-marshal.

  3 Thatchers.

  1 Servant to the storekeepers.

  1 Servant to the assistant surgeon.

  4 Overseers.

25 Sick.

113 Clearing and cultivating the ground.

12 Sawyers.

179

Saturday 24th

Phillip wrote to Nepean   As the iron mills sent out for the purpose of grinding wheat are easily rendered useless and destroyed and will require great labour to grind corn for a considerable number of people, windmills will be wanted, and for the sending out of which I am to request that you, sir, will take the necessary steps, if it is approved of by Mr Secretary Grenville, to whom I have written on the subject. As we have not any good millwright in the colony, I presume some convicts who have been brought up in that branch might be procured. A miller will be necessary, and as he will have a trust reposed in him he should not be a convict.

Monday 26th

Captain William Hill of the New South Wales Corps wrote to Jonathan Wathen of London   In America the officers and settlers had grants of land in proportion to their rank; but those of the marines who are now here, and have borne every hardship, have no such thing, neither is there an intention of giving each their portion. In my humble opinion nothing can be more impolitic. Industry is the first essential to the welfare of any kingdom, consequently all measures that are adopted to promote it are highly commendable and I am well persuaded Britain will not thank our governor for acting, not only on a mean but on an unstable plan, to the great disquiet of every individual in the colony.

Phillip wrote to Sir Joseph Banks   Wedgwood has showed the world that our Welsh clay is capable of receiving an elegant impression, and I return thanks for the cup and medallions. There is a better clay in the country and which I have seen amongst the natives—it will be found by us hereafter.

I have about a thousand cutting of vines now in the ground and have had a few grapes and many as fine figs as ever I tasted in Spain or Portugal. Still my orange trees want a gardener and all my endeavours to send good seeds for his Majesty's garden, without one, will I fear prove fruitless. It is surprising to me how the vines thrive and I am in hopes next year of having a vineyard of five or six acres. Great effort will be made this year and I hope after all our disappointments, that two years more will fix this colony beyond the reach of accidents from the ice, though I almost doubt holding out so long, for I find my health declines fast.

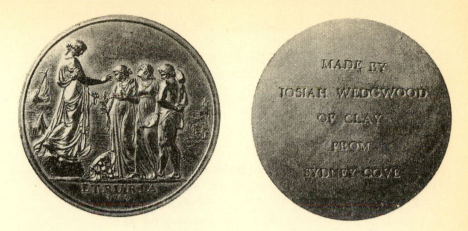

Medallion made from Sydney Cove clay by Josiah Wedgwood in 1789, depicting 'Hope encouraging Art and Labour, under the influence of Peace'. Etruria was the name of one of the Wedgwood factories in Staffordshire.

Tench reported a gradual move from chaos towards order:

> Such was the weakly state of the newcomers that for several weeks little real benefit to the colony was derived from so great a nominal addition to our number. However, as fast as they recovered, employment was immediately assigned to them. The old hours of labour, which had been reduced in our distress, were re-established and the most vigorous measures adopted to give prosperity to the settlement.
>
> New buildings were immediately planned and large tracts of ground at Rose Hill ordered to be cleared and prepared for cultivation. Some superintendents who had arrived in the fleet and were hired by government for the purpose of overlooking and directing the convicts were found extremely serviceable in accelerating the progress of improvement.

AUGUST

Friday 6th

In a letter to Nepean, Phillip reported: 'The number of sick have decreased considerably, the returns of this day being only 220. Deaths since the 27th of June, 89.'

Saturday 7th

A letter from Daniel Southwell to his mother reflects his frustration at having being stationed at the lookout at South Head since February, with very little to do, while Henry Waterhouse, who had joined *Sirius* three weeks after him and was four years his junior, had survived the wreck of the *Sirius* and was now accompanying the governor on expeditions about the settlement:

> I am at this moment at Mr Palmer's, commissary at 11 o'clock at night, in his house by myself and not the heave of a biscuit off of G P's [Governor Phillip's]. I come up to make sure of my packet, of which this to you is one, and he [Phillip] had the conscience to order me down immediately I mentioned my having missed the *Justinian* by being in that out-of-the-way situation at the lookout, and that I humbly hoped he would allow me to make sure of the *Scarborough*.
>
> It was stuck to with modest warmth on my part and at last carried much against his will. He had no better resource than the sly pretence of fearing my being in camp might be prejudicial to my morals: 'What did I want with whores and rogues?' my answer was, warmly, being nettled, 'Nothing', and that I was certain he could have nothing of that kind to bring against my conduct...
>
> Apropos, the governor has this forenoon graciously sent me an invitation to dine, a thing quite out of date a long time, but as I was to eat some kid with Mr P [Palmer] I sent word I was indisposed (he saw my flannel stock) but much obliged etc, of course, and also going down to the lookout to lay by a little. Observe, was it anything worse than a common cold I would not say anything about it in this to you; but I truly assure you that is all, and I am a careful codger.

Friday 20th

Southwell's view of the governor had changed in the past fortnight. He wrote to his mother:

> He treats us with more affability and is all at once so polite as to beg of my only companion, Mr Harris, and self, whenever we come to camp to let him have our company, and I am tomorrow (having been so long a stranger) to wait upon him by particular

invitation, several times repeated and hitherto declined upon account of a cold, and perhaps being a little sulky.

Saturday 21st

The Reverend Richard Johnson wrote to Henry Fricker Last year I cut, I suppose, not much less than a thousand cucumbers, and some that I left for seed have been 16 or 18 inches long and a foot or more in circumference. Have also raised some melons very good-flavoured—water melons and pumpkins too have been raised here very fine and large—all these are put into the ground in the course of next month.

At our first landing I put in some pips of oranges, limes and lemons. There are some of them now two foot high and seem to be very promising. Some guavas too are likely to come to perfection, only I think the climate is not quite hot enough for them. Strawberries we had last summer—not bad. The governor brought out one root of this, which has so increased that now there are scarcely any but who have them in their gardens.

Vines I think will do in time—better if the climate were hotter, but as these do not require the most rich soil, we are in hopes of seeing these turn to some account, and I promise you, if ever wine be made here and not prohibited from being exported, I will send you a specimen and perhaps may drink your health in a bumper of New Holland wine...

Through mercy, we are tolerably well, except that I fear we have by some means or other caught the Scotch Fiddler [probably pubic lice] which at times makes us dance and caper about the room more than I could wish. Hope however soon to be cured of this filthy disorder. My dear Milbah grows every day more and more engaging.

Tuesday 24th

In the criminal court, Hugh Lowe was convicted of stealing a sheep from the commissary, John Palmer. Lowe, who had some experience in farming, was one of 25 convicts sent in the *Guardian* with skills that were needed in the colony. Following the *Guardian's* collision with an iceberg, he was one of a group recommended by Captain Riou for a conditional pardon for the part they played in saving the ship. Despite evidence of his good conduct, Lowe was sentenced to be hanged.

Wednesday 25th

Lowe acknowledged his guilt before he died. Collins wrote:

> Had any lenity been extended to this offender on account of his good conduct in a particular situation, it might have been the cause of many depredations being made upon the stock, which it was hoped his punishment would prevent.

Saturday 28th

Collins A pair of shoes were served to each convict.

☙

Collins The female convicts were employed in making the slops for the men, which had been now sent out unmade. Each woman who could work at her needle had materials for two shirts given her at a time, and while so employed was not to be taken for any other labour.

The storehouse which was begun in July was finished this month, and was got up and covered in without any rain. Its dimensions were 100 feet by 22.

At Rose Hill the convicts were employed in constructing the new town which had been marked out, building the huts, and forming the principal street. The governor, who personally directed all these works, caused a spot of ground for a capacious garden to be allotted for the use of the New South Wales Corps...

In addition to the flagstaff which had been erected on the South Head of the harbour, the governor determined to construct a column of a height sufficient to be seen from some distance at sea, and the stonemasons were sent down to quarry stone upon the spot for the building.

The body of one of the unfortunate people who were drowned at the latter end of July last with Mr Ferguson was found about the close of this month, washed on shore in Rose Bay and very much disfigured. The whale which had occasioned this accident, we were informed, had never found its way out of the harbour but, getting on shore in Manly Bay, was killed by the natives, and was the cause of numbers of them being at this time assembled to partake of the repasts which it afforded them.

SEPTEMBER

Sunday 5th

James Ruse was married to Elizabeth Perry at Rose Hill. Perry had been transported for stealing clothes and money from her employer and came out in the *Lady Juliana*, giving her age as 21. Both signed the register with a cross.

Tuesday 7th

Tench Captain Nepean of the New South Wales Corps and Mr White, accompanied by little Nanbaree and a party of men, went in a boat to Manly Cove, intending to land there and walk on to Broken Bay. On drawing near the shore, a dead whale in the most disgusting state of putrefaction was seen lying on the beach and at least 200 Indians surrounding it, broiling the flesh on different fires and feasting on it...Mr White now called for Bennelong, who, on hearing his name, came forth and entered into conversation. He was greatly emaciated and so far disfigured by a long beard that our people not without difficulty recognised their old acquaintance. His answering in broken English, and inquiring for the governor, however, soon corrected their doubts. He seemed quite friendly, and soon after Colbee came up, pointing to his leg, to show that he had freed himself from the fetter which was upon him when he had escaped from us.

When Bennelong was told that the governor was not far off, he expressed great joy, and declared that he would immediately go in search of him...When the natives saw that the boat was about to depart, they crowded around her, and brought down, by way of present, three or four great chunks of the whale and put them on board of her, the largest of which Bennelong expressly requested might be offered, in his name, to the governor.

Phillip was at the lookout at South Head giving directions for building the 'column or landmark for ships coming in from sea', with a party including Collins and Lieutenant Henry Waterhouse, whose account of the events of the day is included in Bradley's *Voyage*. They were 'returning up the harbour when a boat that was coming up from Collins Cove (after having landed a party who were going to Broken Bay) made signals to speak with us', Waterhouse wrote.

On our going to her, the coxswain informed the governor that Mr White had had a long conference with Bennelong and Colbee, that they had inquired for everybody they knew, particularly for the governor, that he had sent him a piece of whale and said he would come up if the governor would go down for him, in consequence of which the governor went immediately down to the lookout, got everything he thought would be acceptable to them and four muskets, and immediately went to Collins Cove, where they had been seen.

On our way there we found we could make only two of the muskets go off, which we loaded as well as a pistol the governor got at the lookout. When we got to Collins Cove, we saw a number of natives assembled round a fire opposite a whale that had been thrown on shore.

Tench   As they expressed not any consternation on seeing us row to the beach, Governor Phillip stepped out unarmed, attended by one seaman only, and called for Bennelong, who appeared, but notwithstanding his former eagerness would not suffer the other to approach him for several minutes. Gradually, however, he warmed into friendship and frankness and presently after Colbee came up. They discoursed for some time, Bennelong expressing pleasure to see his old acquaintance and inquiring by name for every person whom he could recollect at Sydney, and among others for a French cook, one of the governor's servants, whom he had constantly made the butt of his ridicule, by mimicking his voice, gait, and other peculiarities, all of which he again went through with his wonted exactness and drollery.

He asked also particularly for a lady from whom he had once ventured to snatch a kiss, and on being told that she was well, by way of proving that the token was fresh in his remembrance, he kissed Lieutenant Waterhouse and laughed aloud.

Waterhouse   I frequently heard a man on the right hand side call out Bennelong and told him of something, either what we were doing in the boat or something he had observed, as we kept the boat afloat on her oars (which might reasonably occasion some mistrust as the same precaution was observed when they were forcibly taken away from the same cove where the boat was now lying)...

Bennelong on the governor's going up had a remarkable good spear, which the governor asked him for, but he either would or could not understand him but took it and laid it down in the grass, during all which time perfect harmony subsisted.

The natives now seemed closing round us, which the governor took notice and said he thought we had better retreat as they had formed a crescent with us in the centre. There were then 19 armed men near us and more in great numbers that we could not see.

The governor then assured Bennelong he would return in two days and bring with him the clothes he used to wear and two hatchets (which they are remarkably fond of), one for Colbee and one for himself, with which he seemed much pleased and often repeated it, that it should not be forgot. Just as we were going, Bennelong pointed out and named several natives that were near, one in particular to whom the governor presented his hand and advanced towards him.

Tench   The nearer the governor approached, the greater became the terror and agitation of the Indian. To remove his fear, Governor Phillip threw down a dirk which he wore at his side. The other, alarmed at the rattle of the dirk, and probably misconstruing the action, instantly fixed his lance in his throwing-stick. To retreat, his Excellency now thought, would be more dangerous than to advance. He therefore cried out to the man, *Weree, weree* (bad—you are doing wrong) displaying at the same time every token of amity and confidence. The words had, however, hardly gone forth when the Indian, stepping back with one foot, aimed his lance with such force and dexterity that, striking the governor's right shoulder just above the collar-bone, the point glancing downward came out at his back.

Waterhouse   I immediately concluded the governor was killed, as it appeared to me much lower than it really was, and supposed there was not a chance for any one of us to escape, and turned round to run for the beach as I perceived Captain Collins running that way and calling to the boat's crew to bring the muskets up.

The governor also attempted to run holding the spear with both hands to keep the end off the ground, but owing to the length the end took the ground and stopped him short (I suppose it could not be less than 12 feet long). He then begged me for God's sake to haul the spear out, which I immediately stopped to do and was in the act of doing it, when I recollected I should only haul the barb into his flesh again, which was an inch long. I then determined on breaking it off and bent it down for that purpose, but owing to its length could not effect it. I then bent it upwards, but could not break it owing to the toughness of the wood.

Just at this instant another spear came and just grazed the skin off between the thumb and forefinger of my right hand. I must own it frightened me a good deal and I believe added to my exertions, for the next sudden jerk I gave it, it broke short off; spears were then flying very thick, one of which I perceived fall just at Captain Collins's feet as he was calling to the boat's crew.

The governor attempted to pull the pistol out of his pocket, but I told him the spears were flying so quick that if he stopped he certainly would be speared again. However, he got the pistol out and fired it from the idea that their seeing we had firearms would deter them from throwing any more spears, which I believe had the desired effect, as we all got safe down to the beach, before which time the boat's crew had got between us and the natives and fired a musket, the only one that could be got off. With the help of a seaman, I lifted the governor into the boat, as he was very faint. Captain Collins immediately followed with the boat's crew and put off.

Nagle The doctor not having materials with him to stop the blood, he dare not take the spear out, but cut it off and it remained in him till we pulled the boat to Sydney Cove with all our might. The governor bore it with the greatest patience and as the doctor wrote according to his directions, he made his will and settled his affairs, not expecting to live, while we were pulling him up in the boat.

Waterhouse I supported the governor in my arms all the way up, during which time he was perfectly collected but conscious that a few hours must fix the period of his existence, supposing the spear had got through much lower than it really did and that suffocation must follow the taking the spear out. We got up within two hours to Sydney Cove, when the surgeons were immediately sent for and Mr Balmain attended with his instruments. On his examining the wound, the governor desired him candidly to tell him how many hours he had to settle his affairs...but Mr Balmain made us all happy by confidently assuring the governor he did not apprehend any fatal consequences from the wound. The spear was then extracted.

Although Waterhouse makes no mention of a surgeon until they arrived at Sydney Cove, Nagle's account mentions that there was a doctor in the boat. It may have been John Harris, surgeon of the recently-arrived New South Wales Corps, who was stationed at the lookout on South Head, where Phillip had called on the way to Collins Cove to see Bennelong.

Phillip's account, taken from his official despatches and published in Hunter's *Journal*, gives his explanation for the incident:

> It should be remembered that the man who wounded Governor Phillip was a stranger and might fear their taking him away, as they had carried off others, against which he might not think their numbers a sufficient security... This man had stood for some time peaceably and quietly and the governor certainly was more in his power before he went to call the officers out of the boat than at the time the spear was thrown. It is therefore most likely that the action proceeded from a momentary impulse of fear.

Phillip was speared in Collins Cove, where Bennelong and Colbee had been captured; the boat followed the same procedure, the sailors resting on their oars off the beach; and Phillip was approaching the man who speared him with his arms outstretched. Phillip had not been present when Bennelong and Colbee were taken, so may not have been aware of the similarities. As Collins wrote: 'No other motive could be assigned for this conduct in the savage than the supposed apprehension that he was about to be seized by the governor.'

Monday 13th

A daughter was born to Nancy Yeats and Captain David Collins, judge-advocate of the colony. The child was later christened Marianne Letitia Collins.

Tuesday 14th

Tench The Chaplain and Lieutenant Dawes, having Abaroo with them in a boat, learned from two Indians that Wileemarin was the name of the person who had wounded the governor. These two people inquired kindly how his Excellency did, and seemed pleased to learn that he was likely to recover. They said that they were inhabitants of Rose Hill, and expressed great dissatisfaction at the number of white men who had settled in their former territories. In consequence of which declaration the detachment at that post was reinforced the following day.

Wednesday 15th

Tench On the 15th a fire being seen on the north shore of the harbour, a party of our people went thither, accompanied by Nanbaree and Abaroo. They found there Bennelong and several other natives, and much civility passed which was cemented by a mutual promise to meet in the afternoon at the same place. Both sides were punctual to their engagement, and no objection being made to our landing, a party of us went ashore to them unarmed. Several little presents, which had been purposely brought, were distributed among them and to Bennelong were given a hatchet and a fish.

At a distance stood some children, who, though at first timorous and unwilling to approach, were soon persuaded to advance and join the men. A bottle of wine was produced and Bennelong immediately prepared for the charge. Bread and beef he called loudly for, which were given to him and he began to eat, offering a part of his fare to his countrymen, two of whom tasted the beef, but none of them would touch the bread. Having finished his repast, he made a motion to be shaved, and a barber being present, his request was complied with, to the great admiration of his countrymen, who laughed and exclaimed at the operation. They would not, however, consent to undergo it, but suffered their beards to be clipped with a pair of scissors.

On being asked where their women were, they pointed to the spot, but seemed not desirous that we should approach it. However, in a few minutes, a female appeared not far off and Abaroo was dispatched to her. Bennelong now joined with Abaroo to persuade her to come to us, telling us she was Barangaroo, and his wife...

At the request of Bennelong we combed and cut her hair and she seemed pleased with the operation. Wine she would not taste, but turned from it with disgust, though heartily invited to drink by the example and persuasion of Bennelong. In short, she behaved so well and assumed the character of gentleness and timidity to such advantage, that had our acquaintance ended here, a very moderate share of the spirit of travelling would have sufficed to record that amidst a horde of roaming savages, in the desert wastes of New South Wales, might be found as much feminine innocence, softness, and modesty (allowing for inevitable difference of education), as the most finished system could bestow, or the most polished circle produce.

Thursday 16th

Another meeting was held with Bennelong, who 'inquired with solicitude about the state of the governor's wound'. When they parted, Tench wrote:

We pressed him to appoint a day on which he should come to
Sydney, assuring him that he would be well received and kindly
treated. Doubtful, however, of being permitted to return, he
evaded our request and declared that the governor must first come
and see him, which we promised should be done.

Thursday 16th

Collins   The fishing boats had the greatest success which had yet
been met with; near 4000 of a fish, named by us from its shape only,
the salmon, being taken at two hauls of the seine. Each weighed on
an average about five pounds; they were issued to this settlement,
and to that at Rose Hill.

The fish were probably Australian salmon, although they may have been
tailor, which move in big schools on the east coast and are not unlike
salmon in appearance.

Friday 17th

Phillip   Governor Phillip was so well recovered of his wound as to
be able to go in a boat, on the 17th, to the place where Bennelong
and his wife then resided. He found nine natives on the spot, who
informed him that Bennelong was out a-fishing. The native girl was
in the boat, and her father being among the natives, a hatchet and
some fish were given him, in return for which he gave the governor
a short spear that had been pointed with a knife, which the natives
now used when they could procure one, in preference to the shell.

   The party had just left these people and were going farther in
quest of Bennelong, when they perceived four canoes coming
towards them, in one of which was the person they wanted. On this
they returned to the cove. As soon as Bennelong had laid up his
canoe, he came to the boat and held up both his hands to show
that he had no arms. Presently afterwards the party landed and he
joined them very readily, asked Governor Phillip where he was
wounded, and said that he had beat the man who wounded him,
and whose name he repeated...

   On being asked to dine with Governor Phillip the next day, he
readily consented and promised to bring his wife; he likewise pointed
out a youth and two men to whom hatchets had been given, and
said he would bring them with him also...

Though Bennelong probably might be glad that Governor Phillip was not killed, yet there is no doubt but that the natives throw their spears, and take a life in their quarrels, which are very frequent, as readily as the lower class of people in England strip to box, and think as little of the consequences.

Sunday 19th

Phillip   Governor Phillip went to Rose Hill and returned to Sydney in the evening. The corn looked better than could be expected, but the earth was so parched up by the dry weather that they could not get the remainder of their Indian corn into the ground until some rain fell.

Monday 20th

Several convicts appeared in the magistrates' court at Rose Hill. William Harris was charged with stealing a large quantity of clothes and utensils as part of a plan to escape from the colony. Ann Young, charged with stealing flour, pleaded hunger but was found guilty and sentenced to repay the flour and to additional work for a month on Fridays and Saturdays. James McDonaugh, charged with stealing two pairs of trousers from James Ruse, admitted his guilt and was sentenced to '200 lashes and to wear an iron collar for six months'.

Saturday 25th

Phillip   On the night of the 24th it began to rain and some smart showers fell the next day, which enabled them to sow the remainder of their Indian corn; it was also of great service to the wheat and the vegetables in the gardens.

෮

On a trip in the harbour with a party including Abaroo, the Aboriginal girl who lived with the Reverend Richard Johnson and his wife, Phillip described a visit to Abaroo's people:

> The girl pointed out one of the natives who she said was her father. None of these people showed any signs of fear, though they saw the officers were armed, and the girl was very desirous

of remaining with them. She was now of an age to want to form a connection with the other sex, which she had no opportunity of doing in the clergyman's family where she lived, and very innocently told him, when she asked to go away, that she wanted to be married.

OCTOBER

Saturday 2nd

The Reverend Richard Johnson   Oh, how my mind is daily tossed about, wandering hither and thither and will not come to anything settled and stable...while the governor has one grand mansion at Sydney and another at Rose Hill, I am forced to live in a miserable hut, and that built at my own cost; and as for any place of worship, that is the last thing thought of. Oh for more Christian patience and fortitude.

Friday 8th

Bennelong brought his wife to the settlement, with his sister and three other men.

Tench   On hearing of their arrival, such numbers flocked to view them that we were apprehensive the crowd of persons would alarm them, but they had left their fears behind and marched on with boldness and unconcern. When we reached the governor's house, Bennelong expressed honest joy to see his old friend and appeared pleased to find that he had recovered of his wound...

The ceremony of introduction being finished, Bennelong seemed to consider himself quite at home, running from room to room with his companions and introducing them to his old friends, the domestics, in the most familiar manner. Among these last, he particularly distinguished the governor's orderly sergeant, whom he kissed with great affection, and a woman who attended in the kitchen; but the gamekeeper, Macentire, he continued to hold in abhorrence and would not suffer his approach.

Nor was his importance to his countrymen less conspicuous in other respects; he undertook to explain the use and nature of those things which were new to them. Some of his explanations were whimsical enough; seeing, for instance, a pair of snuffers, he told them that they were 'Nuffer for candle,' which the others not comprehending, he opened the snuffers and holding up the forefinger of his left hand to represent a candle, made the motion of snuffing it. Finding that even this sagacious interpretation failed, he threw down the snuffers in a rage, and reproaching their stupidity, walked away.

Phillip   Blankets and some clothing were given them and each had a belly-full of fish. Bennelong sat down to dinner with Governor Phillip and drank his wine and coffee as usual. The governor bought a spear from one of his visitants and endeavoured to make them understand that spears, lines, birds, or anything they brought should always be purchased. At the same time he promised Bennelong a shield, for which he was to bring a spear in return, as accustoming these people to barter was judged the most likely means of bringing them to reside amongst the colonists.

Tench   It was observed that a soft gentle tone of voice, which we had taught him to use, was forgotten, and his native vociferation returned in full force. But the tenderness which (like Arabanoo) he had always manifested to children, he still retained, as appeared by his behaviour to those who were presented to him.

Saturday 9th

Phillip   When Bennelong came for his present, those who accompanied him, after staying a short time went away, but he stayed to dinner and left the place highly delighted with his shield, which being made of sole leather and covered with tin was likely to resist the force of their spears.

As it was late in the afternoon before Bennelong thought of departing, his wife and sister, with two men, came over in their canoes to fetch him, so that there was every appearance of these people being perfectly reconciled and no doubt could be entertained but that they would visit the settlement as frequently as could be wished.

Collins   Bennelong solicited the governor to build him a hut at the extremity of the eastern point of the cove. This the governor, who was very desirous of preserving the friendly intercourse which seemed to have taken place, readily promised, and gave the necessary directions for its being built.

Tuesday 12th

Phillip A canoe with Bennelong's sister and several young people coming to one of the points of the cove, the girl who had now lived 17 months with the clergyman's wife joined them, and was so desirous of going away that it was consented to. The next day she was seen naked in a canoe, but she put on a petticoat before she joined the clergyman and some others who went to visit her. She appeared to be pleased with having her liberty, and the boy Nanbaree, who was of the party that went to see her, now wished to stay with the natives all night. He was left behind, but the next morning he returned to the surgeon, with whom he lived, and having fared but badly did not seem inclined to go to them again.

Tuesday 19th

Scott The natives come in frequently and the governor has building a house for them at Cattle Point.

Named because the livestock from the First Fleet were landed there, Cattle Point was later named Bennelong Point, after Bennelong's hut was built there. It is now the site of the Sydney Opera House.

Collins The signal for a sail was made at the South Head and shortly after the *Supply* anchored in the cove from Batavia, having been absent from the settlement six months and two days. Lieutenant Ball arrived at Batavia on the 6th of July last, where he hired a vessel, a Dutch snow [the *Waaksamheyd*] which was to sail shortly after with the provisions that he had purchased for the colony. While the *Supply* lay at Batavia the season was more unhealthy than had ever been known before; every hospital was full and hundreds of the inhabitants had died.

Newton Fowell and several seamen from the *Supply* died at Batavia or at sea on the way home.
    When *Supply* left Port Jackson for Batavia in April, it had been intended that she would call at Norfolk Island to take on board William Bradley and leave Newton Fowell, but as Fowell wrote in his last letter to his family: 'The wind blowing fresh from the eastward which was a foul wind for Norfolk and a fair wind to proceed on the voyage, Mr

Ball did not think it proper to lose so fair an opportunity of getting to the northward.'

Newton Fowell was born in Devon, and entered the Navy in 1780, when he was 12 years old. In 1987, his letters were discovered by the Australian historian Nance Irvine when someone she met by chance in England said to her: 'I have some letters at home from a young lieutenant who sailed on the *Sirius* with Captain Philip. Would you like to have a copy?' The letters are now held in the Mitchell Library at the State Library of New South Wales.

Nance Irvine wrote of Newton Fowell:

> The evidence of these letters shows that he had been well drilled in the art of letter writing, taught various interesting subjects such as political history and natural science, perhaps music and dancing, not to forget fencing... Newton died in 1790, a victim of an unknown tropical disease apparently caught on Batavia. We do not know when his family finally learned of his death. But at that time they gathered together his carefully preserved letters, the record of the last three years of his life, and attached this sad note: 'These were the letters of Newton Fowell Second Lieutenant of the *Sirius* who died on his passage from Batavia to N.S.W. August 23, 1790. Universally lamented. He excelled most young men of his age both in body and mind which made his death an inexpressible grief to his parents, John and Mary Fowell.'

Tuesday 26th

Phillip   The native girl, who had left the settlement, returned after being absent 14 days, but though she appeared to have fared badly, and had been beat by her friend Colbee, yet she would not remain at Sydney more than two days, after which she returned to her companions.

Saturday 30th

Ann George, aged about 26, who had been sentenced to seven years' transportation for stealing 'six copper halfpence and three shillings', gave birth to a daughter; the father was Augustus Alt, the colony's surveyor-general.

Phillip Bennelong, with his wife and two children, who appeared to have been adopted by him when their parents died, now lived in a hut built for them on the eastern point of the cove. They were frequently visited by many of the natives, some of whom daily came to the barracks. All of them were very fond of bread, and they now found the advantage of coming amongst the settlers.

Unlike the officers of the Marine Corps in the First Fleet, the officers of the New South Wales Corps were allowed to bring their wives with them. Soon after the return of the *Supply*, Elizabeth Macarthur, who had arrived in the Second Fleet with her husband Lieutenant John Macarthur of the New South Wales Corps, wrote: 'Mr Ball very soon called upon us and complimented me with many little comforts procured at Batavia, which were truly acceptable'.

NOVEMBER

Friday 12th

Tench wrote a review of the colony 'drawn from actual observation... exactly as I find it written in my journal':

> With the natives we are hand and glove. They throng the camp every day and sometimes by their clamour and importunity for bread and meat (of which they now all eat greedily) are become very troublesome. God knows, we have little enough for ourselves! Full allowance (if eight pounds of flour, and either seven pounds of beef, or four pounds of pork, served alternately, per week, without either peas, oatmeal, spirits, butter, or cheese, can be called so) is yet kept up; but if the Dutch snow [the *Waaksamheyd*] does not arrive soon it must be shortened, as the casks in the storehouse, I observed yesterday, are woefully decreased.
>
> The convicts continue to behave pretty well; three only have been hanged since the arrival of the last fleet in the latter end of June, all of whom were newcomers. The number of convicts here diminishes every day, our principal efforts being wisely made at Rose Hill, where the land is unquestionably better than about this place. Except building, sawing, and brickmaking, nothing of consequence is now carried on here.

Saturday 13th

Phillip Early in the morning...16 of the natives visited the settlement and some fish being distributed amongst them, they made a fire in the governor's yard and sat down to breakfast in great good humour. Those that were strangers appeared highly delighted with the novelties that surrounded them...Bennelong, who had been for two days with some of his party at Botany Bay, came along with these people and brought his wife with him. She appeared to be very ill and had a fresh wound on her head, which he gave Governor Phillip to understand she had merited, for breaking a fizgig and a throwing stick.

The governor's reasoning with him on this subject had no effect; he said she was bad, and therefore he had beat her. Neither could it be learned what inducement this woman could have to do an act which she must have known would be followed by a severe beating, for Bennelong either did not understand the questions put to him or was unwilling to answer them. When these people had finished their breakfast, they all went to the hospital to get the women's heads dressed, for, besides Bennelong's wife, a woman who was a stranger had received a blow on the head which had laid her skull bare.

After this business was over, most of them returned and sat down in the yard at the back of Governor Phillip's house; but Bennelong went into the house as usual, and, finding the governor writing, sat down by him. He appeared very much out of humour and frequently said that he was going to beat a woman with a hatchet which he held in his hand. It was impossible to persuade him to say he would not beat her, and after some time he got up, saying that he could not dine with the governor, as he was going to beat the woman. Governor Phillip then insisted on going with him, to which he made no objection, though he was given to understand that he would not be suffered to beat any woman, and they set off for his hut at the point. The governor took his orderly-sergeant along with him, and they were joined by the judge-advocate.

Tench When they reached the house, they found several natives, of both sexes, lying promiscuously before the fire, and among them, a young woman, not more than 16 years old, who at sight of Bennelong, started, and raised herself half up. He no sooner saw her than, snatching a sword of the country, he ran at her and gave her two severe wounds on the head, and one on the shoulder, before interference in behalf of the poor wretch could be made. Our people now rushed in and seized him, but the other Indians continued quiet spectators of what was passing, either awed by Bennelong's superiority, or deeming it a common case, unworthy of notice and interposition. In vain did the governor by turns soothe and threaten him; in vain did the sergeant point his musket at him; he seemed dead to every passion but revenge, forgot his affection to his old friends and, instead of complying with the request they made, furiously brandished his sword at the governor and called aloud for his hatchet to dispatch the unhappy victim of his barbarity. Matters now wore a serious aspect; the other Indians appeared under the control of Bennelong and had begun to arm and prepare their spears, as if determined to support him in his violence.

Phillip Reasoning with him was now out of the question. The savage fury which took possession of him when he found himself kept from the girl, who was lying senseless, is not to be described. He had now got another wooden sword, but the judge-advocate and the sergeant held him and, what passed being observed from the *Supply*, Lieutenant Ball and the surgeon of the hospital came over to the spot armed, and the poor girl was put into the boat without any opposition on the part of the natives...

The girl was removed in the evening from the *Supply* to Governor Phillip's house, where a young man who lived with Bennelong desired to remain with her, and, from the tenderness he shewed her when Bennelong was not present, was supposed to be her husband, though he had not dared to open his lips or even to look dissatisfied when her life was in danger.

Several of the natives came to see this girl and (except the supposed husband) they all appeared very desirous that she might return to the hut, though they must have known that she would be killed; and, what is not to be accounted for, the girl herself appeared desirous of going.

As Tench wrote: 'Inexplicable contradictions arose to bewilder our researches, which no ingenuity could unravel, and no credulity reconcile.'

Wednesday 17th

Continuing his review of the colony, Tench described the settlement at Rose Hill:

The main street of the new town is already begun. It is to be a mile long, and of such breadth as will make Pall Mall and Portland Place hide their diminished heads. It contains at present 32 houses completed, of 24 feet by 12 each, on a ground floor only, built of wattles plastered with clay, and thatched. Each house is divided into two rooms, in one of which is a fireplace and a brick chimney. These houses are designed for men only, and 10 is the number of inhabitants allotted to each; but some of them now contain 13 or 14, for want of better accommodation. More are building; in a cross street stand nine houses for unmarried women, and exclusive of all these are several small huts where convict families of good character are allowed to reside.

The technique of making walls by interlacing pliable branches and plastering them with mud or clay was known in England as 'wattle and daub'. In New South Wales, the acacias used for this purpose in the early buildings were given the common name of 'wattle'.

While at Rose Hill, Tench visited James Ruse, who gave an account of his farming methods:

My land I prepared thus; having burnt the fallen timber off the ground I dug in the ashes and then hoed it up, never doing more than eight or perhaps nine rods in a day, by which means it was not like the government farm, just scratched over, but properly done; then I clod-moulded it and dug in the grass and weeds— this I think almost equal to ploughing. I then let it lie as long as I could, exposed to air and sun, and just before I sowed my seed, turned it all up afresh.

When I shall have reaped my crop, I purpose to hoe it again and harrow it fine, and then sow it with turnip-seed, which will mellow and prepare it for next year. My straw I mean to bury in pits and throw in with it everything which I think will rot and turn to manure. I have no person to help me at present but my wife, whom I married in this country; she is industrious.

Sunday 21st

Tench reported that when Bennelong returned to the settlement with his wife, Barangaroo,

The governor ordered him to be taken to the hospital, that he might see the victim of his ferocity. He complied in sullen silence. When about to enter the room in which she lay, he appeared to have a momentary struggle with himself, which ended his resentment. He spoke to her with kindness and professed sorrow for what he had done, and promised her future protection.

Barangaroo, who had accompanied him, now took the alarm, and as in shunning one extreme we are ever likely to rush into another, she thought him perhaps too courteous and tender. Accordingly she began to revile them both with great bitterness, threw stones at the girl and attempted to beat her with a club. Here terminated this curious history, which I leave to the reader's speculation. Whether human sacrifices of prisoners be common among them is a point which all our future inquiry never completely determined. It is certain that no second instance of this sort was ever witnessed by us.

⸎

A young Aboriginal named Yemmerrawannie, aged about 16, was now living at the settlement.

Tench   This good-tempered lively lad was become a great favourite with us and almost constantly lived at the governor's house. He had clothes made up for him and to amuse his mind he was taught to wait at table. One day a lady, Mrs Macarthur, wife of an officer of the garrison, dined there, as did Nanbaree. This latter, anxious that his countryman should appear to advantage in his new office, gave him many instructions, strictly charging him, among other things, to take away the lady's plate whenever she should cross her knife and fork, and to give her a clean one. This Yemmerrawannie executed, not only to Mrs Macarthur, but to several of the other guests.

At last Nanbaree crossed his knife and fork with great gravity, casting a glance at the other, who looked for a moment with cool indifference at what he had done, and then turned his head another way. Stung at this supercilious treatment, he called in rage to know why he was not attended to as well as the rest of the company. But Yemmerrawannie only laughed; nor could all the anger and reproaches of the other prevail upon him to do that for one of his countrymen, which he cheerfully continued to perform to every other person.

DECEMBER

Thursday 9th

Tench   A sergeant of marines, with three convicts, among whom was Macentire, the governor's gamekeeper (the person of whom Bennelong had, on former occasions, shown so much dread and hatred) went out on a shooting party. Having passed the north arm of Botany Bay, they proceeded to a hut formed of boughs, which had been lately erected on this peninsula for the accommodation of sportsmen who wished to continue by night in the woods... Having lighted a fire, they lay down, without distrust or suspicion.

About one o'clock, the sergeant was awakened by a rustling noise in the bushes near him and, supposing it to proceed from a kangaroo, called to his comrades, who instantly jumped up. On looking about more narrowly, they saw two natives with spears in their hands creeping towards them and three others a little farther behind. As this naturally created alarm, Macentire said, 'Don't be afraid, I know them,' and immediately laying down his gun, stepped forward, and spoke to them in their own language.

The Indians, finding they were discovered, kept slowly retreating, and Macentire accompanied them about a hundred yards, talking familiarly all the while. One of them now jumped on a fallen tree and without giving the least warning of his intention, launched his spear at Macentire and lodged it in his left side. The person who committed this wanton act was described as a young man with a speck or blemish on his left eye. That he had been lately among us was evident from his being newly shaved.

The wounded man immediately drew back and joining his party cried, 'I am a dead man'. While one broke off the end of the spear, the other two set out with their guns in pursuit of the natives, but their swiftness of foot soon convinced our people of the impossibility of reaching them. It was now determined to attempt to carry Macentire home as his death was apprehended to be near and he expressed a longing desire not to be left to expire in the woods. Being an uncommonly robust muscular man, notwithstanding a great effusion of blood, he was able, with the assistance of his comrades, to creep slowly along.

Friday 10th

Tench In the course of the day, Colbee and several more natives came in and were taken to the bed where the wounded man lay. Their behaviour indicated that they had already heard of the accident, as they repeated twice or thrice the name of the murderer, Pemulwy, saying that he lived at Botany Bay. To gain knowledge of their treatment of similar wounds, one of the surgeons made signs of extracting the spear, but this they violently opposed, and said, if it were done, death would instantly follow.

Sunday 12th

Collins   When the spear was extracted, which was not until suppuration took place, it was found to have entered his body under the left arm, to the depth of seven inches and a half. It was armed for five or six inches from the point with ragged pieces of shells fastened in gum. His recovery was immediately pronounced by Mr White to be very doubtful.

Monday 13th

From the first days of the colony the Aboriginal people from the Botany Bay area had been the most aggressive towards the settlement, possibly because of their spiteful encounters with La Pérouse's party at the beginning of 1788. Phillip had been at Rose Hill when Macentire was speared. When he returned to Sydney, the following order was issued:

> Several tribes of the natives still continuing to throw spears at any man they meet unarmed, by which several have been killed or dangerously wounded, the governor, in order to deter the natives from such practices in future, has ordered out a party to search for the man who wounded the convict in so dangerous a manner on Friday last, though no offence was offered on his part, and to make a severe example of that tribe.
>
> At the same time the governor strictly forbids (under pain of the severest punishments), any soldier or other person not expressly ordered out for that purpose ever to fire on any native, except in his own defence, or to molest him in any shape, or to take away any spears or other articles which they may find belonging to those people. The natives will be made severe examples of whenever any man is wounded by them, but that will be done in a manner which may satisfy them that it is a punishment inflicted on them for their own bad behaviour, and of which they cannot be made sensible if they are not treated with kindness while they continue peaceable and quiet.

Phillip ordered that a party consisting of four officers and 40 marines were to be ready to leave 'tomorrow morning at daylight'.

Tench   Just previous to this order being issued...his Excellency informed me that he had pitched upon me to execute the foregoing command...we were, if practicable, to bring away two natives as prisoners and to put to death 10; that we were to destroy all weapons of war, but nothing else; that no hut was to be burned; that all women and children were to remain uninjured...that we were to cut off and bring in the heads of the slain, for which purpose hatchets and bags would be furnished. And finally, that no signal of amity or invitation should be used in order to allure them to us; or if made on their part, to be answered by us, for that such conduct would be not only present treachery, but give them reason to distrust every future mark of peace and friendship on our part.

His Excellency was now pleased to enter into the reasons which had induced him to adopt measures of such severity. He said that since our arrival in the country, no less than 17 of our people had either been killed or wounded by the natives; that he looked upon the tribe known by the name of Bideegal, living on the before-mentioned peninsula, and chiefly on the north arm of Botany Bay, to be the principal aggressors; that against this tribe he was determined to strike a decisive blow, in order at once to convince them of our superiority, and to infuse a universal terror which might operate to prevent further mischief.

Phillip   Many of the natives had recently visited the settlement; they had all been well received, and some of their children frequently remained there for several days without their parents ever seeing them, and if any of them were going where their children would be an encumbrance, they used to leave them at Sydney. Bennelong, Colbee and two or three others now lived at Sydney three or four days in the week, and they all repeatedly desired those natives might be killed who threw spears.

Tench wrote that Phillip told him:

> If I could propose any alteration of the orders under which I was to act, he would patiently listen to me. Encouraged by this condescension, I begged leave to offer for consideration whether, instead of destroying 10 persons, the capture of six would not better answer all the purposes for which the expedition was to be undertaken, as out of this number a part might be set aside for retaliation and the rest, at a proper time, liberated, after having seen the fate of their comrades and being made sensible of the cause of their own detention.
>
> This scheme his Excellency was pleased instantly to adopt, adding, 'If six cannot be taken, let this number be shot. Should you, however, find it practicable to take so many, I will hang

two, and send the rest to Norfolk Island for a certain period, which will cause their country-men to believe that we have despatched them secretly.' The order was accordingly altered to its present form and I took my leave to prepare, after being again cautioned not to deceive by holding signals of amity.

Phillip   On this order appearing, Lieutenant Dawes, whose tour of duty it was to go out with the party, refused that duty by letter to the senior officer of the detachment (Captain Campbell), who finding it impossible to persuade Lieutenant Dawes to obey the order, brought the letter to the governor, who likewise took great pains to point out the consequence of his (Lieutenant Dawes) being put under an arrest. Late in the evening Lieutenant Dawes informed Captain Campbell that the Reverend Mr Johnson thought he might obey the order, and that he was ready to go out with the party, which he did.

Tuesday 14th

They set off at four o'clock in the morning.

Tench   The detachment consisted, besides myself, of Captain Hill of the New South Wales Corps, Lieutenants Poulden and Dawes of the marines, Mr Worgan and Mr Lowes, surgeons, three sergeants, three corporals, and 40 private soldiers, provided with three days' provisions, ropes to bind our prisoners with and hatchets and bags to cut off and contain the heads of the slain. By nine o'clock this terrific procession reached the peninsula at the head of Botany Bay, but after having walked in various directions until four o'clock in the afternoon, without seeing a native, we halted for the night.

Wednesday 15th

Tench   At daylight on the following morning our search recommenced. We marched in an easterly direction, intending to fall in with the south-west arm of the bay about three miles above its mouth, which we determined to scour, and thence passing along the head of the peninsula, to proceed to the north arm and complete our search. However, by a mistake of our guides, at half past seven o'clock, instead of finding ourselves on the south-west arm, we came suddenly upon the sea shore at the head of the peninsula, about midway between the two arms. Here we saw five Indians on the beach, whom we attempted to surround, but they penetrated our design and before we could get near enough to effect our purpose, ran off. We pursued, but a contest between heavy-armed Europeans...and naked unencumbered Indians, was too unequal to last long. They darted into the wood and disappeared.

On our return to our baggage...we observed a native fishing in shallow water...we found it to be our friend Colbee and he joined us at once with his wonted familiarity and unconcern. We asked him where Pemulwy was and found that he perfectly comprehended the nature of our errand, for he described him to have fled to the southward and to be at such a distance, as, had we known the account to be true, would have prevented our going in search of him without a fresh supply of provisions.

When we arrived at our baggage, Colbee sat down, eat, drank, and slept with us from 10 o'clock until past noon. We asked him several questions about Sydney, which he had left on the preceding day, and told us he had been present at an operation performed at the hospital, where Mr White had cut off a woman's leg. The agony and cries of the poor sufferer he depicted in a most lively manner.

The party returned to Sydney the following day.

Friday 17th

Collins   The *Waaksamheyd* anchored in the cove from Batavia, from which place she sailed on the 20th day of last September, meeting on her passage with contrary winds. She was manned principally with Malays, 16 of whom she buried during the passage.

Phillip   The provisions brought in her consisted of 171 barrels of beef, 172 barrels of pork, 39 barrels of flour, 1000 pounds of sugar and 70,000 pounds of rice.

Thursday 23rd

Elizabeth Macarthur   Mrs Colbee, whose name is Daringa, brought in a newborn female infant of hers for me to see...It was wrapped up in the soft bark of a tree, a specimen of which I have preserved. It is a kind of a mantle not much known in England, I fancy. I ordered something for the poor woman to eat and had her taken

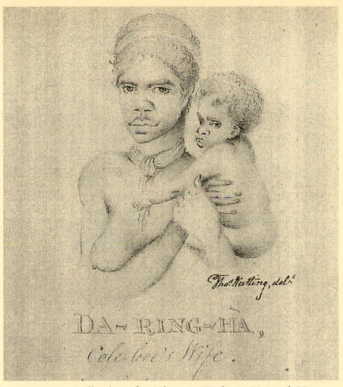

Daringa, Colbee's wife. *Thomas Watling. Natural History Museum, London.*

proper care of for some little while. When she first presented herself to me she appeared feeble and faint. She has since been regular in her visits. The child thrives remarkably well and I discover a softness and gentleness of manners in Daringa truly interesting.

Elizabeth Macarthur is generally referred to as the first 'educated' woman to come to the colony. She kept a journal of the voyage and wrote to her friends in England about all aspects of life in New South Wales—her family's land holdings, local politics, the Aboriginal people and the unique plants and animals. The journal and a collection of her letters is held by the Mitchell Library and were first published in *Historical Records of New South Wales* in 1893; the journal is written in her hand, but the letters were copied by her children from the originals, which have since been lost.

Elizabeth Macarthur, *artist unknown. Dixson Galleries, State Library of New South Wales.*

Friday 24th

From 22 to 24 December, Tench led a second expedition to Botany Bay, 'without our seeing a single native...It ended as those preceding it had done,' he wrote, 'in disappointment and vexation. At nine o'clock we returned to Sydney to report our fruitless peregrination.'

Perhaps Phillip, for once, lost his composure and with it his judgment over the spearing of Macentire. Dawes evidently thought so, but as Collins wrote:

> There was little probability that such a party would be able so unexpectedly to fall in with the people they were sent to punish...The very circumstance, however, of a party being armed and detached purposely to punish the man and his companions who wounded Macentire was likely to have a good effect, as it was well known to several natives, who were at this time in the

town of Sydney, that this was the intention with which they were sent out...Whenever the party was seen by the natives, they fled with incredible swiftness.

Phillip would have known it was unlikely that the marines would be able to catch anyone, let alone to capture 10 and cut off their heads, as he first proposed. He forbade any form of treachery and was quick to accept Tench's less savage proposal. Perhaps he knew it was unlikely that they would be able to capture or kill anyone at all.

Monday 27th

The temperature reached 109 degrees Fahrenheit. Tench wrote: 'Wind north-north-west; it felt like the blast of a heated oven and in proportion as it increased, the heat was found to be more intense, the sky hazy, the sun gleaming through at intervals.'

Tuesday 28th

Phillip Several of the natives who had been pretty constant visitors at Sydney for some weeks were detected stealing potatoes.

A party of marines was sent to 'secure the three natives who had been digging up the potatoes' and 'a club, which at first was taken for a spear, being thrown by one of them, three muskets were fired'. A man known as Bangai was wounded by the shots but managed to escape.

❧

Phillip recorded the number of deaths in the settlement during 1790:

From sickness	142
Lost in the woods	4
Executed	4
Drowned	6
	156

1790 was a year of contrasts and extremes; the first convict was emancipated; the lash came to be counted in thousands instead of hundreds; near-starvation was relieved for a time, but the Second Fleet brought another thousand mouths to feed and massive sickness. When Phillip was speared, he forgave the man who wounded him and wrote that it was 'most likely that the action proceeded from a momentary impulse of fear'; but when his gamekeeper was speared, he ordered a mission of revenge.

Bennelong left the settlement, then came back, and Phillip wrote: 'There was every appearance of these people being perfectly reconciled and no doubt could be entertained but that they would visit the settlement as frequently as could be wished'.

But perhaps Tench was closer to the truth when he wrote in November 1790: 'Our greatest source of entertainment now lay in cultivating the acquaintance of our new friends, the natives... No difficulty but of understanding each other subsisted between us. Inexplicable contradictions arose to bewilder our researches, which no ingenuity could unravel and no credulity reconcile.'

1791
Choice of Their Lands

February	After the hot, dry summer, the streams around Sydney Cove began to dry up.
8 February	An Aboriginal initiation ceremony was held at Farm Cove. A corroboree was also held during the month, on Bennelong Point.
28 March	The *Waaksamheyd* sailed for England with the crew of the *Sirius*. William and Mary Bryant, with their two children and seven other convicts, escaped in a small boat.
30 March	Five grants of land were made, including 30 acres at Rose Hill to James Ruse.
2 April	Shortage of provisions made it necessary to again reduce the weekly ration.
11 April	Phillip led an expedition to find out whether the Hawkesbury and the Nepean were the same river.
24 June	Rain over three days filled the streams and improved the prospect for crops.
9 July	The *Mary Ann*, the first ship of the Third Fleet, arrived with 141 female convicts.
31 August	A return of settlers showed that 37 had been settled in the Parramatta district and 50 at Norfolk Island. During the month, a settler's hut at was burnt down by the Aboriginal people.
21 September	HMS *Gorgon* arrived with provisions, seed, fruit trees and livestock.
16 October	The *Admiral Barrington* arrived, bringing the total of convicts in the Third Fleet to 1881.
11 November	Phillip asked to be replaced as governor, because of ill health.
27 November	Surgeon's returns showed almost 600 sick at Parramatta and Sydney.
18 December	The *Gorgon* sailed for England with the First Fleet marines.

JANUARY

Monday 3rd

Bangai, the Aboriginal man who had been shot and wounded at the end of December, was found dead and, when Phillip accused Benne-long of robbing some fishermen of their catch, Bennelong threatened revenge for Bangai's death and again had to be restrained.

Phillip One of the sentinels was now called in, as it was much feared he would do some violent act...it was suggested by an offi-cer who was in the room that he might not be understood clearly and the governor was very unwilling to destroy the confidence Ben-nelong had for some time placed in him, which the slightest punishment or confinement would have done; he therefore told him to come near, for he was then standing at some distance, but he refused and went away. Bennelong had not left the governor with any intention of returning, for in passing the wheelwright's shop, the workmen being at dinner, he stole a hatchet, with which, though pursued, he got clear off.

Collins It was much to be regretted that any necessity existed for adopting these sanguinary punishments, and that we had not yet been able to reconcile the natives to the deprivation of those parts of this harbour which we occupied. While they entertained the idea of our having dispossessed them of their residences, they must always consider us as enemies, and upon this principle they made a point of attacking the white people whenever opportunity and safety concurred.

It was also unfortunately found that our knowledge of their lan-guage consisted at this time of only a few terms for such things as, being visible, could not well be mistaken, but no one had yet attained words enough to convey an idea in connected terms.

Tuesday 4th

Collins and Alt sat as magistrates at Rose Hill. Robert Russell was one of three convicts found guilty of stealing food. He was sentenced 'to receive 200 lashes on his bare back, with a cat-o'-nine-tails, and wear an iron on his leg for a twelvemonth'.

Saturday 8th

Simon Burn, one of the first convicts to be married in the colony, was involved in a brawl and was brought before Collins and Alt, charged with assaulting two marines. His wife Fanny gave evidence on his behalf. Burn was found guilty and sentenced 'To be turned into a gang', that is, chained together with several other convicts.

Thursday 20th

John Macentire died.

Phillip His death was sudden, as at one time he was thought to be in a very fair way of recovery, being able to walk about. On opening the body, it appeared that the lungs on the left side, which had been wounded, were entirely wasted away; the pleura firmly adhered to the ribs for some inches round the wound; several of the small stones with which the spear had been armed were found adhering to the side and the rib against which the spear had broke was splintered.

Saturday 22nd

Collins reported that the *Supply* sailed for Norfolk Island, 'having some provisions on board for that settlement. She was to bring back Captain Hunter, with the officers and crew of his Majesty's late ship *Sirius*'.

Monday 24th

Tench Two bunches of grapes were cut in the governor's garden from cuttings of vines brought three years before from the Cape of Good Hope. The bunches were handsome, the fruit of a moderate size but well filled out, and the flavour high and delicious.

Wednesday 26th

Collins Our colours were hoisted in the redoubt, in commemoration of the day on which formal possession was taken of this cove three years before.

This is the first recorded celebration of what is now called Australia Day.

Friday 28th

Collins Henry Edward Dodd, the superintendent of convicts employed in cultivation at Rose Hill, died of a decline. He had been ill for some time, but his death was accelerated by exposing himself in his shirt for three or four hours during the night, in search after some thieves who were plundering his garden... The services rendered to the public by this person were visible in the cultivation and improvements which appeared at the settlement where he had the direction. He had acquired an ascendancy over the convicts, which he preserved without being hated by them; he knew how to proportion their labour to their ability, and by an attentive and quiet demeanour had gained the approbation and countenance of the different officers who had been on duty at Rose Hill.

༄

Phillip wrote that Bennelong:

> frequently visited the fishing boats and made many enquiries to know if Governor Phillip was angry and would shoot him; he ventured to go to the hospital and seemed very desirous of knowing if he might come to the governor's house...
>
> Some days afterwards he came to the governor's, who, happening to be in the yard when he came to the gate, ordered him away. He was seen soon afterwards and as he appeared very desirous of being received again, and disclaimed any knowledge of the hatchet or any intention of revenging the death of the native who had been shot, Governor Phillip appeared to believe him and he was permitted to come into the yard, which was always open to the natives, and some bread and fish were given him.
>
> But he was no longer permitted to enter the house; this was putting him on a level with the other natives, and he appeared to feel his degradation, but it did not prevent him from repeating his visits very frequently.

FEBRUARY

Tuesday 3rd

Scott The Dutch snow [*Waaksamheyd*] dropped down the harbour as low as the lookout cove on pretence of going to sea, but I suppose that was the policy of the captain as the governor was about buying her. (A snow was a two-masted, square-sailed vessel, similar to a brig, with a small third mast carrying a trysail.)

Phillip needed the Dutch ship to send home the officers and men who had belonged to the *Sirius*. Tench wrote:

> It had always been the governor's wish to hire the Dutchman... but the frantic, extravagant behaviour of the master of her for a long time frustrated the conclusion of a contract. He was so totally lost to a sense of reason and propriety as to ask £11 per ton, monthly, for her use, until she should arrive from England at Batavia. This was treated with proper contempt and he was at last induced to accept 20 shillings per ton per month...until she should arrive in England, being about the twenty-fifth part of his original demand. And even at this price she was, perhaps, the dearest vessel ever hired on a similar service.

Tuesday 8th

Phillip Two native youths, who had frequently left Governor Phillip's house in order to have their front teeth drawn, had now been absent several days for that purpose. They were seen in a bay down the harbour on the 8th of February, where a considerable number of the natives were assembled, it was supposed not less than a hundred, including women and children. Most of the men were painted and it should seem that they were assembled for the purpose of drawing the front teeth from several men and boys.

Soon afterwards, the two youths returned to the governor's... They had lost their front teeth, and, considering their manner of drawing teeth in this country, it was not surprising to see that one of them had lost a piece of his jaw-bone, which was driven out with the tooth. Both these boys appeared to be in pain, but they would not own it, and seemed to value themselves on having undergone the operation, though why it is performed, or why the females lose a part of the little finger, could not as yet be learnt.

Later, Collins wrote:

> This ceremony occurred twice during my residence in New South Wales and in the second operation I was fortunate enough to

attend them during the whole of the time, attended by a person well qualified to make drawings of every particular circumstance that occurred...It was first performed in the beginning of the month of February 1791, and exactly at the same period in the year 1795 the second operation occurred.

The following description is taken from Collins's 1795 account of the ceremony.

The people from Cammeray [the Cameragal] arrived, among whom were those who were to perform the operation, all of whom appeared to have been impatiently expected by the other natives. They were painted after the manner of the country, were mostly provided with shields and all armed with clubs, spears and throwing sticks...

The place selected for this extraordinary exhibition was at the head of Farm Cove, where a space had been for some days prepared by clearing it of grass, stumps etc; it was of an oval figure, the dimensions of it 27 feet by 18, and was named *yoolahng*. When we arrived at the spot, we found the party from the north shore armed and standing at one end of it; at the other we saw a party consisting of the boys who were to be given up for the purpose of losing each a tooth, and their several friends who accompanied them. They then began the ceremony.

Collins's account is accompanied by eight drawings representing the various scenes of the ceremony, one of which is reproduced here. In the first scene, the 15 young men who were to be initiated were:

seated at the head of the *yoolahng*, while those who were to be the operators paraded several times round it, running upon their hands and feet and imitating the dogs of the country....Every time they passed the place where the boys were seated, they threw up the sand and dust on them with their hands and their feet... We understood that by this ceremony power over the dog was given to them and that it endowed them with whatever good or beneficial qualities that animal might possess.

Two men were at the centre of the second scene:

A stout robust native, carrying on his shoulders a *patagarang* or kangaroo made of grass; the second is carrying a load of brushwood...they at last deposited their load at the feet of the young men and retired from the *yoolahng* as if they were excessively fatigued by what they had done. By this offering of the dead kangaroo was meant the power that was now given them of killing that animal; the brushwood might represent its haunt.

Scene three:

> The actors went down into a valley near the place, where they fitted themselves with long tails made of grass, which they fastened to the hinder part of their girdles, instead of the sword, which was laid aside during the scene. Being equipped, they put themselves in motion as a herd of kangaroos, now jumping along, then lying down and scratching themselves, as those animals do when basking in the sun...This was emblematical of one of their future exercises, the hunting of the kangaroo. The scene was altogether whimsical and curious.

In scene four:

> Quickly divesting themselves of their artificial tails, each man caught up a boy, and, placing him on his shoulders, carried him off in triumph.

Of scene five, Collins wrote:

> I made much enquiry but could never obtain any other answer than that it was very good, that the boys would now become brave men, that they would see well and fight well.

Scene six was dominated by

> Booderro, the native who had throughout taken the principal part in the business...the whole party poised and presented their spears at him, pointing them inwards, and touching the centre of his shield...and it appeared significant of an exercise which was to form the principal business of their lives, the use of the spear.

In the seventh scene:

> They now commenced their preparations for striking out the tooth. The first subject they took out was a boy of about 10 years of age; he was seated on the shoulders of another native who sat on the grass.
>
> [The gum was lanced] then the smallest end of the stick was applied as high up on the tooth as the gum would admit of, while the operator stood ready with a large stone, apparently to drive the tooth down the throat of his patient...They were full 10 minutes about this first operation, the tooth being,

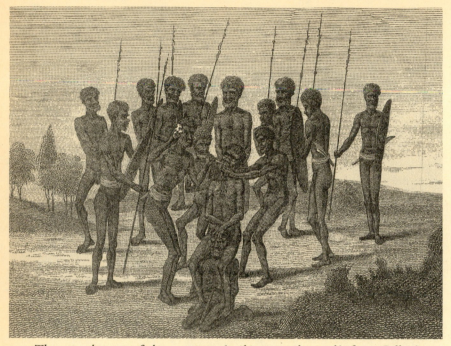

The seventh scene of the ceremony, 'striking out the tooth', from Collins's Account of the English Colony in New South Wales.

unfortunately for the boy, fixed very firm in the gum. It was at last forced out, and the sufferer was taken away to a little distance, where the gum was closed by his friends...

During the whole of the operation the assistants made the most hideous noise in the ears of the patients, sufficient to distract their attention and to drown any cries they could possibly have uttered; but they made it a point of honour to bear the pain without a murmur.

In the final scene the young men are

...arranged and sitting upon the trunk of a tree, as they appeared in the evening after the operation was over...Suddenly, on a signal being given, they all started up and rushed into the town, driving before them men, women, and children, who were glad to get out of their way. They were now received into the class of men, were privileged to wield the spear and the club, and to oppose their persons in combat. They might now also seize such females as they chose for wives.

Collins wrote in conclusion:

> Bennelong's sister and Daringa, Colbee's wife, hearing me express a great desire to be possessed of some of these teeth, procured three of them for me, one of which was that of Nanbaree, Colbee's relation. I found that they had fastened them to pieces of small line, and were wearing them round their necks. They were given to me with much secrecy and great dread of being observed, and with an injunction that I should never let it be known that they had made me such a present, as the Cammeray tribe, to whom they were to be given, would not fail to punish them for it.

Saturday 12th

Phillip The weather was very close and sultry and the natives having fired the country for several miles round, the wind, which blew strong on the 12th, was heated to a very extraordinary degree, particularly at Rose Hill, where the country was on fire for several miles to the northward and southward. Great numbers of parroquets were picked up under the trees, and the bats, which had been seen frequently flying about Rose Hill soon after the evening closed in, and were supposed to go to the southward every night and return to the northward before the day broke, now appeared in immense numbers. Thousands of them were hanging on the branches of the trees, and many dropped down, unable to bear the burning winds.

The head of this bat strongly resembles that of a fox, and the wings of many of them extend three feet 10 inches...The governor had one, a female, that would hang by one leg a whole day without changing its position and in that pendant situation, with its breast neatly covered with one of its wings, it ate whatever was offered it, lapping out of the hand like a cat.

(Phillip also kept a dingo and a collection of kangaroos; in a letter to Sir Joseph Banks he said that kangaroos 'should sleep very warm and have a room to go to in which a good fire should be kept during the cold weather; I have four who always sleep before the fire in the kitchen'.)

Tuesday 15th

At Rose Hill, Collins sat as a magistrate. John Jenkinson was sentenced to 50 lashes for 'boiling wheat in his hut'. John Harrington was sentenced to 25 lashes 'for buying a pair of shoes, the property of Bateman, from a person unknown', and Henry Sayers received 25 lashes for 'taking a knife out of his hut'. A convict whose name is recorded as John Irons, who may also have been known as John Hyon or Hiorne, was found guilty of stealing food and sentenced 'to be locked up in the prison for one month, nightly'.

Friday 25th

Collins James Ruse, the first settler in this country, who had been upon his ground about 15 months, having got in his crop of corn, declared himself desirous of relinquishing his claim to any further provisions from the store and said that he was able to support himself by the produce of his farm. He had shown himself an industrious man and the governor, being satisfied that he could do without any further aid from the stores, consented to his proposal and informed him that he should be forthwith put in possession of an allotment of 30 acres of ground in the situation he then occupied.

Saturday 26th

Collins The *Supply*, after an absence of just five weeks, returned from Norfolk Island, having on board Captain Hunter, with the officers and people of the *Sirius*...

Two pieces of very coarse canvas manufactured at Norfolk Island were sent to the governor, but unless better could be produced from the looms than these specimens, little expectation was to be formed of this article ever answering even the common culinary purposes to which canvas can be applied...

On the *Supply* coming to an anchor, the *Sirius's* late ship's company, whose appearance bore testimony to the miserable fare they had met with in Norfolk Island for several months, were landed and lodged in the military or portable hospital until the *Waaksamheyd* Dutch snow could be got ready to receive them.

Monday 28th

William Bryant, the fisherman, was coming up the harbour with a boatload of fish and with Bennelong's sister, her two children and another little girl in the boat, when a squall of wind upset the boat and it filled with water.

Phillip The young woman had the two children on her shoulders in a moment and swam on shore with them; the girl also swam on shore, as did such of the boat's crew that could swim. Several of the natives, seeing this accident as the boat drove towards the rocks, gave them every possible assistance, without which in all probability one of the crew would have been drowned. After clearing the boat, they collected the oars and such articles as had been driven on shore in different places, and in these friendly offices Bennelong was very assiduous; this behaviour gave Governor Phillip an opportunity of receiving him in a more kindly manner than he had done since his bad behaviour.

⁂

Phillip Though our colonists had never been able to learn the reason for the females losing two joints of the little finger, they now had an opportunity of seeing in what manner that operation is performed. Colbee's wife brought her child to Governor Phillip's house a few days after it was born, and as it was a female both the father and mother had been repeatedly told that if the finger was to be cut off the governor wished to see the operation. The child was now two months old, and a ligature was applied round the little finger at the second joint.

But two or three days afterwards, when she brought the child again, the ligature was either broke or had been taken off. This being mentioned to the mother, she took several hairs from the head of an officer who was present and bound them very tight round the child's finger. After some time a gangrene took place and though the child appeared uneasy when the finger was touched, it did not cry...This bandage was continued until the finger was ready to drop off, when its parents carried it to the surgeon, who, at their request, separated it with a knife.

Later, Collins wrote that it was learned that the top two joints of the little finger were removed because they 'were supposed to be in the way when they wound their fishing lines over the hand'.

During their brief stay at Port Jackson, Hunter and Bradley attended a corroboree. Bradley wrote:

> I went with the governor and a party to Bennelong's house on the east point of the cove [Bennelong Point] to see a dance, according to previous notice given to Bennelong who had assembled

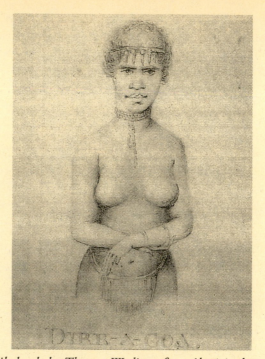

Pencil sketch by Thomas Watling of an Aboriginal woman,
Dirragoa, *with the top two joints of the little finger*
missing. The waistband made from possum fur shows that
Dirragoa was not married. She is also wearing a
headband with kangaroo teeth attached and a necklace of
cut sections of reed. Natural History Museum, London.

many of his friends for the purpose of entertaining us. They
began soon after dark, having several small fires for the purpose
of giving light; they placed us in a ring within which they were
to perform.

Hunter   Their dance was truly wild and savage, yet in many parts
there appeared order and regularity; one man would frequently
single himself out from the dance and running round the whole of
the performers, sing out in a loud voice, using some expressions in
one particular tone of voice which we could not understand; he
would then join the dance, in which it was observed that certain
parties alternately led forward to the front, and there exhibited with

their utmost skill and agility all the various motions which, with them, seemed to constitute the principal beauties of dancing.

One of the most striking was that of placing their feet very wide apart and by an extraordinary exertion of the muscles of the thighs and legs, moving the knees in a trembling and very surprising manner, such as none of us could imitate, which seemed to show that it required much practice to arrive at any degree of perfection in this singular motion...

Their music consisted of two sticks of very hard wood, one of which the musician held upon his breast in the manner of a violin and struck it with the other in good and regular time; the performer, who was a stout strong-voiced man, sung the whole time and frequently applied those graces in music, the piano and forte; he was assisted by several young boys and girls who sat at his feet, and by their manner of crossing the thighs, made a hollow between them and their belly, upon which they beat time with the flat of their hand, so as to make a kind of sound which will be better understood from the manner of its being produced than from any verbal description. [The didgeridoo was not used in the Sydney region. It is used only in northern Australia, where termites create the wooden pipes.] These children also sung with the chief musical performer, who stood up the whole time, and seemed to me to have the most laborious part of the performance. They very frequently, at the conclusion of the dance, would apply to us for our opinions, or rather for marks of our approbation of their performance, which we never failed to give by often repeating the word *boojery*, which signifies good; or *boojery caribberie*, a good dance. These signs of pleasure in us seemed to give them great satisfaction and generally produced more than ordinary exertions from the whole company of performers in the next dance.

Bradley After entertaining us about an hour and they supposed we were going home, Bennelong asked if we would have one more dance, which was agreed to and we then parted, several of the children returning with us.

Neither Bradley nor Hunter say whether the ceremony had any meaning or significance for the Aboriginal people; perhaps they were not able to communicate well enough to find out.

MARCH

Friday 4th

The *Waaksamheyd* was preparing to leave for England at the end of the month. Phillip wrote to Grenville:

> Three stores, sufficient to contain two years' provisions for the settlement, are built here and at Rose Hill; they are of brick and tiled, so that we are no longer under any apprehension of an accident from fire. A barrack is likewise finished at Rose Hill for an hundred men, and the officers' barracks will be finished by the end of May, immediately after which barracks for officers and men will be began at this place.
>
> The want of limestone still obliges us to confine our buildings to a certain height, for although the clay is of a strong, binding nature, we cannot with safety carry the walls of those buildings more than 12 feet above the ground, as the rains are at times very heavy, and should they come on before the clay is thoroughly dry, the walls would be in danger from the great weight of the roof. In their present state they will, however, stand for a great number of years.

Saturday 5th

Phillip to Grenville   In my former letters I have requested instructions relative to those convicts who say that the terms for which they were sentenced are expired, and who, refusing to become settlers, desire to return to England. To compel these people to remain may be attended with unpleasant consequences, for they must be made to work, if fed from the public store, and if permitted to be their own masters they must rob, for they have no other way to support themselves.

The language they hold is that the sentence of the law has been carried into execution, that they are free men and wish to return. I have no means of knowing when the sentences of any of the convicts expire who came out in the first ships...I hope, sir, to receive your instructions on this head by the first ships, for though there has been no very great impropriety in the conduct of any of those who say the time is expired for which they were sentenced, it is more than probable that they will become troublesome as their numbers increase.

Monday 7th

Elizabeth Macarthur wrote to a friend, Bridget Kingdon The *Gorgon*, so long wished for and so long expected, is not yet arrived, and by her unaccountable delay has involved us all in the most mysterious uncertainty and clouded our minds with gloomy apprehensions for her safety...

In my former letter I gave you the character of Mr Dawes and also of Captain Tench. Those gentlemen and a few others are the chief among whom we visit—indeed we are in that habit of intimacy with Captain Tench that there are few days pass that we do not spend some part of together.

Mr Dawes we do not see so frequently. He is so much engaged with the stars that to mortal eyes he is not always visible. I had the presumption to become his pupil, and meant to learn a little of astronomy. It is true I have had many a pleasant walk to his house (something less than a half a mile from Sydney), have given him much trouble in making orrereys [models of the planetary system] and in explaining to me the general principles of the heavenly bodies, but I soon found I had mistaken my abilities, and blush at my error...

I shall now introduce another acquaintance, Mr Worgan to you, a gentleman I have not hitherto named. He was surgeon to the *Sirius*, and happened to be left at this place when that ship met with her fate at Norfolk. It is not improbable this gentleman may himself deliver this letter to you...

I shall now tell you of another resource I had to fill up some of my vacant hours. Our new house is ornamented with a pianoforte of Mr Worgan's. He kindly means to leave it with me, and now under his direction I have begun a new study, but I fear without my master I shall not make any great proficiency. I am told however I have done wonders in being able to play off 'God Save the King' and 'Foot's Minuet', besides that of reading the notes with great facility.

In spite of music I have not altogether lost sight of my botanical studies. I have only been precluded from pursuing that study by the intense heat of the weather, which has not permitted me to walk much during the summer.

The months of December and January have been hotter than I can describe, indeed, insufferably so. The thermometer rising from 100 to 112 which is I believe 30 degrees above the hottest day known in England. The general heat is to be borne, but when we are oppressed by the hot winds we have no other resource but to shut up ourselves in our houses and to endeavour to the utmost of our power to exclude every breath of air. This wind blows from the north and comes as if from an heated oven...

You may be led to question my happiness, but thus much I can with truth add for myself, that...I never was more sincerely happy than at this time. It is true I have some wishes unaccomplished that...would add to my comfort, but when I consider this is not a state of perfection, I am abundantly content.

Friday 11th

Robinson Reid, carpenter of the *Supply*, reported, 'It is my opinion his Majesty's armed tender *Supply* will want, in the course of another year, a total repair, and which cannot be done in this country conveniently.'

Monday 14th

Phillip wrote to Stephens Their lordships will, I presume, have ordered the *Sirius* to be replaced and as from the carpenter's report of the *Supply's* defect, which is enclosed, it is probable that vessel will be ordered to England, I beg leave to observe that two ships will be requisite for the service of this colony, and that the most useful would be ships of from 300 to 400 tons burthen, with flush decks.

Friday 18th

Elizabeth Macarthur wrote to her mother We have not attempted anything in the farming way. Our neighbours succeed so badly that we are not encouraged to follow their example. The government farm did not this year, in grain, return three times the seed that had been sown. This great failure is attributable to a very dry season, but it is a general opinion that this country is not well adapted for corn.

The grape thrives remarkably well. The governor sent me some bunches this season as fine as any I ever tasted, and there is little doubt but in a very few years there will be plenty. We have also very fine melons. They are raised with little or no trouble, the sun being sufficient to ripen them without any forcing whatever and bringing them to a great size and flavour. One day after the cloth was moved when I happened to dine at Government House, a melon was produced weighing 30 pounds.

The Reverend Richard Johnson wrote to Henry Fricker Wish I could give you a pleasing account of our situation here, but must confess I think I meet with things worse than I expected, bad as I might naturally expect them. In almost every respect things are truly wretched and uncomfortable, and when it will be better with us, God only knows...

Water begins to grow very scarce and very bad. Many people have been ill on this account and what has tended to increase their illness has been the very great heat of the weather. The hottest day in England is quite moderate to what we have repeatedly felt it here. Birds, unable to bear the heat, have in great numbers, dropped from the trees and expired...

We are now upon a pretty friendly intercourse with the natives. Numbers of them are coming into the camp daily, or rather are in night and day. This intercourse was principally brought about by means of a little girl which, if I mistake not, I mentioned to you in a former letter. For some time this girl made good improvement in her book, and [I] began to be very partial to her; but since they have come in in common she has not behaved so well or so complying. Once and again she has been off in the woods for some time, but believe she finds things better in camp and with us than amongst her countrymen.

Sunday 20th

Nagle The governor understanding that a number of the ship's company wished to settle in the country, we were all ordered over to the governor's house to inform himself who was most fittest for farmers.

Collins Of the *Sirius's* late ship's company, 10 seamen and two marines chose rather to settle here than return to their friends. Two of the seamen made choice of their lands in this country, the others in Norfolk Island. The majority of them had formed connections with women, for whose sake they consented to embrace a mode of life for which the natural restlessness of a sailor's disposition was but ill-calculated.

Tuesday 22nd

Scott The *Supply* brig sailed for Norfolk with Captain Hill and a detachment consisting of one lieutenant-ensign, one sergeant, one corporal, one drummer and 18 privates to relieve the like number of marines now doing duty on that island.

Also nine seamen and two marines belonging to his Majesty's ship, late *Sirius*, to become settlers on the following encouragement: 18 months provision with 60 acres of land, half an acre of land cleared, a house built, two breeding sows, six hens and one cock, four jackets, four waistcoats, four pair drawers, four pair trousers, four pair shoes, four pair hose, two hats, four shirts and thread needles, bed and blankets etc etc and their time is not to go on till their house is ready.

Wednesday 23rd

Collins wrote to his father   Our climate it is true is healthy and we have no epidemical diseases amongst us, but the constitution of everyone is impaired from the poorness of our living and we generally esteem one year in this country to be equal to two in Europe, so that, as I think five years must elapse before I kiss my native shore, you will find me 10 years older in appearance and constitution.

Of my situation I will say this much; I still live with the governor and continue to be his secretary. Since Major Ross went from hence, tranquillity may be said to have been our guest, but whenever he returns, discord will again drive out tranquillity. Oh! that the *Sirius* when she was lost, had proved his—but no more of that. While here, he made me the object of his persecution, and a day will come, a day of retribution.

Thursday 24th

Phillip wrote to Sir Joseph Banks   Fifty tubs of flowering shrubs are ready to send away when an opportunity offers and as the plants have been some months in the tub and are all very healthy, I hope they will one day reach you by the vessel now ready to sail with the late *Sirius's* ships company...

I hope that you still continue to enjoy health, mine is very indifferent and I find it necessary to return to England, for which purpose I have written to Mr Grenville. A pain in the side from which I have been seldom free for two years has almost worn me out. I think it proceeds from an inflammation in the kidney and that it was brought on by cold, but a long voyage may be of service, and as this colony which has given me as many anxious hours and in which I feel myself so much interested is not immediately in the state in which I would wish to leave it, I shall have no objection to return here if my health permits.

In a later note, Phillip added: 'I am sorry that I cannot send you a head. After the ravages made by the smallpox, numbers were seen in every part, but the natives burn the bodies. Some may be found hereafter.' Presumably, if Tench's expedition of revenge for the death of Macentire had been successful at least one of the heads would have been sent to Banks.

Saturday 26th

John Palmer, the commissary, prepared a 'State of the Settlement', including details of the ration:

> Present weekly ration issued at Port Jackson the 26th March 1791 viz. to men, four pounds of flour, five pounds of rice, seven pounds of beef or four pounds of pork; to women and to children above 10 years of age, two-thirds of the above; to children above two years of age, half of the man's ration. To children under two years of age, quarter of the man's ration.

Bradley reported that:

> The state of the number of people in the settlement is as follows:

Governor	1
Commissioned officers	14
Non-commissioned officers	24
Surgeon's mate	1
Drummers	8
Privates	164
Wives of soldiers	36
Children of soldiers	59
Staff	8
Civil	6
Free men and women	16
Men convicts	789
Women convicts	203
Children of convicts	50
Natives	6
At Sydney and Rose Hill	1,385

Soldiers on their passage to Norfolk Island	24
Surgeon's mate and 10 settlers from the *Sirius*	11
At Norfolk Island as before specified	627
Total	2,047

Sunday 27th

The crew of the *Sirius* left the settlement.

Hunter Everything being embarked, we left Sydney Cove in the *Waaksamheyd* transport and sailed down the harbour, when we were accompanied by the governor and most of the civil and military officers in the settlement. When we passed the lower point of the Cove, all the marines and the New South Wales Corps who were off duty came down and cheered our people, by way of taking leave and wishing us a good passage.

Easty She weighed anchor and ran down the harbour. She was again cheered by the marines which was returned by the ship's company and there was two parties of men separated which had spent four years together in the greatest love and friendship as ever men did in such a distant part of the globe, both by officers and men. She was then accompanied down the harbour by all the marine officers, which when they parted she saluted them with nine guns, which was the last honour as could be conferred on them.

The American seaman Jacob Nagle was among those who left in the *Waaksamheyd* to return to England. He married 'a lively handsome girl' in London in 1795, but she and their child died of yellow fever in Lisbon in 1802. That year, Nagle left the British navy. He served in various merchant ships for the next 23 years, returning to America at the end of that time and spent the declining years of his life, often in poor health, living with various members of his family, telling his stories and doing odd jobs where he could. He died in Ohio in 1841, in his 80th year.

Others who sailed in the *Waaksamheyd* included Daniel Southwell and midshipman Henry Waterhouse; surgeon George Worgan, who left his piano in the care of Elizabeth Macarthur; John Hunter, who was to return as governor in 1795; Midshipman George Raper and William Bradley. Raper, Bradley and Hunter were three of the artists of the first settlement and would have worked on their drawings of the colony during the voyage. It was not uncommon then for artists to copy each other's work, and several of their illustrations are remarkably similar.

No doubt Hunter and Bradley worked on the manuscripts of their books while they were at sea. Hunter would also have had time to reflect on the court-martial over the loss of the *Sirius* which he faced on arrival in England.

William Bradley was a thoughtful, introspective soul; he described the capture of Bennelong and Colbee as 'by far the most unpleasant service I ever was ordered to execute', and when he was stranded, with the rest of *Sirius*'s crew, on Norfolk Island in March 1790, he soon decided to quit the Ross-inspired bickering of the officers' mess and live apart from them, where he was some months later joined by Hunter (who brought with him a hogshead of wine saved from the wreck, which may have helped to pass what must have seemed unsatisfactory times).

Jacob Nagle provides a glimpse of a more relaxed Bradley on the voyage home; at the Cape of Good Hope he 'gave the ship's company a frolic, being rejoiced to think we were so near England after five years' absence...giving us as much as we pleased to drink and carousing on the quarterdeck and dancing and shouting, so great a noise on board of us, the captain of the *Swan*, man-of-war, thought there was a mutiny on board of us.'

Back in England, Bradley had a distinguished career in the navy, rising to the rank of rear-admiral in 1812, when he was retired. But soon after this he had bouts of mental illness and in 1814 he was himself sentenced to transportation for attempting to defraud the Post Office; the sentence was waived on condition that he live in exile, and he lived much of the remainder of his life in France. He died in 1833. His wife Sarah had died before him; they had three daughters and a son who died as a cadet in the service of the East India Company.

Like the other officers of the First Fleet who kept journals, Bradley knew he was making history, and in view of the care taken with the manuscript and the illustrations, it seems almost certain that he prepared it with publication in mind. But Bradley's book was not published at the time; perhaps publishers thought the market was too crowded, perhaps it was thought to be too introspective and technical, perhaps there are other reasons. *A Voyage to New South Wales* was eventually published 177 years after it was completed, in a facsimile edition published in 1969 for the Public Library of New South Wales, funded by the William Dixson Foundation.

George Worgan, surgeon of the *Sirius*, was married to Mary Lawry of Liskeard, in Cornwall, soon after his return to England, and during the next 10 years they had four children. Worgan remained in the navy until 1800 and after that was involved in teaching and writing about farming. He died in Cornwall in 1838 at the age of 80.

Worgan must have spoken well of the colony that he had helped to establish; it is thought that two of his sons went to live in New South Wales; a William Worgan arrived as a settler on the *Elizabeth* in April 1830 and a John Worgan was clerk to the Bench of Magistrates at Hyde Park Barracks from September 1830 to August 1836.

Daniel Southwell was promoted to lieutenant in 1794, while serving in the *Royal William*. He was serving in HMS *Aurora* in 1797, when he died in hospital in Lisbon at the age of 31.

Henry Waterhouse returned to the settlement in 1795 as second captain of the *Reliance*, the ship which brought John Hunter back to New South Wales. He took the *Reliance* to the Cape of Good Hope in 1796, returning with the first cargo of merino sheep, and he was given a grant of land in the colony, but he went back to England in 1800 and left the navy soon after. He died in 1812, aged 42.

Midshipman George Raper served in the famous 100-gun HMS *Victory* in 1792, was commissioned a lieutenant in 1793 and saw action in various ships before he was invalided home from Gibraltar with fever in 1796. He died in 1797, aged 28. His will makes reference to drawings and directs that his papers should be 'put in my painting case and delivered to my dearest and beloved mother'. The paintings were acquired by the British Museum in 1962.

Thomas Brooks, bosun of the *Sirius*, and his wife Deborah also left the settlement in the *Waaksamheyd*. Phillip was once said to have had 'a sneaking kindness for' Deborah Brooks, but no reference to the relationship has appeared in the writings from the first settlement.

Monday 28th

The fisherman William Bryant, with his wife Mary, their two young children and seven other convicts, escaped from the colony. Easty wrote that they:

took a king's boat of six oars with a large quantity of provisions which they had got from time to time by work, and a new seine for fishing, with a large quantity of carpenter's tools of all sorts for enlarging the boat, with beds and mathematic instruments and compass, new sails and masts and oars and six stand of arms and everything that was necessary for making their escape, which was executed between the hours of nine and 12.

It was supposed that they intended for Batavia, but having no vessel in the harbour there was no pursuing them so they got clear off, but it's a very desperate attempt to go in an open boat for a run of about 16 or 17 hundred leagues and in particular for a woman and two small children, the oldest not above three years of age.

But the thoughts of liberty from such a place as this is enough to induce any convicts to try all schemes to obtain it, as they are the same as slaves all the time they are in this country. Although their times are expired for which they are sentenced by law, there is no difference between them and a convict that is just cast for transportation.

Wednesday 30th

Collins Mr Schaeffer, who came out from England as a superintendent of convicts, finding himself, from not speaking the language (being a German) inadequate to the just discharge of that duty, gave up his appointment as a superintendent and accepted of a grant of land and an allotment of 140 acres were marked out for him on the south side of the creek leading to Rose Hill.

On the same side of the creek, but nearer to Rose Hill, two allotments of 60 acres each were marked out for two settlers from the *Sirius* [Robert Webb and William Reid]. On the opposite side, the governor had placed a convict, Charles Williams, who had recommended himself to his notice by extraordinary propriety of conduct as an overseer, giving him 30 acres, and James Ruse received a grant of the same quantity of land at Rose Hill.

These all the settlers at this time established in New South Wales, but the governor was looking out for some situations in the vicinity of Rose Hill for other settlers, from among the people whose sentences of transportation had expired.

In the magistrates' court at Rose Hill, before David Collins, Robert Hunt was convicted of stealing corn and sentenced 'to wear an iron collar for two years of seven pounds weight'. William Cross confessed to stealing corn, driven by hunger, and was sentenced to wear an iron collar round his neck for a year.

Collins The depradations committed on the Indian corn at Rose Hill were now so frequent and so extensive that it became absolutely necessary to punish such offenders as were detected with a severity that might deter others; to this end, iron collars of seven pounds weight were ordered as a punishment for flagrant offenders, who were also linked together by a chain, without which precaution they would still have continued to plunder the public grounds...It must be remarked, however, that all these thefts were for the procuring of provisions and that offences of any other tendency were very seldom heard of.

APRIL

Saturday 2nd

Collins The supplies of provisions which had been received in the last year not warranting the continuing any longer at the ration now issued, the governor thought it expedient to make a reduction of flour, rice and salt provisions. Accordingly, on the first Saturday in this month, each man, woman, and child above 10 years of age was to receive:
    3 pounds of flour, 1 pound being taken off
    3 pounds of rice, ditto
    3 pounds of pork, ditto
    or when beef should be served,
    4½ pounds of beef, 2½ pounds being taken off...
Of this allowance the flour was the best article; the rice was found to be full of weevils, the pork was ill-flavoured, rusty, and smoked, and the beef was lean, and by being cured with spices, truly unpalatable.

Tench Notwithstanding the incompetency of so diminished a pittance, the daily task of the soldier and convict continued unaltered. I never contemplated the labours of these men without finding abundant cause of reflection on the miseries which our nature can overcome.

Monday 11th

Tench An expedition was undertaken in order to ascertain whether or not the Hawkesbury and the Nepean were the same river…Our party was strong and numerous: it consisted of 21 persons, viz. the governor, Mr Collins and his servant, Mr White, Mr Dawes, the author, three gamekeepers, two sergeants, eight privates and our friends Colbee and Boladeree. These two last were volunteers on the occasion, on being assured that we should not stay out many days, and that we should carry plenty of provisions. Bennelong wished to go, but his wife [Barangaroo] would not permit it…

Every man (the governor excepted) carried his own knapsack, which contained provisions for 10 days; if to this be added a gun, a blanket and a canteen, the weight will fall nothing short of 40 pounds. Slung to the knapsack are the cooking kettle and the hatchet, with which the wood to kindle the nightly fire and build the nightly hut is to be cut down…

Our method on these expeditions was to steer by compass, noting the different courses as we proceeded and counting the number of paces, of which 2,200, on good ground, were allowed to be a mile. At night when we halted, all these courses were separately cast up and worked by a traverse table in the manner a ship's reckoning is kept…This arduous task was always allotted to Mr Dawes, who, from habit and superior skill, performed it almost without a stop, or an interruption of conversation; to any other man, on such terms, it would have been impracticable.

Phillip After passing several deep ravines and going round the heads of others over a barren country for an hour, the land grew better and was tolerable till one o'clock, when it grew again bad and rocky. The natives informed them that this part of the country was inhabited by the Bidjigals, but that most of the tribe were dead of the smallpox…[That night] soon after the fires were lighted, the voice of a native was heard in the woods, hunting his dog, and as Colbee and Boladeree were very desirous of having an interview with him, though they said the tribe of Buruberongal, who were bad men and their enemies resided near the spot, they frequently hallooed, and were answered by the stranger.

Tench After some whooping and shouting on both sides, a man with a lighted stick in his hand advanced near enough to converse with us. The first words, which we could distinctly understand were, 'I am Colbee, of the tribe of Cadigal'. The stranger replied, 'I am

Bereewan, of the tribe of Buruberongal'. Boladeree informed him also of his name and that we were white men and friends, who would give him something to eat. Still he seemed irresolute. Colbee therefore advanced to him, took him by the hand, and led him to us.

By the light of the moon we were introduced to this gentleman, all our names being repeated in form by our two masters of the ceremonies, who said that we were Englishmen, and *budyeree* (good), that we came from the sea coast, and that we were travelling inland. Bereewan seemed to be a man about 30 years old, differing in no respect from his countrymen with whom we were acquainted. He came to us unarmed, having left his spears at a little distance. After a long conversation with his countrymen, and having received some provisions, he departed highly satisfied.

Tuesday 12th

Tench Started this morning at half past six o'clock, and in two hours reached the river. The whole of the country we passed was poor and the soil within a mile of the river changed to a coarse deep sand, which I have invariably found to compose its banks in every part, without exception, that I ever saw. The stream at this place is about 350 feet wide, the water pure and excellent to the taste, the banks are about 20 feet high and covered with trees, many of which had been evidently bent by the force of the current in the direction which it runs, and some of them contained rubbish and driftwood in their branches at least 45 feet above the level of the stream...Supposing ourselves to be higher on the stream than Richmond Hill, we agreed to trace downward...

At four o'clock we halted for the night, on the bank of the creek [Cattai Creek]. Our natives continued to hold out stoutly. The hindrances to walking by the river side, which plagued and entangled us so much, seemed not to be heeded by them, and they wound through them with ease. But to us they were intolerably tiresome; our perplexities afforded them an inexhaustible fund of merriment and derision; did the sufferer, stung at once with nettles and ridicule, and shaken nigh to death by his fall, use any angry expression to them, they retorted in a moment, by calling him by every opprobrious name which their language affords. (Their general favourite term of reproach is *gonin pata*, which signifies an eater of human excrement—our language would admit a very concise and familiar translation. They have, besides this, innumerable others, which they often salute their enemies with.)

Wednesday 13th

Tench   About two o'clock we reached the head of the creek; passed it, and scrambled with infinite toil and difficulty to the top of a neighbouring mountain, whence we saw the adjacent country in almost every direction for many miles. I record with regret that this extended view presented not a single gleam of change which could encourage hope, or stimulate industry, to attempt its culture. We had, however, the satisfaction to discover plainly the object of our pursuit, Richmond Hill, distant about eight miles, in a contrary direction from what we had been proceeding upon.

It was now determined that we should go back to the head of the creek and pass the night there and in the morning cut across the country to that part of the river which we had first hit upon yesterday, and thence to trace upward, or to the left...

Our fatigue today had been excessive, but our two sable companions seemed rather enlivened than exhausted by it. We had no sooner halted and given them something to eat than they began to play ten thousand tricks and gambols. They imitated the leaping of the kangaroo, sang, danced, poised the spear and met in mock encounter...They had become, however, very urgent in their inquiries about the time of our return and we pacified them as well as we could by saying it would be soon, but avoided naming how many days.

Their method of testifying dislike to any place is singular: they point to the spot they are upon, and all around it, crying 'Weeree, weeree' (bad) and immediately after mention the name of any other place to which they are attached, (Rose Hill or Sydney for instance) adding to it 'Budyeree, budyeree' (good). Nor was their preference in the present case the result of caprice, for they assigned very substantial reasons for such predilection: 'At Rose Hill,' said they, 'are potatoes, cabbages, pumpkins, turnips, fish and wine; here are nothing but rocks and water.' These comparisons constantly ended with the question of 'Where's Rose Hill; where?' on which they would throw up their hands and utter a sound to denote distance, which it is impossible to convey an idea of upon paper.

Thursday 14th

Tench   We started early, and reached the river in about two hours and a half...we continued our progress until it was again interrupted by a creek, over which we threw a tree and passed upon it. While this was doing, a native, from his canoe, entered into conversation with us and immediately after paddled to us with a frankness and confidence which surprised everyone.

He was a man of middle age, with an open cheerful countenance, marked with the smallpox and distinguished by a nose of uncommon magnitude and dignity; he seemed to be neither astonished nor terrified at our appearance and number. Two stone hatchets and two spears he took from his canoe and presented to the governor, who in return for his courteous generosity gave him two of our hatchets and some bread, which was new to him, for he knew not its use, but kept looking at it until Colbee shewed him what to do, when he eat it without hesitation. We pursued our course and to accommodate us our new acquaintance pointed out a path and walked at the head of us. A canoe, also with a man and a boy in it, kept gently paddling up abreast of us.

Phillip The old man called himself Gombeeree, and said the child's name was Jimbah; they were of the tribe of Buruberongal. Colbee and Boladeree, in describing that tribe on the second day's journey, had called them climbers of trees, and men who lived by hunting. Certainly, no persons can better deserve the appellation of climbers if we may judge from what was seen of Gombeeree, who, for a biscuit, in a very few minutes cut his notches in the bark of a tree and mounted it with surprising agility, though an old man. These notches are cut in the bark little more than an inch deep, which receives the ball of the great toe; the first and second notches are cut from the ground; the rest they cut as they ascend and at such a distance from each other that when both their feet are in the notches the right foot is raised nearly as high as the middle of the left thigh.

When they are going to raise themselves a step, their hatchet is held in the mouth, in order to have the use of both their hands, and when cutting the notch the weight of the body rests on the ball of the great toe. The fingers of the left hand are also fixed in a notch cut on the side of the tree for that purpose, if it is too large to admit their clasping it sufficiently with the left arm to keep the body close to the tree. In this manner do these people climb trees whose circumference is 10 or 15 feet or upwards, after an opossum or a squirrel, though they rise to a height of 60 or 80 feet before there is a single branch.

Tench What we were able to learn from them was that they depend but little on fish, as the river yields only mullets, and that their principal support is derived from small animals which they kill, and some roots (a species of wild yam chiefly) which they dig out of the earth. If we rightly understood them, each man possesses two wives. Whence can arise this superabundance of females?

Neither of the men had suffered the extraction of a front tooth. We were eager to know whether or not this custom obtained among them, but neither Colbee nor Boladeree would put the question for us and, on the contrary, showed every desire to waive the subject. The uneasiness which they testified whenever we renewed it, rather served to confirm a suspicion which we had long entertained, that this is a mark of subjection imposed by the tribe of Cameragal (who are certainly the most powerful community in the country) on the weaker tribes around them...

Although our natives and the strangers conversed on a par and understood each other perfectly, yet they spoke different dialects of the same language; many of the most common and necessary words used in life bearing no similitude, and others being slightly different...It deserves notice that all the different terms seemed to be familiar to both parties, though each in speaking preferred its own.

Friday 15th

Tench The return of light aroused us to the repetition of toil. Our friends breakfasted with us and...soon after they bade us adieu in unabated friendship and good humour. Colbee and Boladeree parted from them with a slight nod of the head, the usual salutation of the country, and we shook them by the hand, which they returned lustily. At the time we started, the tide was flowing up the river, a decisive proof that we were below Richmond Hill. We had continued our march but a short time when we were again stopped by a creek [South Creek], which baffled all our endeavours to cross it and seemed to predict that the object of our attainment, though but a very few miles distant, would take us yet a considerable time to reach, which threw a damp on our hopes. We traced the creek until four o'clock, when we halted for the night.

Tench observed that Colbee and Boladeree were 'thoroughly sick of the journey, and wished heartily for its conclusion; the exclamation of "Where's Rose Hill; where?" was incessantly repeated, with many inquiries about when we should return to it'.

Saturday 16th

Tench   It was this morning resolved to abandon our pursuit, and to return home, at hearing of which our natives expressed great joy. We started early and reached Rose Hill about three o'clock, just as a boat was about to be sent down to Sydney. Colbee and Boladeree would not wait for us until the following morning, but insisted on going down immediately, to communicate to Bennelong and the rest of their countrymen the novelties they had seen. The country we passed through, was, for the most part, very indifferent, according to our universal opinion.

✑

Phillip   The dry weather still continued, and though they had a few showers, the quantity of rain which fell in the month of April was not sufficient to bring the dry ground into proper order for sowing the grain; a few acres, however, of what was in the best condition were sown with wheat the last week in the month. This long continuance of dry weather not only hurt their crops of corn very much, but the gardens likewise suffered greatly, many being sown a second and a third time, as the seed never vegetated from the want of moisture in the soil; this was a double misfortune, for vegetables were not only growing scarce, but seed also.

Collins   So great a desire for tobacco prevailed among these people that a man was known to have given the greatest part of his week's provisions for a small quantity of that article, and it was sold, the produce of the place, for 10 and even 15 shillings per pound...

At Sydney, the house for the surveyor-general was covered in and the carpenters were employed in finishing that for the clergyman. Bricks were also brought in for a house for the principal surgeon, to be built near the hospital on the west side.

MAY

Sunday 8th

Phillip   Bennelong and Colbee, with their wives, dined at the governor's on the 8th of May and came in as usual to have a glass of wine and a dish of coffee, after which they left house to go and sleep at Bennelong's hut on the point. But in the middle of the night Governor Phillip was called up by the cries of the young girl whom he had formerly rescued from Bennelong. She, it seems, had gone to sleep in a shed at the back of the governor's house, and Bennelong, Colbee, and two others got over the paling and were endeavouring to carry her off, which the sentinels prevented.

Sunday 15th

Phillip Bennelong and Colbee were not seen for a week and the latter appearing first, when he was accused, said he was asleep at the time and laid the blame on Bennelong, who coming soon after and not being able to make any excuse, or to deny being in the yard, appeared sullen. And when Governor Phillip told him that he was angry and that the soldiers should shoot him if ever he came again to take any woman away, he very coolly replied that then he would spear the soldier. At the same time he said he was very hungry, and as no advantage would have followed punishing him, he was ordered something to eat.

Tuesday 24th to Sunday 29th

Tench Mr Dawes and myself, accompanied by a sergeant of marines and a private soldier, determined on another attempt, to ascertain whether it [Richmond Hill] lay on the Hawkesbury or Nepean... This excursion completely settled the long contested point about the Hawkesbury and Nepean; we found them to be one river.

Monday 30th

Phillip The *Supply* had now so far exceeded the time in which she generally made the voyage to and from Norfolk Island that fears were entertained for her safety, but they were removed by her arrival on the 30th of May. As she was the only vessel in this country, it was not without great concern that Governor Phillip found the necessary repairs she wanted would require more time than he could have wished her to remain in the harbour.

ↄpopↄ

Tench The natives continued to complain of being robbed of spears and fishing tackle. A convict was at length taken in the fact of stealing fishing-tackle from Daringa, the wife of Colbee. The governor ordered that he should be severely flogged in the presence of as many natives as could be assembled, to whom the cause of punishment should be explained. Many of them, of both sexes, accordingly attended.

Arabanoo's aversion to a similar sight has been noticed, and if the behaviour of those now collected be found to correspond with it, it is, I think, fair to conclude that these people are not of a sanguinary and implacable temper. Quick indeed of resentment, but not unforgiving of injury, there was not one of them that did not testify strong abhorrence of the punishment and equal sympathy with the sufferer. The women were particularly affected; Daringa shed tears and Barangaroo, kindling into anger, snatched a stick and menaced the executioner. The conduct of these women, on this occasion, was exactly descriptive of their characters. The former was ever meek and feminine, the latter fierce and unsubmissive.

JUNE

Thursday 2nd

Tench The name of the settlement at the head of the harbour, Rose Hill, was changed by order of the governor, to that of Parramatta, the native name of it.

According to Elizabeth Macarthur, the native word meant 'head of the river', but another translation was 'place where eels lie down'.

Saturday 4th

Collins On his Majesty's birthday an extra allowance of provisions was issued to the garrison and settlements…and to make it a cheerful day to everyone, all offenders who had, for stealing Indian corn, been ordered to wear iron collars, were pardoned.

Monday 13th

William Fraser, the convict blacksmith, was buried. Collins wrote: 'He was an excellent workman and was supposed to have brought on an untimely end by hard drinking, as he seldom chose to accept of any article but spirits for work done in his extra hours.'

Fraser had received 25 lashes in January 1789 for telling Sergeant Martin Connor, 'You can kiss my arse,' but Tench, too, had a high opinion of his skill:

> Fraser was an iron manufacturer, bred at Sheffield, of whose abilities, as a workman, we had witnessed many proofs. The governor had written to England for a set of locks to be sent out for the security of the public stores, which were to be so constructed as to be incapable of being picked. On their arrival his Excellency sent for Fraser and bade him examine them, telling him at the same time that they could not be picked. Fraser laughed, and asked for a crooked nail only, to open them all. A nail was brought and in an instant he verified his assertion...
>
> But it was not only in this part of his business that he excelled; he executed every branch of it in superior style. Had not his villainy been still more notorious than his skill, he would have proved an invaluable possession to a new country. He had passed through innumerable scenes in life and had played many parts. When too lazy to work at his trade, he had turned thief in 50 different shapes, was a receiver of stolen goods, a soldier and a travelling conjurer. He once confessed to me that he had made a set of tools for a gang of coiners, every man of whom was hanged.

Tuesday 21st

Tench The extreme dryness...had operated so far in the beginning of June that we we dreaded a want of water for common consumption, most of the little reservoirs in the neighbourhood of Sydney being dried up. The small stream near the town was so nearly exhausted (being only the drain of a morass) that a ship could not have watered at it, and the *Supply* was preparing to sink casks in a swamp, when rain fell and banished our apprehensions.

Friday 24th

Phillip   On the 21st of June they had rain, which continued until the morning of the 24th and at times was very violent; indeed, more rain fell in three days than had done in many months past, so that the low grounds were thoroughly soaked.

∽

Collins   Since the establishment of that familiar intercourse which now subsisted between us and the natives, several of them had found it their interest to sell or exchange fish among the people at Parramatta, they being contented to receive a small quantity of either bread or salt meat in barter for mullet, bream, and other fish. To the officers who resided there this proved a great convenience and they encouraged the natives to visit them as often as they could bring them fish.

There were, however, among the convicts some who were so unthinking, or so depraved, as wantonly to destroy a canoe belonging to a fine young man, a native, who had left it at some little distance from the settlement and, as he hoped, out of the way of observation, while he went with some fish to the huts. His rage at finding his canoe destroyed was inconceivable and he threatened to take his own revenge, and in his own way, upon all white people.

Three of the six people who had done him the injury, however, were so well described by someone who had seen them, that, being closely followed, they were taken and punished, as were the remainder in a few days after.

The instant effect of all this was that the natives discontinued to bring up fish, and Boladeree, whose canoe had been destroyed, although he had been taught to believe that one of the six convicts had been hanged for the offence, meeting a few days afterwards with a poor wretch who had strayed from Parramatta as far as the Flats, he wounded him in two places with a spear. This act of Boladeree's was followed by the governor's strictly forbidding him to appear again at any of the settlements. The other natives, his friends, being alarmed, Parramatta was seldom visited by any of them, and all commerce with them was destroyed.

How much greater claim to the appellation of savages had the wretches who were the cause of this, than the native who was the sufferer?

Phillip Hawks and crows were now frequently seen in great numbers, though at times several months would pass without one of either species being seen. At Parramatta, after the wheat was sown, the crows were very troublesome, and though frequently fired at they did great damage.

JULY

Saturday 9th

Easty This morning at seven o'clock the signal was made at the South Head for the *Mary Ann*, a ship from England with 144 women convicts.

Mary Ann was the first ship of the Third Fleet.

Collins This ship sailed alone, but we were informed that she was to be followed by nine sail of transports, on board of which were embarked...2050 male and female convicts, the whole of which was to be expected in the course of six weeks or two months, together with his Majesty's ship *Gorgon*.

Tench To demonstrate the effect of humanity and justice, of 144 female convicts embarked on board, only three had died, and the rest were landed in perfect health, all loud in praise of their conductor. The master's name was Munro and his ship, after fulfilling her engagement with government, was bound on the southern fishery...

By the governor's letters we learned that such convicts as had served their period of transportation were not to be compelled to remain in the colony, but that no temptation should be offered to induce them to quit it...that those who might choose to settle in the country should have portions of land, subject to stipulated restrictions, and a portion of provisions assigned to them on signifying their inclinations, and that it was expected that those convicts who might be possessed of means to transport themselves from the country would leave it free of all encumbrances of a public nature.

Wednesday 13th

Collins Patrick Burn, a person employed to shoot for the commanding officer of the marine detachment, died...and the hut that he had lived in was burnt down in the night a few hours after his decease by the carelessness of the people, who were Irish and were sitting up with the corpse, which was with much difficulty saved from the flames, and not until it was much scorched.

Monday 18th

Phillip It being the intention of government that, as the time for which the convicts were sentenced expired, they should be permitted to become settlers, those who chose to accept this bounty were received as such, and lands were granted them in the following proportions, viz. 30 acres to the single men, 50 acres to those who were married and 10 acres more for every child. It had been proposed to victual and clothe them from the public store for 12 months from the time they became settlers, but to encourage those who first offered themselves, Governor Phillip promised to clothe and support them for 18 months from the public stores.

They were to have the necessary tools and implements of husbandry, with seeds and grain to sow the ground the first year. Two young sow pigs were also to be given to each settler, which was all the governor's stock would afford...

On these conditions, 27 convicts were admitted settlers; 12 of them were fixed at the foot of Prospect Hill, four miles from Parramatta, and 15 at some ponds, an eligible situation about two miles to the northward of those settlers who were placed on the creek leading to Parramatta.

In laying out the different allotments, an intermediate space, equal to what was granted the settler, was retained between every two allotments, for the benefit of the Crown, and as this set them at some distance from each other, and there being a wood between every two settlers in which the natives might conceal themselves, if they were inclined to mischief, several muskets were distributed amongst the settlers, and they took possession of their allotments on the 18th of July and began to erect their huts.

Thursday 21st

Scott wrote that Private William Godfrey, charged with stealing wine while he was on guard duty at the public cellar, 'was tried by a battalion court-martial for disobedience of orders and neglect of duty; sentenced to receive 800 lashes and to be drummed out of the Corps of Marines. Received 300 the same day and drummed out'.

AUGUST

Monday 1st

Phillip   The *Matilda* transport anchored at Sydney with clothing, provisions and 205 male convicts...although this ship had made so good a passage, she buried 24 convicts, 20 were sick and many were in so emaciated a state that scarcely any labour could be expected from them for some months.

Saturday 20th

Collins   About noon on the 20th the *Atlantic* transport anchored in the cove...She had on board a sergeant's party of the new corps as a guard to 220 male convicts, 18 of whom died on the passage. The remainder came in very healthy, there being only nine sick on board.

Sunday 21st

Phillip   The *Salamander* arrived...she brought out 12 privates belonging to the New South Wales Corps and 154 male convicts, with stores and provisions. Most of the convicts on board this ship were in a weak, emaciated state and they complained that they had not proper attention paid to them.

Tuesday 23rd

Phillip   A number of natives...came to Governor Phillip's house, amongst whom some bread was dividing, when he was informed that Boladeree was on the opposite side of the cove with a number of the natives, and that he was armed, as were most of his companions.

Whether his coming in, after what had passed, proceeded from an opinion that Governor Phillip would not punish him, or from supposing himself safe whilst surrounded by so many of his countrymen, it was thought necessary to order him to be seized, as soon as those who were then in the yard eating what had been given them should be gone...

Having finished their meal, and received some fish-hooks, they set off, immediately after which a party of soldiers were ordered out to secure Boladeree...They came up with several natives, who joined them in a friendly manner, and, whilst they were talking to the sergeant, one of them attempted to wrest a firelock from a soldier and immediately afterwards a spear was thrown, supposed to be by Boladeree. Two muskets were then fired, by which a native was wounded in the leg, but unfortunately it was neither the man who attempted to take the musket nor the person who threw the spear.

Soon afterwards the natives were said to be assembled near the brickfields; an officer was therefore ordered out with a strong party to disperse them and to make a severe example of them if any spears were thrown. But they never saw a native, for the boy Nanbaree, true to his countrymen, on seeing the soldiers form on the parade, ran into the woods and, stripping himself that he might not be known, joined the natives and put them on their guard.

Orders were given that Boladeree 'was to be taken whenever an opportunity offered'. Collins wrote: 'Those who knew Boladeree regretted that it had been necessary to treat him with this harshness, as among his countrymen we had nowhere seen a finer young man.'

Sunday 28th

Easty   This day arrived the *William and Ann* with 200 men convicts and 16 privates and one sergeant and one corporal of the New South Wales Corps.

∽

More convicts were settled in the Parramatta area during August. A return in Phillip's journal in *Hunter* shows that, in all, there were 13 settlers at The Ponds and six at the Northern Boundary Farms, to the north-east of Parramatta in the Ryde area, 12 had settled at Prospect Hill, four miles west of Parramatta, three north of 'the creek leading to Parramatta' and three more south of the river. There were 50 settlers on Norfolk Island.

Phillip's journal in *Hunter* also records that:

a large body of the natives appeared in the grounds of one of the new settlers of Prospect Hill, who, alarmed at the sight of a number of natives (by his account more than a hundred) fired off his musket and retreated. This, of course, encouraged them, and they advanced and set fire to his hut, which was nearly finished. On hearing the report of a musket, another settler took up his arms, and, running to the spot, fired on the natives, who retired to some distance. As soon as this affair was known at Parramatta, a party of soldiers were detached, who, getting sight of about 50 of the natives, obliged them to disperse.

This circumstance induced Governor Phillip to deviate from the royal instructions, which pointed out in what manner the allotments of land were to be made, and as the only means of enabling the settlers to defend themselves against similar accidents, he granted all those intermediate lands, which had been reserved for the use of the Crown, to the settlers.

By this means, all the land would be cleared of timber, so that the natives could find no shelter, and, in all probability, there would be little danger from them in future. However, a non-commissioned officer and three privates were detached to each settlement, with orders to remain there until the lands were cleared.

Phillip Bennelong's wife was now very near her time, which gave our colonists an opportunity of seeing the preparations the women of New South Wales make on these occasions. She had two nets hanging from her neck, one of which being new, Governor Phillip was desirous of obtaining, and it was given him after she had taken a large piece of the bark of the tea-tree out of it, nicely folded up, and which was intended to lay her infant upon. This seems to be the only preparation which is made by lying-in women in that country...

Bennelong, however, desired to have a blanket for the child, which was given him, and the next day a net made in the English manner, which appeared more acceptable to his wife than the one she had parted with. He told Governor Phillip that his wife intended doing him the honour of being brought to bed in his house, but the governor at length persuaded him that she would be better accommodated at the hospital.

The women do not appear to suffer any great inconvenience while in this state, and they all seem best pleased with having boys; Bennelong often said his was to be a son.

This child of Bennelong and Barangaroo was called Dilboong, but Barangaroo did not live for long after it was born. In an appendix which does not give dates or make it clear whether the child was a girl or a boy, Collins wrote that when Barangaroo died, Bennelong:

> determined at once to burn her and requested Governor Phillip, Mr White and myself to attend him. He was accompanied by his own sister, Carrangarrang, Collins [an Aboriginal man who had taken Collins's name], Yemmerrawannie and one or two other women. Collins prepared the spot whereon the pile was to be constructed by excavating the ground with a stick to the depth of three or four inches and on this part so turned up were first placed small sticks and light brushwood; larger pieces were then laid on each side of these and so on till the pile might be about three feet in height... When wood enough had been procured some grass was spread over the pile and the corpse, covered with an old blanket, was borne to it by the men and placed on it with the head to the northward. A basket with the fishing apparatus and other small furniture of the deceased was placed by her side, and Bennelong having laid some large logs of wood over the body, the pile was lighted by one of the party...
>
> The following day he invited us to see him rake the ashes of his wife together... he formed with a piece of bark a tumulus that would have done credit to a well-practised gravedigger, carefully laying the earth round, smoothing every little unevenness and paying a scrupulous attention to the exact proportion of its form... when all was done he asked us 'if it was good', and appeared pleased when we assured him that it was.

Bennelong 'spoke about finding a nurse from among the white women to suckle his child', but Dilboong must also have died soon after; 'The ceremony of sleeping at the grave of the deceased... was observed by Bennelong after the death of his little child Dilboong', Collins wrote, 'he and two or three others passing the night in the governor's garden, not very far from the spot where it was buried.'

Collins does not give the cause of Barangaroo's death, but Colbee's wife, Daringa, also died at about this time. Collins wrote that:

> She died of a consumption brought on by suckling a little girl who was at her breast when she died... When the body was placed in the grave the bystanders were amazed to see the father himself place the living child in it with the mother. Having laid the child down, he threw upon it a large stone and the grave

was instantly filled in by the other natives. The whole business was so momentary that our people had not time or presence of mind sufficient to prevent it, and on speaking about it to Colbee, he, so far from thinking it inhuman, justified the extraordinary act by assuring us that as no woman could be found to nurse the child it must die a much worse death than that to which he had put it.

In a footnote, Collins added that Colbee's child 'seemed to have partaken of its mother's illness. I think it could not have lived'.

SEPTEMBER

Thursday 1st

Phillip Although few of the convicts were sick when they were first landed from the transports, yet many of them were extremely weak from long confinement and a few days carried numbers of them to the hospital. The surgeon's returns on the 1st of September were 285 convicts under medical treatment. Several soldiers and seamen were likewise in the hospital with a fever of a bad sort, which was supposed to be brought on board by the convicts.

Wednesday 21st

Easty reported the arrival of 'H.M. Ship *Gorgon* of 44 guns…she brought Governor King passenger and stores and provisions for the settlement'. Philip Gidley King had been appointed governor of Norfolk Island.

Mary Ann Parker, wife of John Parker, captain of the *Gorgon* As soon as the ship anchored several officers came on board, and shortly after Governor King, accompanied by Captain Parker, went on shore and waited on his Excellency Governor Phillip with the government dispatches. They were welcome visitors and I may safely say that the arrival of our ship diffused universal joy throughout the whole settlement.

The *Gorgon* was in Port Jackson for three months, unloading supplies and waiting for the Marine Corps to embark for the journey back to

England, and during this time Mrs Parker joined in the activities of the governor and his officials. She later wrote a book, titled *A Voyage Round the World in the Gorgon Man of War*, which was published by Debrett in 1795.

According to Collins, the *Gorgon* had on board 'three bulls, 23 cows, 68 sheep, 11 hogs, 200 fruit trees, a quantity of garden seed and other articles for the colony. Unfortunately the bulls and seven of the cows died, but a bull calf, which had been produced on board, arrived in good condition'.

Thursday 22nd

William Neate Chapman, whose parents were friendly with both King and Phillip and who had come out with King in the *Gorgon*, wrote to his mother: 'I am sorry to inform you Governor Phillip, when we got to Port Jackson, was not very well. His health now is very bad, he fatigues himself so much. He fairly knocks himself up and won't rest till he is not able to walk.'

Monday 26th

Collins The *Active* from England, and the *Queen* from Ireland, with convicts of that country, arrived and anchored in the cove...these ships had been unhealthy and had buried several convicts in their passage...they in general complained of not having received the allowance intended for them, but their emaciated appearance was to be ascribed as much to confinement as to any other cause. The convicts from the *Queen*, however, accusing the master of having withheld their provisions, an enquiry took place before the magistrates.

The *Queen* brought the first load of convicts from Ireland.

Scott Received a letter from friend Mooney and a box containing one loaf sugar, two pounds tea, two pair shoes, two pair for wife, two quires paper, half a hundred quills, one paper of ink powder and a frock for [his daughter] Betsy.

Collins By the arrival of these ships several articles of comfort were introduced among us, there being scarcely a vessel that had not brought out something for sale. It could not, however, be said that they were procurable on easier terms than what had been sold here in the last year. The Spanish dollar was the current coin of the colony, which some of the masters taking at five shillings and others at four shillings and sixpence, the governor, in consideration of the officers having been obliged to receive the dollars at five shillings sterling when given for bills drawn in the settlement, issued a proclamation fixing the currency of the Spanish dollar at that sum.

❧

Phillip   A number of emus had been seen lately, and this appears to be the season in which they breed, as a nest was found near some fresh water at the head of the harbour, containing 14 eggs... The patagarang and baggaray [grey kangaroo and red kangaroo] frequently supplied our colonists with fresh meals, and Governor Phillip had three young ones which were likely to live.

OCTOBER

Tuesday 4th

The Reverend Richard Johnson wrote to Henry Fricker   After being here for near four years you may reasonably suppose that we have by this time become more settled. In some respects I am happy to inform you we are so, as we have lately removed out of our old little cabbage-tree cottage and are now in a house as comfortable and convenient as I can wish.

My garden too is in a flourishing state, but yet in some other respects, and especially in my public line, I am little better off than ever. No church is yet built or even begun of, and the only places that we can procure for the purpose of public worship is an old storehouse—a barrack etc; I have frequent promises and assurances made me however, that in a little time a church shall be built both here at Sydney and also at Parramatta.

Thursday 13th

Collins wrote that the *Albemarle* arrived:

with 250 male and six female convicts, her proportion of stores and provisions and one sergeant, one corporal, one drummer and 20 privates of the new corps. The convicts of this ship had made an attempt, in conjunction with some of the seamen, to seize her on the 9th of April, soon after she had sailed from England, and they would in all probability have succeeded but for the activity and resolution shown by the master, Mr George Bowen, who, hearing the alarm, had just time to arm himself with a loaded blunderbuss, which he discharged at one of the mutineers, William Syney (then in the act of aiming a blow with a cutlass at the man at the wheel) and lodged its contents in his shoulder.

The ringleaders in the mutiny, Syney and another convict, Owen Lyons, were hanged 'at the foreyard arm'. No doubt they had good reason to mutiny; George Barrington, who had arrived in the *Active*, wrote that when the convicts from the *Albemarle* went on shore:

> their appearance was truly deplorable, the generality of them being emaciated by disease, and those who laboured under no bodily disorder from the scantiness of their allowance were in no better plight... Upon their landing they were entirely new clothed from the King's store and their old things were all burnt, in order to prevent any infectious disorder that might have been in the ship from being introduced into the colony.

Barrington was thought to have been the son of an English army officer and had been educated at Dublin Grammar School. He ran away from school and at the age of 16 joined a band of strolling players and later became well known as a London pickpocket. In 1790 he was charged with stealing a gold watch and chain at Enfield racecourse, convicted and sentenced to seven years' transportation. After the conviction he apparently changed his ways, because he was treated with respect and given responsibility in the new colony. His account of his adventures, *A Voyage to New South Wales,* published in London in 1795, is colourful and informative, although it is not regarded as being reliable.

Phillip received a letter from Lord Grenville:

> Lord Sydney has transmitted to me a private letter... wherein you have expressed a desire to be permitted to return to England. I am much concerned that this situation of your private affairs should have been such as to render this application necessary at a time when your services in New South Wales are so extremely important to the public.

I cannot, therefore, refrain from expressing my earnest hope that you may have it in your power so to arrange your private concerns that you may be able, without material inconvenience, to continue in your government for a short time longer.

Friday 14th

The *Britannia* arrived with 129 male convicts, 13 soldiers, one of their wives and three children, as well as stores and provisions. Her captain, Thomas Melville, wrote to the owners to confirm his arrival at Port Jackson, adding that,

> Within three leagues of the shore, we saw sperm whales in great plenty; we sailed through different shoals of them from twelve o'clock in the day till after sunset, all round the horizon as far as I could see from the masthead. In fact, I saw a very great prospect in making our fishery upon this coast and establishing a fishery here. Our people were in the highest spirits at so great a sight and I was determined, as soon as I got in and got clear of my live lumber, to make all possible dispatch on the fishery on this coast.
>
> On our arrival here, I waited upon his Excellency Governor Phillip and delivered my letters to him. I had the mortification to find he wanted to despatch me with my convicts to Norfolk Island, and likewise wanted to purchase our vessel to stay in the country, which I refused to do. I immediately told him the secret of seeing the whales, thinking that would get me off going to Norfolk Island, that there was a prospect of establishing a fishery here, and might be of service to the colony, and left him.
>
> Waited upon him two hours afterwards with a box directed to him; he took me into a private room, he told me he had read my letters and that he would render me every service that lay in his power; that next morning he would despatch every longboat in the fleet to take our convicts out and take our stores out immediately, which he did accordingly, and did everything to dispatch us on the fishery. Captain King used all his interest in the business; he gave his kind respects to you.

Sunday 16th

Barrington, who had been appointed superintendent of convicts at Parramatta, wrote:

Left Sydney Cove about eight o'clock in the morning, and arrived at Parramatta about noon...After a short walk we arrived at the house appropriated for me; it is a compact little cottage with four rooms in it, the situation is most delightful, being in the midst of pleasant gardens. The convicts' houses form a line in front, at some distance; they have each a small garden and those who have been industrious seem very comfortable, as their day's work is not so hard as many working men's in England.

Collins The *Admiral Barrington*, the last of the 10 sail of transports, anchored in the cove...The whole number of convicts now received into the colony [in the Third Fleet], including 30 on board the *Gorgon*, were male convicts 1695, female convicts 186 and children nine. There were also eight free women (wives of convicts) and one child...upwards of 200 convicts, male and female, did not reach the country.

Monday 17th

Richard Owen, master of the *Queen* transport and Robert Stott, second mate, were summoned to attend court on a complaint made by the convicts of 'not having received the ration of provisions that was directed by contract to be furnished them during the passage'. Evidence was given that Stott had tampered with the weights which were used to issue rations and that Owen and Stott had given favours and stood over convicts involved in issuing rations. The enquiry was adjourned until the following day.

Barrington [at Parramatta] proceeded through the different gangs of people at their respective occupations and found them much more attentive to their business and respectful to those over them than I could possibly have imagined. Some were employed in making bricks and tiles, others building storehouse, huts etc, a great number clearing the grounds, bringing in timber, and making roads. Others at their different callings, such as smiths, gardeners, coopers, shoemakers, tailors, bakers, attendants on the sick etc.

Collins wrote to his father I should be extremely happy to comply with your command to return to England with the marines in the *Gorgon*; I am full as anxious to embrace my family again as they can be to receive me, but there are one or two insurmountable objections against it. The nature of my civil appointment is such, that, there being no person in the colony who could succeed me, I must be relieved from England—of course, that cannot happen until I have made application for that purpose. This however I shall do very pointedly by the *Gorgon*.

A second objection is, and to me stronger than any that could be urged; Major Ross takes his passage in that ship, and with him I would not sail were wealth and honours to attend me when I landed. A third objection is, I could not reconcile it to my mind to leave Governor Phillip, with whom I have now lived so long that I am blended in every concern of his.

Tuesday 18th

The case against the master and second mate of the *Queen* was resumed. There was little doubt that large quantities of provisions had been in effect stolen from the convicts, many of whom suffered death and illness as a result. The magistrates' finding was: 'On a full consideration of the evidence that has been laid before us, we are of opinion that the ration of provisions directed by the contract...to be furnished to the convicts embarked on board the *Queen*, transport, has not been supplied them'. But as they were not able to establish how much had been stolen, they submitted their finding to 'the governor's consideration, with our request that he will be pleased to take such steps as he shall think necessary'. Phillip referred the matter to Lord Grenville, but no evidence has emerged that any action was taken.

Tuesday 25th

King, who had been waiting in Sydney Cove for transport to Norfolk Island to take up his position as governor, wrote to Sir Joseph Banks:

> The natives are now on the most sociable terms with us and Bennelong, the native who was so long in the governor's family, goes with me to Norfolk and as it is a voluntary offer of his own, I hope we shall be able to instruct him in English...
>
> There is a circumstance which will add greatly to the consequence of this settlement, which is the whale fishery. Most of the whalers here have changed their plan of fishing on the west coast of America. Four of them sailed yesterday, under a full persuasion of being able to load their ships in six or eight weeks and not go 30 leagues from hence. It is needless for me to point out the very obvious advantages which will accrue to this colony

if the fishery succeeds and which I think there is little doubt of. The most experienced among the masters of the whalers has declared that he saw more sperm whales in one day off the Pigeon House [in southern New South Wales, near Ulladulla] than he had seen in six years' fishing on the coast of Brazil.

Wednesday 26th

Easty   This day sailed the *Atlantic* [for Norfolk Island] with Governor King and Captain Paterson with some soldiers of the New South Wales Corps and the settlers and to proceed from thence to Bengal for provisions for this settlement.

King had mentioned that Bennelong was going with him to Norfolk Island, and William Chapman confirmed it, writing that Bennelong had 'brought all his spears and fishgig, stone hatchet, bones for pointing his spears and his basket to be packed up for him. The governor is to give him two nankeen [trousers], three dresses, six white shirts and a trunk to keep them in, which pleases him very much'. However, there is no mention of Bennelong at Norfolk Island, and he is referred to in Phillip's journal in *Hunter* as being at Sydney Cove on 14 December, when he took the surgeon to see Boladeree and persuaded Phillip to allow Boladeree to be brought into the settlement to be cured.

Monday 31st

Collins   On the last day of this month, James Downey [probably James McDonaugh] was found hanging in his hut. The cause of this rash action was said to have been the dread of being taken up for a theft which, according to some information he had received, was about to be alleged against him. He came out in the First Fleet, had served his term of transportation, had constantly worked as a labourer in the bricklayer's gang and was in general considered as a harmless fellow.

✍

Mary Ann Parker   Upon our first arrival at Parramatta, I was surprised to find that so great a progress had been made in this new settlement, which contains above one thousand convicts, besides the military. There is a very good level road of great breadth that runs nearly a mile in a straight direction from the landing place to the governor's house, which is a small convenient building placed upon a gentle ascent and surrounded by about a couple of acres of garden ground; this spot is called Rose Hill. On both sides of the road are small thatched huts at an equal distance from each other.

After spending the day very agreeably at the governor's, we repaired to the lodging which had been provided for us, where we had the comfort of a large wood fire and found everything perfectly quiet, although surrounded by more than one thousand convicts. We enjoyed our night's repose and in the morning, without the previous aid of toilet or mirror, we set out for the governor's to breakfast, and returned with the same party on the ensuing day...

Here we have feasted upon oysters just taken out of the sea; the attention of our sailors, and their care in opening and placing them round their hats, in lieu of plates, by no means diminishing the satisfaction we had in eating them. Indeed, the oysters here are both good and plentiful; I have purchased a large three-quart bowl of them, for a pound and a half of tobacco, besides having them opened for me into the bargain.

NOVEMBER

Saturday 5th

Phillip wrote to Grenville   Of those convicts whose sentences are expired, some who are seamen or carpenters will be carried away by the transports, but by far the greatest part of those people must remain, discontented and desirous of seizing the first opportunity which offers of escaping.

Amongst the many great advantages which would attend settlers coming out who had some property of their own, their finding employment for this class of people would be one, for such settlers would separate them from the convicts, which cannot well be done while they are employed by the Crown, and probably most of them would soon be reconciled to remain in the country.

Thursday 10th

Easty   This day arrived the *Britannia* from a cruise, having caught a whale, the first ever caught on this coast. She was entitled to a £1,000 bounty for the first fish.

The captain of the *Britannia*, Thomas Melville, wrote:

> We went out, in company with the *William and Ann*, the eleventh day after our arrival. The next day after we went out we had very bad weather, and fell in with a very great number of sperm whales. At sun-rising in the morning we could see them all round the horizon. We run through them in different bodies till two o'clock in the afternoon, when the weather abated a little, but a very high sea running. I lowered away two boats, and Bunker [captain of the *William and Ann*] followed the example; in less than two hours we had seven whales killed, but unfortunately a heavy gale came on from the south-west, and took the ship aback with a squall, that the ship could only fetch two of them...
>
> We saw whales every day for a week after, but the weather being so bad we could not attempt to lower a boat down. We cruised 15 days in all...and having no prospect of getting any good weather, I thought it most prudent to come in and refit the ship and complete my casks and fill my water, and by that time the weather would be more moderate.

Friday 11th

Phillip wrote to Lord Sydney   From what I suffer, lately more frequently than ever, from a violent pain in the left kidney, I am anxious to return, for I am not without hopes of finding some relief in London and that I shall still have a few more years in which I would not wish to remain idle.

Lord Grenville's request, that I would remain some time longer, would have been complied with most readily had I no other cause for wishing to return but what proceeded from a desire of settling some private affairs. I should have thought it my duty to have remained if it was judged to be necessary, but the complaint I have renders me at times unable either to ride or walk.

I wrote to Lord Grenville by the last ship and requested leave of absence from the government, but did not then wish to give it up, and which I now fear may occasion my remaining longer than it would have been necessary was another governor to be appointed, and which is what I shall ask, for I give up all thoughts of ever returning to this part of the world after I once leave it.

Tuesday 15th

Collins wrote to his father   The numbers of convicts which have been poured in upon us by the arrival of the transports having reduced the supplies now arrived to only five months' flour for the whole, two pounds of flour were last Saturday taken off, and one of the transports has been taken again into government employ and sent to Calcutta to purchase a quantity of peas and flour for the settlement.

Friday 18th

Phillip wrote to Nepean For cross-cut saws, axes, iron pots and combs we are much distressed. You will see by the return that there are now 2570 male and 608 female convicts with 161 children to be clothed. Nothing was sent out proper for shirts or shifts for the convicts. Two or three hundred iron frying pans will be a saving of spades.

Of those who have been received from Ireland in the *Queen* transport, from 15 to 20 have taken to the woods, and though several of them have been brought in when so reduced that they could not have lived a second day if they had not been found, some of those very men have absconded a second time, and must perish.

Such is their ignorance that some have left the settlement to go to China, which they suppose to be at the distance of only 150 miles. Others, to find a town they supposed to be a few days' walk to the northward. As these people work daily in the woods, the preventing such desertions is impossible, but this is an evil which will cure itself...

Iron mills and querns for grinding Indian corn are very much wanted, and a windmill is now become absolutely necessary.

Tench said of the convicts who had fled the settlement to walk to China:

I trust that no man would feel more reluctant than myself to cast an illiberal national reflection, particularly on a people whom I regard, in an aggregate sense, as brethren and fellow citizens and among whom I have the honour to number many of the most cordial and endearing intimacies which a life passed on service could generate—but it is certain that all these people were Irish.

Elizabeth Macarthur In June Mr Macarthur and myself were removed to Rose Hill with Captain Nepean's company, at which place we remained until about a fortnight since Mr Macarthur was again ordered to Sydney with the command of a detachment of about 60 men...

Captain Parker, commander of the *Gorgon*, brought his wife with him; a very amiable intelligent woman, we have spent many pleasant days together. One of the agents of transports has also his wife with him, so that our little circle has been of late quite brilliant; we are constantly making little parties in boats up and down the various inlets of the harbour, taking refreshments with us and dining out under an awning upon some pleasant point of land or in some of the creeks or coves in which for 20 miles together these water abound. There are so many ladies in the regiment that I am not likely to feel the want of female society as I first did.

Thursday 24th

Phillip wrote to Lord Grenville Several officers of the civil and military departments being desirous of having grants of land, which they would cultivate for their own advantage while they remain in the country, and convey the property to children or other persons when they return to Europe, I am to request your lordship will furnish me with such information on this head as your lordship may judge necessary for my guidance.

Friday 25th

Collins wrote to his brother George I still live where I did, with the governor; we go on in the old way, looking out for supplies from England, sending to other settlements for provisions and living in the meantime upon a reduced ration. This is literally the case; whenever we meet and by a winter's fire I can show you my journal, I will convince you that three-fourths of the time we have been in the country we have not had the full allowance of provisions as directed by government.

We have received upwards of 2,000 people by the fleet that has lately arrived and the supply of provisions which they brought with them was calculated to serve them for nine months, but as we had the same number of people in the colony before they were added, and not an ounce of provisions for them being sent out, it gives us only four months' supply for the whole...

I write by the *Gorgon* to be relieved, or be permitted to return on leave—I matter not which, so as I do but get home. I am tired and disgusted, passed over when it came to my turn to be put on full pay, I feel my services neglected and much fear however highly I may set their value, others may think differently of them.

In fact, the adventurers to New South Wales, from being the objects of admiration, curiosity and their compassion are become, I am clearly of opinion, wherever they are thought of, the objects of cavil and murmur and discontent. The expenses we cost the mother country are enormous and as yet there has not been any prospect of a return to compensate.

Saturday 26th

Henry Lidgbird Ball, commander of the *Supply* Having received orders from Governor Phillip to get the *Supply* ready for sea, I had everything in readiness by the 25th of November and early the next morning we weighed anchor and stood out of Sydney Cove...I had a kangaroo on board, which I had directions to carry to Lord Grenville as a present for his Majesty.

Ball probably took Sarah Partridge, whose term of transportation had expired, and Ann Maria, his daughter with Sarah Partridge, back to England with him on board the *Supply*.

Tench The *Supply*, ever the harbinger of welcome and glad tidings, proclaimed by her own departure that ours was at hand. On the 26th of November she sailed for England. It was impossible to view our separation with insensibility; the little ship which had so often agitated our hopes and fears, which from long acquaintance we had learned to regard as part of ourselves, whose doors of hospitality had been ever thrown open to relieve our accumulated wants and chase our solitary gloom.

In 1792, after the return voyage to England, *Supply* was sold for £500, renamed *Thomas and Nancy* and used to carry coal in the Thames.

Sunday 27th

Phillip From the debilitated state in which many of the convicts were landed from the last ships, the number of sick were greatly increased, the surgeon's returns on the 27th being upwards of 400 sick at Parramatta and the same day medicines were distributed to

192 at Sydney. To the number of sick at Parramatta upwards of 100 may be added, who were so weak that they could not be put to any kind of labour, not even to that of pulling grass for thatching the huts. Forty-two people died in the month of November and in these people nature seemed fairly to be worn out; many of them were so thoroughly exhausted that they expired without a groan and apparently without any kind of pain.

∽

Collins By the dry weather which prevailed our water had been so much affected, beside being lessened by the watering of some of the transports, that a prohibition was laid by the governor on the watering of the remainder at Sydney, and their boats were directed to go to a convenient place upon the north shore.

To remedy this evil the governor had employed the stone-mason's gang to cut tanks out of the rock, which would be reservoirs for the water large enough to supply the settlement for some time.

These were the tanks or reservoirs for which the Tank Stream was named.

Phillip gave details of the land 'in cultivation at Parramatta in November 1791...measured by David Burton, the public gardener, who observed that the soil in places is remarkably good and only wants cultivation to be fit for any use, for the ground that has been the longest in cultivation bears the best crops'. The acreages shown by Burton were:

351 in maize.
  44 in wheat.
    6 in barley.
    1 in oats.
    2 in potatoes.
    4 not cultivated, but cleared.
    5 mostly planted with vines.
    6 the governor's garden, mostly sown with maize and wheat.
  80 garden ground belonging to individuals.
  17 land in cultivation by the New South Wales Corps.
150 cleared and to be sown with turnips.
  92 ground in cultivation by settlers.
  28 ground in cultivation by the civil and military.
<u>134</u> enclosed and the timber thinned for feeding cattle.
<u>920</u>

Tench The hour of departure to England for the marine battalion drew nigh. If I be allowed to speak from my own feelings on the occasion, I will not say that we contemplated its approach with mingled sensations: we hailed it with rapture and exultation.

DECEMBER

Friday 2nd

Phillip wrote to Banks The plants for the King's garden are all on board, except two or three tubs coming from Parramatta, and in very high perfection, most of them have flowered in the tubs. You will receive 60 tubs which contain 221 plants; seeds are sowed likewise in all the tubs and I am certain that Captain Parker will see that great care is taken of them while on board…

The young kangaroo sent by the *Supply*, will, I hope, live to be presented to his Majesty and I shall send another by the *Gorgon* for the same purpose…I send you a drawing of the waratah, several plants of which are in the tubs. I am getting drawings of all the plants and animals, they are done correctly, and about 200 are finished…

We have now many thousand young vines, here and at Norfolk Island. I had two or three bunches of grapes the year before last, and last year several good bunches; at present the old vines in my garden are loaded with very fine fruit. One orange and two fig trees are also in good fruit, and if I except the banana, I do not know any fruit which has been tried that does not thrive as well here as it does in any part of the world…

I think that my old acquaintance Bennelong will accompany me whenever I return to England and from him when he understands English, much information may be attained, for he is very intelligent.

Tench, who was preparing to conclude his second book, *A Complete Account of the Settlement at Port Jackson*, summed up the settlement's progress in a 'Description of the existing state of the colony, as taken by myself, a few days previous to my embarkation in the *Gorgon* to sail for England':

Went up to Rose Hill. Public buildings here have not greatly multiplied since my last survey. The storehouse and barrack have been long completed, also apartments for the chaplain of the regiment and for the judge-advocate, in which last criminal courts, when necessary, are held; but these are petty erections... The great road from near the landing place to the governor's house is finished, and a very noble one it is, being of great breadth and a mile long in a straight line; in many places it is carried over gullies of considerable depth, which have been filled up with trunks of trees, covered with earth.

All the sawyers, carpenters and blacksmiths will soon be concentred under the direction of a very adequate person of the governor's household [probably Henry Brewer]; this plan is already so far advanced as to contain nine covered sawpits, which change of weather cannot disturb the operations of, an excellent work shed for the carpenters and a large new shop for the blacksmiths; it certainly promises to be of great public benefit.

Monday 5th

Easty This morning arrived the *Queen* from Norfolk Island with Major Robert Ross Commandant of Marines and the troops from that place.

The marines were to join the *Gorgon* to return to England; Ralph Clark was with them, but he made no diary entries during his brief stay at Sydney Cove. Later, he wrote, 'Since the day before I left Norfolk have not been able to do anything...while on board the *Queen* I was seasick the whole of the way from Norfolk to Port Jackson and the few days I remained there was so busy in getting the accounts of the men settled that I had not time.'

Another passenger returning to Port Jackson in the *Queen* was Mary Branham. At the age of 14 she had been convicted for stealing a large quantity of clothes and taking them to a pawn shop, for which she was sentenced to seven years' transportation. Three years later she was sent to Botany Bay in the *Lady Penrhyn*, where she had a son in July 1788, fathered by a seaman, William Curtis. In March 1790 she went to Norfolk Island and she now returned, her term of transportation expired and with a second child, a daughter. The father was Ralph Clark.

Wednesday 7th

Tench Went to Schaeffer's farm. I found him at home, conversed with him, and walked with him over all his cultivated ground. He had 140 acres granted to him, 14 of which are in cultivation, 12 in maize, one in wheat, and one in vines and tobacco. He has besides 23 acres on which the trees are cut down but not burnt off the land. He resigned his appointment and began his farm last May and had at first five convicts to assist him; he has now four. All his maize, except three acres, is mean. This he thinks may be attributed to three causes: a middling soil, too dry a spring, and from the ground not being sufficiently pulverised before the seed was put into it. The wheat is thin and poor; he does not reckon its produce at more than eight or nine bushels. His vines, 900 in number, are flourishing, and will, he supposes, bear fruit next year. His tobacco plants are not very luxuriant. To these two last articles he means principally to direct his exertions. He says (and truly) that they will always be saleable and profitable.

Thursday 8th

Tench Ruse now lives in a comfortable brick house, built for him by the governor. He has 11 acres and a half in cultivation and several more which have been cleared by convicts in their leisure hours, on condition of receiving the first year's crop. He means to cultivate little besides maize; wheat is so much less productive. Of the culture of vineyards and tobacco he is ignorant and, with great good sense, he declared that he would not quit the path he knew for an uncertainty.

His live stock consists of four breeding sows and 30 fowls. He has been taken from the store (that is, has supplied himself with provisions) for some months past, and his wife is to be taken off at Christmas, at which time, if he deems himself able to maintain a convict labourer, one is to be given to him...

Before I bade adieu to Rose Hill, in all probability for the last time of my life, it struck me that there yet remained one object of consideration not to be slighted; Barrington had been in the settlement between two and three months and I had not seen him. I saw him with curiosity. He is tall, approaching to six feet, slender, and his gait and manner bespeak liveliness and activity. Of that elegance and fashion with which my imagination had decked him (I know not why) I could distinguish no trace.

Great allowance should, however, be made for depression, and unavoidable deficiency of dress. His face is thoughtful and intelligent; to a strong cast of countenance he adds a penetrating eye and a prominent forehead; his whole demeanour is humble, not servile. Both on his passage from England and since his arrival here his conduct has been irreproachable. He is appointed high-constable of the settlement of Rose Hill, a post of some respectability and certainly one of importance to those who live here.

Tuesday 13th

The Reverend Richard Johnson wrote to Mr J. Stonard   There have been and are great differences amongst our officers here; yesterday a duel was fought between Major R. [Ross] and a Captain Hill. I wish that after the marines are gone home we may be more peaceable, but I fear whether dissensions will not prevail as bad as ever. Fortunately neither party was wounded yesterday and after two fires on each side, the seconds interfered and settled the differences.

Scott   Major Ross, two captains, one lieutenant, one captain-lieutenant, quartermaster, adjutant, three first lieutenants, three second lieutenants, nine sergeants, eight corporals, six drummers and 50 privates embarked on board the *Gorgon* for a passage to England, together with 21 women and 43 children of the marines and 4 convict children brought home by the officers.

Friday 16th

Collins wrote to Lord Grenville   From information which I have received by His Majesty's Ship *Gorgon*, I find that some private affairs require my attendance in England. I have therefore to request your lordship will be pleased to permit me to return, and to hope that my request for that purpose may not be deemed improper by your lordship.

The whalers *Matilda* and *Mary Ann* had returned to Port Jackson. The *Matilda* had not seen any whales, the *Mary Ann* had killed nine, enough to give them 30 barrels of oil, before bad weather closed in.

Collins   These ships sailed again immediately...and returned on the 16th without killing a fish. The masters attributed their bad success to currents and, giving up all hopes of a fishery here, they determined, after refitting, to quit the coast.
     The *Salamander* and *Britannia* whalers came in at the same time, and with like ill fortune. Melville, the master of the *Britannia*, who

had been formerly so sanguine in his hopes of a fishery, seemed now to have adopted a different opinion and hinted to some in the colony that he did not think he should try the coast any longer.

Tench's description of the colony included some observations on the Aboriginal people:

Longevity, I think, is seldom attained by them. Unceasing agitation wears out the animal frame and is unfriendly to length of days. We have seen them grey with age, but not old; perhaps never beyond 60 years...

The women are proportionally smaller than the men. I never measured but two of them, who were both, I think, about the medium height. One of them, a sister of Bennelong, stood exactly five feet two inches high; the other, named Gooreedeeana, was shorter by a quarter of an inch.

But I cannot break from Gooreedeeana so abruptly. She belonged to the tribe of Cameragal, and rarely came among us. One day, however, she entered my house, to complain of hunger. She excelled in beauty all their females I ever saw; her age, about 18; the firmness, the symmetry, and the luxuriancy of her bosom might have tempted painting to copy its charms; her mouth was small and her teeth, though exposed to all the destructive purposes to which they apply them, were white, sound and unbroken. Her countenance, though marked by some of the characteristics of her native land, was distinguished by a softness and sensibility unequalled in the rest of her countrywomen, and I was willing to believe that these traits indicated the disposition of her mind.

I had never before seen this elegant timid female, of whom I had often heard, but the interest I took in her led me to question her about her husband and family. She answered me by repeating a name, which I have now forgotten and told me she had no children. I was seized with a strong propensity to learn whether the attractions of Gooreedeeana were sufficiently powerful to secure her from the brutal violence with which the women are treated and as I found my question either ill understood, or reluctantly answered, I proceeded to examine her head, the part on which the husband's vengeance generally alights. With grief I found it covered by contusions and mangled by scars.

The poor creature, grown by this time more confident from perceiving that I pitied her, pointed out a wound just above her left knee, which she told me was received from a spear, thrown at her by a man who had lately dragged her by force from her home to gratify his lust. I afterwards observed that this wound had caused a slight lameness, and that she limped in walking. I could only compassionate her wrongs and sympathise in her misfortunes. To alleviate her present sense of them, when she took her leave, I gave her, however, all the bread and salt pork which my little stock afforded.

Tench asked:

Have these people any religion, any knowledge of or belief in a deity? Any conception of the immortality of the soul?

He answered with:

the following instance; Abaroo was sick; to cure her, one of her own sex slightly cut her on the forehead, in a perpendicular direction, with an oyster shell, so as just to fetch blood; she then put one end of a string to the wound, and, beginning to sing, held the other end to her own gums, which she rubbed until they bled copiously. This blood she contended was the blood of the patient, flowing through the string, and that she would thereby soon recover. Abaroo became well and firmly believed that she owed her cure to the treatment she had received. Are not these, I say, links, subordinate ones indeed, of the same golden chain? He who believes in magic confesses supernatural agency.

Sunday 18th

Collins On board of the *Gorgon* were embarked the marines who came from England in the first ships, as valuable a corps as any in his Majesty's service. They had struggled here with greatly more than the common hardships of service and were now quitting a country in which they had opened and smoothed the way for their successors and from which, whatever benefit might hereafter be derived, must be derived by those who had the easy task of treading in paths previously and painfully formed by them.

Scott The *Gorgon* sailed with a fair wind.

Sergeant James Scott and his wife Jane left in the *Gorgon* with their children Elizabeth, born on the voyage out, and William, born in 1790.

Scott continued to serve as a sergeant of marines at Portsmouth, where he died in 1796.

Others who left in the *Gorgon* included Major Robert Ross and Ralph Clark, both of whom had been stationed on Norfolk Island for the previous 21 months, Watkin Tench, and William Dawes.

Ross continued in the marines but died in Kent in June 1794, at the age of 54. His son, Alexander John Ross, who had arrived in the colony as a private marine at the age of eight and was promoted to second lieutenant a year later, returned to England with his father and distinguished himself in action in France in 1798, but died two years later at the age of 20.

In February 1788 Ralph Clark had written in his diary: 'I never will have any thing, any woman whatever except yourself, my dear wife, I will be true to my Betsey, my love for you will keep me so', but when he sailed into Sydney Cove from Norfolk Island in December 1791 he had brought with him Mary Branham (who although she was only about 21 had served her term of transportation) and their five-month-old daughter, Alicia. Mary Branham does not appear in the colony's records after that date and it is possible that she and the child went back to England with Clark, although she would not have lived with him there.

Clark returned to Betsey Alicia and young Ralph, but he did not stay there long. In 1793 he embarked in the HMS *Tartar* for the West Indies, leaving Betsey carrying a second child. In 1794 he was serving in HMS *Sceptre* in Haiti, fighting the French; young Ralph was a midshipman aboard the same ship. Ralph Clark died there, from yellow fever, on 18 June 1794 and the same disease killed his son 11 days later. Probably neither knew that Betsey Alicia had died in childbirth earlier in the same year.

Watkin Tench married Anna Maria Sargent, of Devonport in Cornwall, some years after he returned to England; they had no children of their own, but adopted the four orphaned children of his wife's sister. Tench served in various ships, was a prisoner of war in France, and was promoted through the ranks to lieutenant-general. He retired in 1821 to live in Devonport, not 20 miles from his friend George Worgan at Liskeard. He died in Devonport in May 1833, at the age of 74.

William Dawes was respected throughout the colony. His decision to leave with the rest of the Marine Corps in 1791, after he had indicated in 1788 that he would stay, is attributed to his disillusionment at the ill-conceived and unsuccessful excursion ordered by Phillip to revenge the death of John Macentire, Phillip's 'gamekeeper'; he went with the party against his better judgment and, even though it was entirely unsuccessful, he later regretted it. However, there may have been other factors in his decision not to stay; most of his fellow officers returned to England with him on the *Gorgon* in December 1791 and the discomforts of life in the colony are well documented.

Dawes had been provided with instruments from the Board of Longitude with which to observe a comet that the Astronomer Royal had calculated would be seen in the southern hemisphere in 1789. The comet did not appear, but Dawes busied himself with a study of the Aboriginal people and their language and for a time he worked closely with an Aboriginal girl, Patyegarang, another spelling of *patagarang*, the word for the grey kangaroo.

Dawes kept a notebook, titled *Vocabulary of the Language of N. S. Wales, in the Neighbourhood of Sydney*. From an entry in this book which reads in part, 'At this time Patyegarang was standing by the fire naked, and I desired her to put on her clothes', it has been inferred that he and Patyegarang were lovers.

His career after he left New South Wales was distinguished by valuable service in Sierra Leone, where he became governor, and significant achievements in limiting the slave trade and dealing with its victims in Antigua, West Indies, where he died in 1836.

Sunday 25th

Collins From the state of the provision stores, the governor, on Christmas Day, could only give one pound of flour to each woman in the settlement. On that day divine service was performed here and at Parramatta, Mr Bain, the chaplain of the new corps, assisting Mr Johnson in the religious duties of the morning. There were some among us, however, by whom even the sanctity of this day was not regarded, for at night the marine store was robbed of two-and-twenty gallons of spirits.

Saturday 31st

Collins At Parramatta...many of the convicts there not having any part of their ration left when Tuesday or Wednesday night came, the governor directed, as he had before done from the same reason, that the provisions of the labouring convicts should be issued to them daily. This measure being disapproved of by them, they assembled in rather a tumultuous manner before the governor's house at Parramatta on the last day of the month to request that their provisions might be served as usual on the Saturdays.

The governor, however, dispersed them without granting their request and as they were heard to murmur and talk of obtaining by different means what was refused to entreaty...he assured them that as he knew the major part of them were led by eight or 10 designing men to whom they looked up, and to whose names he was not a stranger, on any open appearance of discontent, he should make immediate examples of them...This was the first instance of any tumultuous assembly among these people, and was now to be ascribed to the spirit of resistance and villainy lately imported by the newcomers from England and Ireland.

✍

The relationship of the settlers to the new land had improved, as convicts and marines who wished to stay made 'choice of their lands' and began the business of private farming. The Third Fleet brought almost 1,900 more people into the colony and the settlements at Sydney Cove and Parramatta took on an air of substance and permanency.

Communication with the Aboriginal people also improved during the year; some of the Europeans attended a corroboree held at Bennelong Point and an initiation ceremony held at Farm Cove; some of the Aboriginal people spent much of their time at Sydney Cove, where they used Bennelong's hut and Government House as gathering places; Yemmerrawannie 'almost constantly lived at the governor's house'.

But Collins wrote early in the year: 'We had not yet been able to reconcile the natives to the deprivation of those parts of this harbour which we occupied. While they entertained the idea of our having dispossessed them of their residences, they must always consider us as enemies.' When the convicts who had served their terms were settled in the Parramatta area in July, Phillip wrote that 'very few days elapsed before a large body of the natives appeared'; they set fire to one of the settlers' huts.

As the settlement expanded, that situation was not likely to improve.

1792
A House as I Wish For

14 February	The *Pitt* arrived with Major Francis Grose, commandant of the NSW Corps.
31 March	Eighty-eight deaths were recorded during the month, with more expected in April.
11 April	Heavy rain and high winds damaged buildings and crops.
14 April	The ration was reduced to three pounds of flour, two pounds of maize and four pounds of pork.
12 May	The weekly ration was again reduced.
6 June	Remaining supplies were estimated at one month's flour and two months' salt meat.
20 June	The *Atlantic* arrived with supplies and livestock from Calcutta.
26 July	The *Britannia* arrived with supplies and provisions from England.
24 October	The *Britannia* sailed for Rio and the Cape to buy provisions and livestock for the officers, at their own expense.
30 November	Five convicts petitioned Phillip for the appointment of a Catholic priest.
11 December	The *Atlantic* sailed for England, carrying Phillip, Bennelong, Yemmerrawannie and the remaining First Fleet marines.

JANUARY

Of the original writers, only Collins and Easty remained in 1792; however, Phillip's despatches remain a source of information; the diarist Richard Atkins was to arrive in the *Pitt* in February 1792 and there are contributions from George Barrington and the letters of the Reverend Richard Johnson and Surgeon John White.

Monday 9th

The judge-advocate, David Collins, the Reverend Richard Johnson and the surveyor-general, Augustus Alt, heard 18 cases at Parramatta. There was one acquittal; 15 cases resulted in sentences totalling 1950 lashes. Thomas Francis was charged with 'going to Sydney without leave' and sentenced to wear 'an iron on the leg for six months'; Robert Miles, charged with stealing potatoes, was sentenced to be 'on a chain with the rest'.

☙

Collins The convicts having assembled [at Parramatta] at the latter end of the last month in an improper and tumultuous manner, the governor now thought proper to issue a proclamation directing that in case of any riot or disturbance among the convicts, everyone who was seen out of his hut would (if such riot or disturbance should happen in the night or during the hours of rest from labour, or if he were absent from his labour during the hours of work) be deemed to be aiding and assisting the rioters, and be punished accordingly.

FEBRUARY

Friday 3rd

Collins Eight settlers from the marines received their grants of land, situated on the north side of the harbour near the Flats, and named by the governor the Field of Mars.

All were privates in the marine company of the First Fleet; the grants were 80 acres each. Phillip named the area after Mars, the Roman god of war, because the first settlers in the area were all soldiers.

Tuesday 14th

The *Pitt* arrived in Sydney Cove. Easty wrote that she 'saluted the town with 13 guns'. Collins wrote:

> She had on board Francis Grose, Esq, the lieutenant-governor of the settlements and major-commandant of the New South Wales Corps, one company of which, together with the adjutant and surgeon's mate, came out with him. She brought out 319 male and 49 female convicts, five children and seven free women, with salt provisions [salt meat] calculated to serve that number of people 10 months, but which would only furnish the colony with provisions for 40 days.

Grose replaced Major Robert Ross as lieutenant-governor. Born in 1754, Grose joined the army at the age of 21, had been wounded during the American War of Independence and probably obtained his appointment in New South Wales through his friendship with Evan Nepean.

> **Collins** The whole of the New South Wales Corps, except one company, being now arrived, the numbers requisite for the different duties were settled, and one company...was fixed for the duty at Parramatta, a like number for Norfolk Island, and the remainder were to do duty at Sydney, the headquarters of the corps.

The New South Wales Corps consisted of four companies, three of which were raised by Major Grose, who had recruited more than 300 men. Grose had the right to sell the captaincies and lieutenancies for what he could get for them, which meant that soldiers who would not otherwise have been made officers were able to buy their commissions, and some of them outlaid the money with a view to making a profit from the transaction.

The fourth company of the corps was raised by Phillip, under the captaincy of the marine officer, George Johnston, from members of the First Fleet marine corps who wished to stay, and from emancipated convicts.

Wednesday 29th

The Reverend Richard Johnson wrote to Phillip We have been here now above four years, and the first time we had public service at Port Jackson I found things much more comfortable for myself and for the congregation…than I did last Sunday, for then we had the advantage of the trees to shelter us from the sun, but now we were wholly exposed to the weather, first to the rain, which I was fearful would have made me dismiss the people, and afterwards to the wind and sun.

On this account, sir, it cannot be wondered at that persons, whether of higher or lower rank, come so seldom and so reluctantly to public worship. I have, not seldom, found very great inconveniences attending it myself…

I neither wish or mean to interfere with anything that does not concern myself, but as the clergyman of the colony and as intrusted with the spiritual charge of those unhappy people around us, I submit it to your Excellency's own consideration whether, before the approaching winter, some place should not be thought of and built both here and at the new settlement for the purpose of carrying on public worship.

✑

Collins Permission having been obtained, a shop was opened at a hut on shore for the sale of various articles brought out in the *Pitt*, and notwithstanding a fleet of transports had but lately sailed hence, notwithstanding the different orders which had been sent to Bengal and the high price at which every thing was sold, the avidity with which all descriptions of people grasped at what was to be purchased was extraordinary.

MARCH

Saturday 17th

Easty At six o'clock the troops in garrison was under arms when Major Francis Grose's commission for lieutenant-governer of this island was read and the troops was reviewed by his Excellency the governor. The colours of the New South Wales [Corps] was displayed for the first time on this ground.

Wednesday 21st

The Reverend Richard Johnson wrote to Dr William Morice, the secretary of the Society for the Propagation of the Gospel in Foreign Parts It is now a considerable time since his Excellency our governor told me that he expected the schoolmasters out from England. None however have yet arrived. There being several children of age to be instructed, I proposed to his Excellency to have a person appointed at different places to instruct them to read. To this he readily consented, and myself was appointed to superintend them. We have now one school established at Sydney and another at Parramatta—a school mistress appointed for each. These teach the children belonging to the convicts gratis, the military, officers etc making them some little acknowledgment for their trouble.

APRIL

Monday 2nd

Although there was much sickness and they were again short of provisions, the new lieutenant-governor, Major Francis Grose of the New South Wales Corps, took an optimistic view. He wrote to Nepean:

> I am at last, thank God, safely landed with my family at this place, and, to my great astonishment, instead of the rock I expected to see I find myself surrounded with gardens that flourish and produce fruit of every description. Vegetables are here in great abundance and I live in as good a house as I wish for. I am given the farm of my predecessor, which produces a sufficiency to supply my family with everything I have occasion for. In short, all that is wanting to put this colony in an independent state is one ship freighted with corn and black cattle. Was that but done, all difficulties would be over.

Monday 9th

William Pugh, the convict servant of Captain George Johnston, was charged with stealing from Johnston a white linen shirt valued at six shillings, 20 pounds of flour valued at 10 shillings and eight Spanish dollars worth 40 shillings; Pugh admitted to stealing the shirt and the money. Johnston himself gave evidence of Pugh's good character, saying 'he had always behaved very well and he never found anything missing until now', but Pugh was found guilty and sentenced to receive 300 lashes.

The trial was observed by Richard Atkins, who had arrived as a paying passenger in the *Pitt*. The son of a baronet, Atkins, 47 years old, was well educated and well presented, but he had disposed of a considerable amount of the family's money and had apparently come to New South Wales to escape his creditors.

Atkins kept an intermittent and somewhat eccentric diary, now held in the National Library, containing a mixture of weather and legal notes, poetry, philosophy and occasionally shrewd observations about the settlement. He wrote that the trial:

> was conducted with the greatest propriety, and except a jury... was conformable to the English law and custom. An Englishman would with reason spurn the idea of giving up life unless sanctioned by the verdict of an English jury, yet I cannot but conceive strict justice may be done him as well by six officers whom we must suppose men of some education, attended by the judge-advocate, as by a jury consisting of 12 ignorant farmers or tradesmen who know nothing but what belongs to their own line of trade.

Wednesday 11th

Atkins A continual deluge of rain all night attended with violent gusts of wind from the south-west and south-east. It has continued all this day without intermission and done a great deal of damage to the gardens and huts...

There has been a violent battle between the natives of Botany Bay and this place in which many were wounded on both sides. The subject of dispute was one of the natives of Botany Bay having mentioned the name of a person deceased belonging to this clan. For so trifling a cause do men murder each other, but is it not the same in Europe? Read the history of civilised nations and we shall find it so.

Thursday 12th

Atkins The rain still continues, but with less violence than before; the wind veering from the south-east to south-west. The colony very sickly. Eighty-eight died in the course of the last month and in all probability this will exceed it. It has pleased God almighty to inflict on me these last three weeks more sickness than I have experienced these last 30 years.

Collins At Parramatta the gale had done much damage; several huts which were built in low grounds were rendered almost inaccessible and the greater part of the wattled huts suffered considerably. A large portion of the cleared ground was laid under water and such corn as had not been reaped was beaten down.

Saturday 14th

Collins recorded another change to the weekly ration: 'Three pounds of flour and two pounds of maize, with four pounds of pork, were served to each man, and three pounds of flour and one pound of maize, with four pounds of pork, were served to each woman in the settlement. The children received the usual proportion.'

Tuesday 17th

Atkins Mild and regular weather, the sea breeze sets in generally about one o'clock. This evening I walked by myself to the brickfields about a mile from the camp, for so Sydney is called from its having been the spot they pitched their tents on their first landing. A very good road is made the whole way to it through the wood, where trees of an immense size border it on both sides, their lofty and wide spreading branches look beautiful...The underwood is mostly flowering shrubs, some of whom are now in blossom of the most vivid and beautiful colours imaginable, and many of them most delicately formed.

Wednesday 18th

Atkins Some continuance of fine weather. The convicts dying very fast, merely through want of nourishment. The Indian corn served out is of little use in point of nourishment; they have no mills to grind it and many are so weak that they cannot pound it. At present there is not more than eight weeks' ration of flour at three pounds per man in the store. Oh, shame, shame!

Friday 20th

Atkins This morning breakfasted with the governor, who received me with his usual politeness. People may exclaim against him as much as they please, but I much doubt whether those who find much fault would not run into much greater errors themselves. His situation is by no means a desirable one in point of duty, for except the civil and military departments he has nothing but a set of rascals to deal with who require a watchful eye to make them do their duty.

The overseers are themselves convicts and are not to be depended on. At Parramatta some of them are rigid to a degree, which proceeds from a fear of being thought too indulgent and probably from what will almost universally operate upon weak minds—a thirst for power and dominion over the rest of our fellow creatures.

Saturday 21st

Atkins This day at six o'clock set off for Parramatta in the governor's gig with the judge-advocate. The feelings of humanity is sorely wounded to see the number of poor wretches whose emaciated looks denote poverty and misery in the extreme, brought as prisoners for stealing a few cobs of Indian corn. Hunger is the general plea, but unfortunately in this country it cannot be admitted, for was it, no private property could be secure. Indeed, to act as a magistrate here with efficacy, you must in a great degree lay aside that philanthropy and goodwill towards men that adorns human nature.

Friday 27th

The *Waaksamheyd*, carrying Hunter and the crew of the *Sirius*, including William Bradley, Jacob Nagle, George Worgan and George Raper, had left Port Jackson on 28 March 1791 and anchored at Portsmouth on 22 April 1792.

On the last page of Bradley's journal, the entry for this day reads: 'A court-martial was held on board of *Brunswick* to try Captain Hunter, the officers and crew of the *Sirius* for the loss of the said ship. When it appeared that everything was done that could be done, Captain Hunter, the officers and crew were honourably acquitted.'

Saturday 28th

Atkins Continuance of fine weather. This day went to Parramatta with Captain Collins. A number of poor wretches brought before him for stealing Indian corn; 'tis dreadful but they must be punished.

✑

Collins The natives had not lately given us any interruption by acts of hostility. Several of their young people continued to reside among us and the different houses in the town were frequently visited by their relations. Very little information that could be depended upon respecting their manners and customs was obtained through this intercourse and it was observed that they conversed with us in a mutilated and incorrect language formed entirely on our imperfect knowledge and improper application of their words.

Collins also wrote:

The mortality in the last month had been extremely great. Distressing as it was, however, to see the poor wretches daily dropping into the grave, it was far more afflicting to observe the countenances and emaciated persons of many that remained soon to follow their miserable companions...

The weakest of the convicts were excused from any kind of hard labour; but it was not hard labour that destroyed them, it was an entire want of strength in the constitution to receive nourishment, to throw off the debility that pervaded their whole system, or to perform any sort of labour whatever. This dreadful mortality was chiefly confined to the convicts who had arrived in the last year; of 122 male convicts who came out in the *Queen* transport from Ireland, 50 only were living at the beginning of this month.

MAY

Wednesday 9th

Collins Mr Richard Atkins, who came out in the *Pitt,* and who had been sworn a justice of the peace, went up to Parramatta to reside there, the constant presence of a magistrate being deemed by the governor indispensable at that settlement.

Saturday 12th

The flour ration was halved and the ration of maize was increased.

Collins As maize or Indian corn was now necessarily become the principal part of each person's subsistence, hand-mills and querns were set to work to grind it coarse for every person both at Sydney and at Parramatta; and at this latter place, wooden mortars, with a lever and a pestle, were also used to break the corn, and these pounded it much finer than it could be ground by the hand-mills; but it was effected with great labour.

Sunday 13th

Atkins Went to church. As I mean to make every person attend divine service, I think it necessary to set the example. It is proper everywhere, but more particularly so here. Dined with the governor.

Friday 18th

Collins A party of the tribe inhabiting the woods, to the number of 15 or 16, was observed coming out of a hut at the middle settlement, dressed in such clothing as they found there and taking with them a quantity of corn in nets. The person who saw them imagined at first from their appearance they they were convicts, but perceiving one of them preparing to throw a spear at him, he levelled his piece, which was loaded with small shot, and fired at him. The native instantly dropped his spear and the whole party ran away, leaving behind them the nets with the corn, some blankets and one or two spears. It was supposed that the native was wounded.

Monday 21st

Atkins This morning at daylight set off with the governor to visit the settlers...At the Ponds are about 10 settlers, each distinct from the other. Though they have not begun cultivating the ground above 10 months, they are for the most part...very comfortably lodged, have plenty of vegetables, Indian corn for their families as well as to keep, some two, some three pigs; many have from one to two acres of ground under wheat and from eight to 10 acres cleared which will be ready for a crop next year.

In short they are in every particular much better situated than they could possibly be in England. Indeed too much praise cannot be given to the governor for (I may say) the paternal care and encouragement he gives to all and each of them who deserve it.

Saturday 26th

Atkins Yalloway, a native, has been killed and burnt and it is supposed on account of his attachment to us; jealousy was the cause.

Sunday 27th

Collins Information was received from Parramatta that a convict who was employed in well-digging at Prospect Hill, having come in from thence to receive some slops which were issued, was on his return met midway and murdered, or rather butchered by some of the natives. When the body was found, it was not quite cold and had at least 30 spear wounds in it.

The head was cut in several places and most of the teeth were knocked out. They had taken his clothing and provisions and the provisions of another man which he was carrying out to him. The natives with whom we had intercourse said that this murder was committed by some of the people who inhabited the woods, and was done probably in revenge for the shot that was fired at the natives who some time before were stripping the hut.

✦

Collins At Sydney a tank that would contain about 7,996 gallons of water, with a well in the centre 15 feet deep, was finished and the water let into it. Brick huts were in hand for the convicts in room of the miserable hovels occupied by many, which had been put up at their first landing.

Barrington The following list of articles and prices in the infantine country of New South Wales may at some future time, if not at present, be deemed an object of curiosity. The list included:
Flour from 6d to 1s per pound.
Hens, laying ones, from 7s to 10s each.
Chickens from 2s 6d to 3s 6d.
Eggs 3d each.
Fresh pork 1s per pound.

Potatoes 3d per pound.
Cabbages 1d each.
Sows £3 to £4 4s each.
Growing pigs £1 to £2 10s each.
Sucking pigs 10s each.
Coffee 2s to 2s 6d per pound.
Brazil tobacco 3s to 5s per pound.
Tobacco grown in the country 1s 6d to 2s 6d per pound.
Soap from 1s 6d per pound.

JUNE

Friday 1st

Collins   With infinite satisfaction it was observed at the beginning
of the month that the mortality and sickness among the people had
very much decreased. This was attributed by the medical gentlemen
to the quantities of fresh meat which had been obtained at Parramatta by the people who were employed to shoot for the hospital,
a sufficiency having been brought in at one time to supply the sick
with fresh meat for a week, and for the remainder of the month in
the proportion of twice or three times a week. Great quantities of
vegetables had also been given to those who were in health, as well
as to the sick, both from the public ground at the farther settlement
(which had been sown and produced some most excellent turnips),
and from the governor's garden.

Saturday 2nd

Atkins   Walked to the new settlement and shot some beautiful para-
keets etc of which there are certainly greater variety in this country
than in the whole known world besides; plants, insects etc are likewise here in the greatest variety.

The parrots which were so common in the Rose Hill area were at first
called 'Rose Hill parrots', which was abbreviated to 'Rosehiller' and later
to 'rosella'.

Wednesday 6th

Collins   There was only a sufficiency of flour in store to serve till
the 2nd of July, and salt provisions till the 6th of August following,

at the ration then issued, and neither the *Atlantic* storeship from Calcutta nor the expected supplies from England had arrived.

Saturday 9th

Atkins It was mentioned above that Yalloway, a native, was murdered and burnt by another native. It appears to be a general determination that the friends of the murdered person revenge his death by the murder of the guilty person or upon any relation they may have an opportunity of doing it on. The wife of Yalloway, a few days after her husband's death, met a young girl, a relation of the murderer, and immediately took a large stone and beat her over the head till her skull was fractured in many places, and she died a few hours after. Upon this being mentioned to some of the natives they were not in the least surprised at it, but said it was a natural consequence.

Saturday 16th

Atkins It had been usual for the governor on his Majesty's birthday to show some respect to it by giving a general amnesty to all those who wore irons, except those whose crimes were too deep a dye, or those that from the frequency of crimes there was no reformation to be expected. As he neglected it on that day, he appointed this for the purpose.

All the convicts were assembled and he told them that he was sorry the ration was so small, he desired them to be patient, orderly and to do their duty with cheerfulness, that he expected ships in every day, that then they should receive the benefit of their good behaviour. He then extended his lenity to the poor objects in irons, and the whole finished in the greatest order.

Afterwards we walked up the hill from whence we saw distinctly mountains called the blue ones at about 25 miles distance. The whole face of the country appears one artistic wood.

Tuesday 19th

Atkins The difficulties, almost insurmountable, at getting at truth among a set of people used to every species of vice and Newgate chicanery is amazing. Nothing but perseverance with a firm resolution of getting at it, if attainable, can operate.

Wednesday 20th

Collins To the inexpressible joy of all ranks of people in the settlements, the *Atlantic* storeship anchored safely in the cove with a cargo of rice, soujee [flour] and dhal, from Calcutta, having been much longer performing her voyage than was expected, owing to some delays at Calcutta in settling and arranging the contracts for the supply of provisions which had been required.

JULY

Monday 2nd

Atkins It rained all night; this will I hope secure us a good crop of wheat, though it is more likely to fail from the excessive heats than from the want of rain except bringing it up well above the ground. The rain as usual comes from the south-east.

This week's ration is two pounds of pork, four pounds of Indian corn, one pint bad rice, one and a half pounds of a species of flour called in Bengal 'soujee' and one pound of dhal or pea flour. We had a report from the natives that five ships were seen to the southward.

Tuesday 3rd

Atkins Rainy weather; was sent for to Sydney to attend a civil court and got very wet.

Saturday 14th

Atkins The pork served to us this day very bad from Bengal. Only a few casks was brought by way of sample; it is found from this specimen it will not keep, as it is putrid. Indeed our ration is much too small for working men, and more especially as this is the busy time of the year in getting the wheat in and preparing the ground for the Indian corn etc.

Monday 16th

Collins   Phillip granted an absolute remission of the term for which Elizabeth Perry had been sentenced. This woman came out in the *Neptune* in 1790 and had married James Ruse, a settler. The good conduct of the wife and the industry of the husband, who had for some time supported himself, his wife, a child and two convicts, independent of the public store, were the reasons assigned in the instrument which restored her to her rights and privileges as a free woman.

Thursday 26th

Easty   This day arrived the *Britannia*, Captain Raven, from London, laden with provisions and stores for the settlement. She has been six months on her passage.

(This was not the same ship that had arrived in October 1791 under Captain Melville.)

Collins   The *Britannia* was the first of three ships that were to be despatched hither, having on board 12 months' clothing for the convicts, four months' flour and eight months' beef and pork for every description of persons in the settlements, at full allowance, calculating their numbers at 4639, which it was at home supposed they might amount to after the arrival of the *Pitt*.

It was still a matter of uncertainty in England, even at the departure of the *Britannia*, whether the merchants of Calcutta had supplied this country with provisions, and under the idea that some circumstance might have prevented them, this supply was ordered to be forwarded.

Friday 27th

Collins   In the consequence of the arrival of the *Britannia*, the commissary was…directed to issue, until further orders, the following weekly ration; To each male four pounds of maize, three pounds of soujee, seven pounds of beef, or in lieu thereof four pounds of pork, three pints of peas or dhal and half a pound of rice. Two-thirds of the man's ration was directed to be issued to each woman, and to every child above 10 years of age, one half of the man's ration…

Thus happily was the colony once more put upon something like a full ration of provisions, a change in our situation that gave universal satisfaction, as at the hour of the arrival of the *Britannia* there were in the public store only 24 days' salt provisions for the settlement at the ration then issued. With this new ration all entertained new hopes and trusted that their future labours would be crowned with success.

AUGUST

Friday 17th

Collins reported that the unmerchantable articles which had arrived from Calcutta on 20 June in the *Atlantic*,

consisting of soujee, dhal and rice, were sold at public auction, and though wholly unfit for men to eat, yet being not too bad for stock, were quickly purchased and in general went off at a great price...This cargo might be termed an experiment, to which it was true we were driven by necessity, and it had become the universal and earnest wish that no cause might ever again induce us to try it.

Tuesday 28th

Atkins The Governor with his usual goodness has given me three and a half acres of ground fit for Indian corn for stock.

℞

Collins During the month the governor thought it necessary to issue some regulations to be observed by those convicts whose sentences of transportation had expired. The number of people of this description in the colony had been so much increased of late that it had become requisite to determine with precision the line in which they were to move...

They were, therefore, called upon to declare their intentions respecting their future mode of living. Those who wished to be allowed to provide for themselves were informed that, on application to the judge-advocate they would receive a certificate of their having served their several periods of transportation, which certificate they would deposit with the commissary as his voucher for striking them off the provision and clothing lists, and once a week they were to report in what manner and for whom they had been employed.

Such as should be desirous of returning to England were informed that no obstacle would be thrown in their way, they being at liberty to ship themselves on board of such vessels as would give them a passage; and those who preferred labouring for the public and receiving in return such ration as should be issued from the public stores, were to give in their names to the commissary, who would victual and clothe them as long as their services might be required.

Of those, here and at Parramatta, who had fulfilled the sentence of the law, by far the greater part signified their intention of returning to England by the first opportunity.

SEPTEMBER

Tuesday 11th

Atkins   Walked out to Toongabbie…All hands busily employed getting in the Indian corn and though the ration is tolerable good, yet, though the seed is steeped in urine, some of the convicts cannot refrain from stealing and eating it.

Friday 28th

Atkins   For these three weeks past there has been a great decrease of crimes, I should hope from a conviction that honesty is the best policy. Indeed I must say that, considering they are people that have most of them forfeited their lives to their country, they behave wonderfully well.

✍

Several convicts absconded from Parramatta, taking with them the provisions of their huts, intending, it was supposed, to get on board the *Britannia*.

Collins It had been found that the masters of ships would give passages to such people as could afford to pay them from £10 to £20 for the same, and the perpetrators of some of the thefts that were committed appeared to have had that circumstance in view, as one or two of the huts, whose proprietors were known to have amassed large sums of money for people in their situations, were broken into.

OCTOBER

Tuesday 2nd

Phillip wrote to Dundas Of the present state of this settlement, I have the satisfaction of assuring you that the soil and its produce more than answer the expectations which I have formerly given. Our last year's crop of maize, notwithstanding the long drought, was 4844 bushels, of which 2649 bushels have been issued as bread for the colony, 695 bushels reserved for seed and other purposes, and not less than 1500 bushels were stolen from the grounds, notwithstanding every possible precaution was taken to prevent it.

From the time the corn began to ripen to the time it was housed, the convicts were pressed by hunger and great quantities were stolen and concealed in the woods; several convicts died from feeding on it in its crude state when carrying the grain to the public granary. But in speaking of these people, it is but just to observe that I can recollect very few crimes during the last three years but what have been committed to procure the necessaries of life.

Wednesday 3rd

Collins The *Britannia*...returned to the cove on the 3rd of this month for the purpose of fitting for the Cape of Good Hope, the officers of the New South Wales Corps having engaged the master to proceed thither and return on their account with a freight of cattle and such articles as would tend to the comfort of themselves and the soldiers of the Corps, and which were not to be found in the public stores.

Mr Raven, the master, let his ship for the sum of £2,000, and eleven shares of £200 each were subscribed to purchase the stock and other articles. The ship was well calculated for bringing cattle, having a very good between-decks, and artificers from the corps were immediately employed to fit her with stalls proper for the reception and accommodation of cows, horses etc. A quantity of hay was put on board sufficient to lessen considerably the expense of that article at the Cape and she was ready for sea by the middle of the month.

Thursday 4th

Grose wrote to Phillip The situation of the soldiers under my command, who at this time have scarcely shoes to their feet, and who have no other comforts than the reduced and unwholesome rations served out from the stores, has induced me to assemble the captains of my corps for the purpose of consulting what could be done for their relief and accommodation.

Amongst us we have raised a sufficient sum to take up the *Britannia* and as all money matters are already settled with the master, who is also an owner, I have now to request you will interest yourself in our favour, that you will, by representing the necessities of my soldiers, protect this ship from interruption as much as you can, and that you will assist us to escape the miseries of that precarious existence we have hitherto been so constantly exposed to.

Phillip replied I think that there can be little doubt but that an ample supply of provisions from Europe will arrive before the *Britannia* can return to this port, and there is every reason to expect that a very few months will remove the inconvenience the colony labours under...I am sorry that I cannot, with propriety, take any official step in this business.

Phillip wrote to Dundas I have not received any instructions respecting the quantity of land which may be intended to be given to an officer on such officer's becoming a settler, nor under what circumstances an officer might be permitted to settle. This is mentioned as an ensign in the New South Wales Corps has been desirous of becoming a settler if he could have been permitted to retire on his half pay.

It is, sir, likewise necessary to observe that the officers in the New South Wales Corps have supposed, on coming to this country, that lands might be granted them, with indulgences similar to those which have been granted to settlers; and I am very far from wishing to throw the smallest obstacle in the way of officers obtaining grants of land, but in the present state of this colony the numbers employed on the public buildings in procuring the materials, and in other occupations equally necessary, does not leave more than 450 for agriculture, and from that number those convicts must be taken who are to be given to officers or settlers, which will increase the number of those who do not labour for the public and lessen those who are to furnish the colony with the necessaries of life.

At present 51 convicts are allowed to the major-commandant of the New South Wales Corps and those under his command in this place, and convicts in proportion are allowed those on duty at Norfolk Island.

The officers, civil and military, have land which they cultivate; but as the grounds which they have chosen are mostly within the limits of what is marked out for building on hereafter, or on the land which is to remain as common land for the township, no lease or grant has been given with such grounds, and the officers understand that they are to give them up when wanted for the public service.

Sunday 7th

Easty This day arrived the *Royal Admiral,* Indiaman, Captain Bond, laden with convicts, provisions and stores for the settlement; she had four months' passage from England and five weeks only from the Cape of Good Hope.

Collins On board of the *Royal Admiral* came stores and provisions for the colony; one sergeant, one corporal and 19 privates belonging to the New South Wales Corps; a person to be employed in the cultivation of the country, another as a master miller and a third as a master carpenter, together with 289 male and 47 female convicts...

Captain Bond brought on with him Thomas Watling, a male convict, who found means to get on shore from the *Pitt* when at that port [the Cape of Good Hope] in December last, and who had been confined by the Dutch at the Cape Town from her departure until this opportunity offered of sending him thither.

Thomas Watling, an artist and coach painter from Dumfries in southern Scotland, had been charged with forging notes of the Bank of Scotland and, facing a death sentence, had asked to be transported. In sentencing him, the Lord Advocate of Scotland said: 'He is a young man, unmarried, and an ingenious artist; he will be an acquisition to the new colony at Botany Bay.'

At Sydney Cove, Watling was assigned to Surgeon John White, who, after the success of his first book about the settlement was working on a second account. White employed him to provide illustrations for his book and when White did not need him he let him work for others who could use his talents. Watling apparently did not enjoy the arrangement, writing to an aunt that his drawings were 'such as may be expected from genius in bondage to a very mercenary, sordid person', and that he was 'lent about as an household utensil to his neighbours'.

The main collection of Thomas Watling's work is held in the Natural History Museum in London, part of the British Museum. In *Art of the First Fleet*, the art historian Bernard Smith wrote of it: 'The

Detail from Watling's undated North-west view, taken from the Rocks above Sydney, *showing Bennelong's hut, Pinchgut, and the flagstaff and lookout at South Head in the early 1790s. Dixson Gallieries, State Library of New South Wales.*

drawings of ethnographic and natural history interest form the largest and most detailed collection of the period.' There are 488 drawings in the collection, 123 of which are signed by Watling; many of the others are the work of at least one other artist. Bernard Smith wrote:

> The most prolific of all First Fleet draughtsmen has not yet been identified but has become known, for convenience, as the Port Jackson Painter, since most of the work that reveals the characteristic traits of his style is of plants, animals, native peoples and events that are associated with the Port Jackson neighbourhood. It should be stressed that the Port Jackson Painter should not be considered, until identified, as an individual artist, but as a cluster of stylistic traits. That cluster may embrace the work of more than one artist.

Some of the hundreds of drawings attributed to the Port Jackson Painter are probably the work of Thomas Watling. Others may be by John Hunter, who, as Surgeon White noted, had 'a pretty turn for drawing'; other candidates include Surgeon White himself and a convict named Francis Fowkes, who had been a midshipman in the navy and would have received training in draughtsmanship.

One of the main contributors to the collection was almost certainly Phillip's ageing protégé, the eccentric Henry Brewer. The British seaman Edward Spain, who had served with Phillip and Brewer, wrote that when they were in the East Indies in HMS *Europe* in 1783, Phillip had given Admiral Sir Edward Hughes 'some original drawings of places we had touched at on our passage out, drawn by Mr Henry Brewer, his clerk, who was well skilled in drawing, and he…always obliged him to draw two sets for this purpose. When we arrived at Madras, Captain Phillip showed one set to the commander in chief. If he seemed to praise them, he pressed him to accept of them thinking thereby to pave the way to any favour he might have occasion to ask.' When Phillip was appointed governor, Spain wrote: 'Mr Brewer was just such a man as the governor wanted. What excellent plans, drafts and views of places he could draw, which I can send home to my patrons.'

Brewer, of course, had other things to do; as provost-marshal he was responsible for seeing that the orders of the court were carried out, he directed the night-watch and he was involved in planning and supervising the colony's buildings. He was also known to drink heavily, but from the evidence available it seems very likely that many of the illustrations which have survived from the first few years of the settlement are the work of this unusual man.

Monday 8th

Phillip prepared a 'Return of settlers and persons to whom lands have been granted, at and near Parramatta:

Settler, late superintendent of convicts	1
Settlers, late of the marines	8
Settlers, seamen late of his Majesty's ship *Sirius*	2
Settlers, convicts whose sentence of transportation have expired	53
An assistant surgeon (Mr Thomas Arndell)	1
An emancipated convict, who acts as assistant surgeon	1

Thursday 11th

Phillip wrote to Dundas You are, sir, pleased to express your regret at my being obliged to return to England on account of my health... How far that part of your letter to which the above alludes may have been intended to convey to me his Majesty's permission to return, I am doubtful, and although I am inclined to think it has been written with that intention...still, sir, I fear there is a possibility of its being expected that I should remain until permission to quit the government is more fully and clearly expressed, and as there appears to be a wish that I should remain in this country some time longer, I shall wait the arrival of the next ships.

Monday 22nd

Grose wrote to the Under-Secretary for War, Matthew Lewis I think it requisite to request your interference in behalf of the officers and soldiers who are doing duty at this place. Unwilling as I always shall be to complain, I but with little reluctance set about the subject of this letter being confident that the Secretary of State will be better pleased to remove the grievance than to hear it has happened. I need not inform you that the necessaries of life are not often to be purchased and that the ration allowed by government is the soldiers' chief and almost only support.

Now whenever it happens that a short allowance is issued to the felons, the soldiers' ratio is also reduced and that without the smallest difference or distinction—the captain of a company and the convict transported for life divide in share and share alike whatever is served out...and what makes our situation the more unpleasant is that the governor does not feel himself authorised to indulge with grants such as would wish either for comfort or amusement to cultivate a small quantity of ground.

I have frequently applied to Governor Philip on this business, who in answer to my representations assures me he has more than once written to the Secretary of State, that unfortunately he has never received any reply whatever...

I rather hope the Governor has not forgotten by this packet to make some representations in our favour for I am convinced he both perceives and laments the difficulties that perplex the officers as much as I can, but for fear of accidents, I have ventured to solicit your protection.

Wednesday 24th

Easty This day sailed the *Britannia* from this place for Rio de Janeiro and the Cape of Good Hope to fetch a cargo of provisions and stock for the gentlemen and officers of the settlement, taken up at their own expense.

∽

A letter written by a convict, James Lacey, who had arrived in the *Royal Admiral* on 7 October, showed that some of the convicts were improving their conditions:

> Our situation here is much better than we was led to expect from the accounts we had received of the settlement. The convicts, those I mean who choose to apply themselves to industry, are much better off than the labouring people in England, few of them being without a garden, pigs, poultry etc etc, but then the slightest crime is punished in a very exemplary manner. A tradesman enjoys many advantages and as such I am fortunate in being employed at my business.

George Thompson, a seaman in the *Royal Admiral*, described in his journal the conditions in the colony. At Toongabbie, he wrote: Their hours of work are from five in the morning till eleven; they then leave off till two in the afternoon, and work from that time till sunset. They are allowed no breakfast hour because they have seldom anything to eat. Their labour is felling trees, digging up the stumps, rooting up the shrubs and grass, turning up the ground with spades or hoes and carrying the timber to convenient places. From the heat of the sun, the short allowance of provision and the ill-treatment they receive from a set of merciless wretches (most of them of their own description) who are their superintendents, their lives are rendered truly miserable.

At night they are placed in a hut, perhaps 14, 16 or 18 together (with one woman, whose duty is to keep it clean and provide victuals for the men while at work) without the comfort of either beds or blankets, unless they take them from the ship they come out in, or are rich enough to purchase them when they come on shore. They have neither bowl, plate, spoon or knife but what they make of the green wood of this country, only one small iron pot being allowed to dress their poor allowance of meat, rice etc; in short, all the necessary conveniences of life they are strangers to and suffer everything they could dread in their sentence of transportation...

The women have a more comfortable life than the men. Those who are not fortunate enough to be selected for wives (which every officer, settler, and soldier is entitled to, and few are without) are made hut-keepers; those who are not dignified with this office are set to make shirts, frocks, trousers, etc for the men, at a certain number per day, occasionally to pick grass in the fields, and for a very slight offence are kept constantly at work the same as the men.

Thompson also observed that 'the natives...are very quick in learning to speak English and will repeat any sentence after you immediately, particularly any tune. When in their canoes they keep constantly singing while they paddle along. They have the French tune of "Malbrook" very perfect; I have heard a dozen or twenty singing it together.' The song was probably 'Malbrouck', a burlesque song originating in Normandy about John Churchill, the first Duke of Marlborough, sung to the tune of 'For He's a Jolly Good Fellow'.

Collins The month closed with a circumstance that excited no small degree of concern in the settlement; Governor Phillip signified a determination of quitting his government and returning to England in the *Atlantic*. To this he was induced by perceiving that his health hourly grew worse, and hoping that a change of air might contribute to his recovery. His Excellency had the satisfaction, at the moment that he came to this resolution, of seeing the public grounds wear every appearance of a productive harvest.

On 11 October, Phillip had written to Dundas, seeking confirmation of permission to leave. It had not arrived, but apparently he could wait no longer.

NOVEMBER

Thursday 1st

Collins   The *Philadelphia* brigantine, Mr Thomas Patrickson master, anchored in the cove…Lieutenant-Governor King, on his passage to this country in the *Gorgon* in the month of July 1791 had seen Mr Patrickson at the Cape of Good Hope, and learning at that time from the *Lady Juliana* and *Neptune* transports, which had just arrived there from China, that the colony was in great distress for provisions, suggested to him the advantage that might attend his bringing a cargo to this country on speculation. On this hint Captain Patrickson went to England, and thence to Philadelphia, from which place he sailed the beginning of last April with a cargo consisting chiefly of American beef, wine, rum, gin, some tobacco, pitch and tar…

The governor directed the commissary to purchase such part of the *Philadelphia's* cargo as he though was immediately wanting in the colony, and 569 barrels of American cured beef, each barrel containing 193 pounds, and 27 barrels of pitch and tar were taken into store, the expense of which amounted to £2,829 11s…a great part of his cargo that was not taken by the government was disposed of among the officers and others of the settlement, and the governor hired his vessel to take provisions to Norfolk Island, giving him £150 for the run.

The *Philadelphia* was the first American ship to arrive in the colony.

Friday 2nd

Surgeon-General White wrote to Phillip   The peculiarly unfortunate and deranged state of my affairs, in consequence of the failure of my agent…prompts me to trouble your Excellency on the present occasion to entreat leave of absence for a short time to return to England in order to place the wreck of my little fortune in more security than it now is, and which is morally impossible for me to do without being present.

The detachment of marines that accompanies you to Europe and your own poor state of health, which I am truly sorry makes your departure from hence for the re-establishment of it so absolutely necessary, induces me the more readily to entreat your Excellency's permission to return in the *Atlantic*, from a wish to offer you my services and aid on the passage as well as them, who no doubt in so long a voyage will require some medical assistance.

Three convicts were emancipated, including George Barrington, of whom Collins wrote:

> On his arrival the governor employed him at Toongabbie, and in a situation which was likely to attract the envy and hatred of the convicts, in proportion as he might be vigilant and inflexible. He was first placed as a subordinate and shortly after as a principal watchman, in which situation he was diligent, sober and impartial and had rendered himself so eminently serviceable that the governor resolved to draw him from the line of convicts, and, with the instrument of his emancipation, he received a grant of 30 acres of land in an eligible situation near Parramatta.

Monday 5th

White wrote again to Phillip   As your Excellency does not feel yourself at liberty to grant the request made in my letter of the 2nd instant, wherein I fully stated my reasons for such a procedure, I have therefore to entreat your Excellency will on your arrival be pleased to move his Majesty's principal Secretary of State to grant me leave of absence, in order to adjust the deranged state of my affairs... Should my prayers, strengthened by your intercession in my behalf not succeed, I hope my entreating permission to retire on my half pay will not by your Excellency or any other servant of the Crown be considered an unreasonable request.

Tuesday 13th

Collins   The *Royal Admiral* sailed for Canton. Of the private speculation brought out in this ship, they sold at this place and at Parramatta to the amount of £3,600 and left articles to be sold on commission to the amount of £750 more.

Sunday 18th

Ann Inett, who had had two children with Philip Gidley King during their time at Norfolk Island, was married to the Second Fleet convict Richard John Robinson, by the Reverend Richard Johnson, at

Parramatta. (In England in 1789, Robinson had been among more than 100 convicts under a sentence of death who were offered a pardon on condition of transportation for life. Such was the reputation of the colony that eight of them at first refused the offer, saying they would prefer death to transportation to New South Wales.)

Collins The *Kitty* transport anchored in the cove from England... There arrived in this ship two chests containing 3,870 ounces of silver, in dollars, amounting to £1,001. This remittance was sent out for the purpose of paying such sums as were due to the different artificers who had been employed in this country. It was also applied to the payment of the wages due to the superintendents, who had experienced much inconvenience from not receiving their salaries here, and indeed the want of public money had been very much felt by every one in the colony.

There were also 27 male convicts on board the *Kitty*, described by Dundas as 'artificers and handy-craftsmen', sent in reply to Phillip's requests.

Saturday 24th

Atkins From this day to the 28th was employed with the governor in getting his insects etc ready. We shall all feel a great loss, except one description of people, in his going away. I am in hopes that everything will go well. For myself, I have lost a good friend in the governor.

Friday 30th

John Brown, Simon Burn, Mary McDonald, Joseph Morley and Thomas Tynan, all Roman Catholics and recent settlers, wrote to the governor:

> We, the undernamed, with the most humble respect, take the liberty of representing to your Excellency the inconvenience we find in not being indulged heretofore with a pastor of our religion...
> We therefore humbly implore your Excellency's assistance, on your return to England, to represent it to his Majesty's ministry that it may be taken into consideration, as our present opinion

is that nothing else could induce us ever to depart from his Majesty's colony here unless the idea of going into eternity without the assistance of a Catholic priest.

⁒

Collins At Parramatta a brick hospital consisting of two wards was finished this month and the sick were immediately removed into it. The spot chosen for this building was at some distance from the principal street of the town and convenient to the water and, to prevent any improper communication with the other convicts, a space was to be enclosed and paled in round the hospital, in which the sick would have every necessary benefit from air and exercise.

At the other settlement [Toongabbie] they had begun to reap the wheat which was sown in April last and for want of a granary at that place it was put into stacks. From not being immediately thrashed out, there was no knowing with certainty what the produce of it was; but it had every appearance of turning out well. The ear was long and full and the straw remarkably good.

DECEMBER

Monday 3rd

Collins The governor, as one of his last acts in the settlement, ordered one pound of flour to be added to the weekly ration, which by means of this addition stood on his departure at three pounds of flour, five pounds of rice, four pounds of pork or seven pounds of beef, three pounds of dhal and six ounces of oil.

Wednesday 5th

Collins The wind blew strong from the northward of west; the country, to add to the intense heat of the atmosphere, was everywhere on fire. At Sydney, the grass at the back of the hill on the west side of the cove, having either caught or been set on fire by the natives, the flames aided by the wind which at that time blew violently spread and raged with incredible fury. One house was burnt down, several gardens with their fences were destroyed and the whole face of the hill was on fire, threatening every thatched hut with destruction.

Easty   This day the remainder part of the detachment of marines under the Command of Lieutenant John Poulden embarked on board the *Atlantic* transport for England, amidst all the acclamations of a large concourse of people, when every mark of joy and respect [was] shown by the New South Wales Corps. After being four years and 10 months and eight days on shore in the country when we have been three parts of our time on short allowance and hardships, very much has been undergone, as must be expected by settling a new colony.

Forty-seven of the Marine Corps remained as settlers, either in New South Wales or at Norfolk Island, and 57 had joined the New South Wales Corps.

Collins wrote to Dundas   Some very urgent private and family affairs requiring my presence in England, I have to request you will be pleased to grant me permission to return from this country for the purpose of attending to them. I have the honour of assuring you, Sir, that this application entirely meets the concurrence of Governor Phillip, and that nothing but the most pressing motives would induce me to relinquish my further services in this country, in which I have now resided within a few weeks of five years, during which time I have been in the constant execution of my duty—a circumstance that will of itself, I hope, be allowed to operate in favour of my present application.

Monday 10th

Easty   This day Arthur Phillip, governor and commander in chief and captain-general in and over his Majesty's territories in New South Wales embarked on board the *Atlantic* for England, when the New South Wales Corps was under arms and paid him all the marks of honour.

Collins   With the governor there embarked, voluntarily and cheerfully, two natives of this country, Bennelong and Yemmerrawannie, two men who were much attached to his person and who withstood at the moment of their departure the united distress of their wives and the dismal lamentations of their friends, to accompany him to

England, a place that they well knew was at a great distance from them. One or two convicts also who had conducted themselves to his satisfaction, and whose periods of transportation were expired, were permitted by the governor to return to England in the same ship with himself.

The *Atlantic* had likewise on board various specimens of the natural productions of the country; timber, plants, animals, and birds. Among the animals were four fine kangaroos and several native dogs.

Tuesday 11th

Easty, who returned to England with Phillip in the *Atlantic*, wrote:

> This morning at three o'clock began to weigh anchor and at seven under way; sailed out of the cove accompanied by all the principal officers of settlement, the wind at south-west, a light breeze. At nine o'clock between the heads, officers parted from us and gave three cheers and returned the same...
>
> As to the state of the colony at this present time, seems far better than at any time since the settlement was made, as several ships have lately arrived from Europe. And likewise having had a good season, very good crops of corn are expected, the wheat was fit for cutting and the Indian corn looked very promising.
>
> The country is everywhere covered with wood where fit for cultivation, and by a great deal of trouble and fatigue that it's cleared, as everything must be done by men as there is no cattle in the country. Fine clay for bricks so that buildings are carried on here fast. All the convicts are in bricked huts, but not a place dedicated to divine worship amidst all the work, a thing to be lamented by a serious mind.

✎

At the time Phillip left there were 3101 new settlers in the colony, 1256 at Sydney Cove and 1845 at Parramatta. There were 1703 acres under crops or cleared ready for planting. The population of Norfolk Island at this time was 1121.

Vista de la Colonia de Paramata, a view of Parramatta by Fernando Brambila, described by Collins as a 'landscape painter on board the Atravida'; one of the two Spanish ships which visited the colony in March and April 1793. The 'great road from near the governor's house to the landing place' can be seen. The governor's house is partly hidden on the left. Naval Museum, Madrid.

So Arthur Phillip sailed out through the Heads for the last time, accompanied by Bennelong and Yemmerrawannie. It was hot, and Easty tells us there was a light breeze from the south-west, which would have made for good sailing.

If Phillip was still keeping a journal, what would he have written? From what we know of him, probably not a great deal. 'Attended by Major Grose at the head of the New South Wales Corps, embarked on the 10th. Under way at daylight on the 11th', followed perhaps by a discourse on the need for more free settlers, or a hymn of praise for the behaviour of the convicts.

But what did he think? What did he feel?

No doubt he was ill, but the frequent references to his need to return to England give the impression that he was worn down mentally, too. What he felt most was probably relief, and gratitude at the prospect of a six-month sea voyage without day to day responsibility for everything that went wrong in a very imperfect world.

Phillips's most important tasks were to reconcile the settlers to the new land and to reconcile the Aboriginal people to the settlers.

Grose, expecting a rock, had found 'gardens that flourish' and 'as good a house as I wish for'. True, he objected to the fact that 'the captain of a company and the convict transported for life divide in share and share alike whatever is served out'. That was an aspect of colonial life that was soon to change, to the benefit of the soldiers.

But there was a realisation that at least some of those who had been transported were relatively well off. A letter written by a convict, James Lacey, in October, observed: 'The convicts, those I mean who choose to apply themselves to industry, are much better off than the labouring people in England, few of them being without a garden, pigs, poultry etc etc.' The settlement by this time was secure.

Reconciliation with the Aboriginal people has been talked about since 1788. In July that year Phillip wrote to Lord Sydney: 'When I have time to mix more with them every means shall be used to reconcile them to live amongst us.' In September he said: 'I am sorry to have been so long without knowing more of these people', and he observed that 'they certainly are not pleased with our remaining amongst them'. Collins wrote in 1791: 'While they entertained the idea of our having dispossessed them of their residences, they must always consider us as enemies.'

In 1792 Collins wrote: 'Several of their young people continued to reside among us and the different houses in the town were frequently visited by their relations. Very little information that could be depended upon respecting their manners and customs was obtained through this intercourse and it was observed that they conversed with us in a mutilated and incorrect language formed entirely on our imperfect knowledge and improper application of their words.'

What Collins said about dispossession is indisputable. Nevertheless, the British probably did have something to offer the Aboriginal people. The inability to make them see this, arising from the failure to communicate, is the main failure of Phillip's administration.

Not that it was Phillip's fault; if the British government had paid more than lip service to reconciliation, if they had sent people to make sure it happened, rather than beads and mirrors and instructions to people who already had too much to do, then perhaps we would not still be talking about reconciliation today. And perhaps the fault was not all on one side; it would have helped if the Aboriginal people had been as willing to communicate as the British and if they had been able to accept that the British might have had something to offer them.

It's easy to say now what should have been done 200 years ago. It may not have been possible—eventually the whole continent was at stake, not just the Sydney region, and the differences between the cultures and what they wanted from the continent were vast—but if it was to happen, the process had to start during the first few years of the settlement; the sad truth is that by the time Phillip left the settlement the opportunity had gone.

Aftermath

The colony's first weddings were celebrated on Sunday, 10 February 1788, two weeks after the fleet arrived in Sydney Cove. William Parr was married to Mary McCormack, Simon Burn to Frances Anderson, William Bryant to Mary Braund, William Haynes to Hannah Green and Henry Kable to Susannah Holmes. All five couples were convicts and only three of the 10 people could write their names in the register, the others signing with a cross.

Referred to as 'the noted swindler', William Parr, from Liverpool, was transported for seven years and arrived in the colony aged about 23. Mary McCormack, also from Liverpool, was convicted of receiving stolen goods in 1786, her age given as 32. Parr was sentenced to 200 lashes in 1788 for 'attempting to sow discontent' and again in 1790 for theft, but by 1791 the Parrs were settled on 50 acres near Parramatta. Watkin Tench visited them (and Simon Burn and Frances Anderson, who had been married at the same time) in December 1791 and wrote: 'Parr and Burn are men of great industry. They both have good houses which they hired people to build for them. Parr told me that he has expended 13 guineas on his land, which nevertheless he does not seem pleased with.' There is no further record of the Parrs and it is likely that they went back to England.

Simon Burn and Frances (also known as Fanny) Anderson were aged about 34 and 30 respectively when they arrived in New South Wales in 1788. They had no children. Burn worked as a timber-getter, lost an eye splitting timber, and in April 1790 was boss of a group of labourers. He was involved in a brawl and put in chains early in 1791, but in August that year he was settled on 50 acres near Parramatta and, with William Parr, was mentioned favourably by Watkin Tench in December 1791, although Tench's view was contradicted by Collins, who wrote that Burn 'and his wife were too fond of spirituous liquors to be very industrious'. In November 1792, Burn was one of a group of settlers who wrote to the governor asking for his assistance in having a

Catholic priest appointed to the colony. Two years later, on 5 December 1794, Collins wrote that 'Simon Burn, a settler, had been stabbed to the heart about eight o'clock in the evening...of which wound he died in an hour. The man who perpetrated this atrocious act was a convict named Hill, a butcher by trade.' It emerged at the trial that Hill and Burn had been drinking together all day and Burn was stabbed when he tried to prevent Hill from beating the woman who was living with him. Fanny was Irish; she buried her husband 'in a corner of his own farm, attended by several settlers of that and the neighbouring districts, who celebrated the funeral rites in a manner and with orgies suitable to the disposition and habits of the deceased'. Fanny married again in January 1795.

William and Mary Bryant had a daughter, Charlotte, born on the voyage out from England, and a son, Emanuel, born in April 1790. Bryant, a Cornishman and a fisherman by trade, was put in charge of the fishing operations at Sydney Cove, but in February 1789 he was convicted of selling fish on his own account, sentenced to 100 lashes and 'deprived of the direction of the fish and the boat, to continue in the boat and to be turned out of the hut he is now in'. In March 1791 the Bryants, with their children and seven other convicts, stole a six-oared boat, provisions and equipment and rowed out of Sydney Harbour, bound for Batavia.

When the *Gorgon* arrived in Cape Town in March 1792 on the way home to England, they found Mary and Charlotte Bryant and four of the other convicts who had escaped. William and Emanuel had died in Batavia.

Tench Six of these people, including the woman and one child, were put on board of us to be carried to England; four had died and one had jumped overboard at Batavia. The particulars of their voyage were briefly as follows. They coasted the shore of New Holland...until they reached the Gulf of Carpentaria, they saw no natives or canoes differing from those about Port Jackson. But now they were chased by large canoes fitted with sails and fighting stages, and capable of holding 30 men each. They escaped by dint of rowing to windward. On the 5th of June 1791 they reached Timor and pretended that they had belonged to a ship, which, on her passage from Port Jackson to India, had foundered and that they only had escaped. The Dutch received them with kindness and treated them with hospitality, but their behaviour giving rise to suspicion, they were watched, and one of them at last, in a moment of intoxication,

betrayed the secret. They were immediately secured and committed
to prison...I confess that I never looked at these people without
pity and astonishment...and I could not but reflect with admiration
at the strange combination of circumstances which had again
brought us together, to baffle human foresight and confound human
speculation.

Charlotte Bryant died at sea on the way to England. Mary Bryant,
James Martin, John Butcher (also known as Samuel Broom), William
Allen and Nathaniel Lilley reached England by the *Gorgon* in July 1792,
where they were placed in custody. Their case was taken up by the
author James Boswell and they were pardoned and released in 1793.

William Haynes had been sentenced to death at the Old Bailey for the
theft of one shilling and ninepence, commuted to transportation for
seven years. Hannah Green had been sentenced to transportation for
seven years for stealing hats. The records show that Haynes, sometimes
spelled Haines, an artificer (probably a carpenter or perhaps what is
now called a handyman) was in possession of a 25-acre grant at Concord in 1795, was found not guilty of assault in 1796 and was buried
on 9 July 1801. In the same year Hannah, her term expired, is recorded
as having returned to England.

Susannah Holmes and Henry Kable had a child, born in Norwich
prison, when they arrived with the First Fleet in 1788. At their marriage in February 1788, both signed with a cross. Kable became involved
in the night-watch in 1791, and in 1794 he was granted 30 acres at
Petersham and began a career of successful but often unscrupulous dealing. In 1799 he was appointed chief constable of the colony and,
although he was demoted for illegally importing pigs in 1802, his
empire flourished, probably because of his involvement in the rum
trade. In 1803 he was running the first coach service from Sydney to
Parramatta. In 1806 he employed five convicts and was reported to
hold 215 acres and to own 10 horses, 17 cattle, four oxen, 260 sheep
and 20 hogs. He and Susannah had 11 children, four of whom died
in infancy. In July 1788, Kable had won damages of £15 in the civil
court from the master of the *Alexander*, Duncan Sinclair, over the loss
of a parcel during the voyage to Botany Bay. Later, he used the courts
ruthlessly; Hunter wrote that 'several masters of ships have been
ruined...with constant litigation and infamous prosecutions in the
courts'. Susannah died in 1825. Henry lived until 1846, by which time
the family was also involved in shipping, hotels and the seal trade.

Private John Easty's journal for May 1793 reads: 'Came to anchor at Spithead after an absence of six years and 10 days and on the 24th landed to our unspeakable joy in old England.' His published journal includes a petition to Lord Spencer (First Lord of the Admiralty) written in November 1796, asking for compensation for short rations received while serving in New South Wales, which had been promised 'on our return to England to be paid or settled for, according to the rules of his Majesty's service'. By then he had left the marines and was working for a firm of grocers in London. Apparently he did not get any satisfaction, because he wrote a similar letter to the colonial secretary, Lord Hobart, in 1801. Nothing more is known about John Easty's life.

Of the 1373 people identified as having arrived with the First Fleet, 754 were convicts or their children, and virtually all the remaining 619 were ships' crew, marines or their families, or officials.

Analysis of the records in Mollie Gillen's *The Founders of Australia* shows that 572 of those people were documented as having left the colony, about 100 of whom were convicts. A further 533 were documented as having died in New South Wales, Tasmania or Norfolk Island. There was no record of death or departure for the remaining 268 people, most of whom would have been convicts and would have died in New South Wales.

Overall, of the 619 ships' crew and marines, probably about 100 stayed in Australia, including the 70 marines who eventually joined the New South Wales Corps. Of the 754 convicts, more than 600 would have lived their lives out in Australia.

Despite his earlier requests to return to England to 'adjust the deranged state of my affairs', John White, surgeon-general to the settlement, was one of the last of the First Fleet officers to leave the colony. He stayed until December 1794, sailing home in the storeship *Daedalus*, leaving a son in the colony named Andrew Douglas White, born in September 1793. The child's mother was Rachel Turner, transported in the Second Fleet for stealing clothes and material from her mistress, Rebecca Comber, in 1787. (At Turner's trial it was inferred that she had been framed by Mrs Comber because of the attention paid to her by Mr Comber; this brought her a reprimand from the bench for attempting to 'destroy the domestic peace of your master and mistress'.)

Rachel Turner later married a boat-builder, Thomas Moore, and by the time she died in 1838 they were among the colony's biggest land-holders. Her son with Surgeon White went to England to join his father in 1800, was educated there and joined the Royal Engineers, fought at the Battle of Waterloo and returned to Australia in 1823.

White continued in the service in England until 1820, when he was superannuated on half pay. He was married twice and died in 1832, leaving an estate of £12,000.

White was replaced as principal surgeon by William Balmain, with whom he had fought a duel in June 1788. Balmain lived with Margaret Dawson, who had been sentenced to death in 1786, at the age of 15, for stealing clothes, jewellery and money from her master and mistress. Her master appealed for clemency and her sentence was reduced to transportation. She and Balmain had a daughter born in 1797 and a son born in 1800. They went back to England in 1801 and although they did not marry, they continued to live together. Balmain died in London in November 1803, aged 41, a few days before Margaret Dawson gave birth to their second son.

Before they left New South Wales, Balmain had received several grants of land, including 550 acres at what was then known as 'the Petersham district', part of which is now the suburb which bears his name.

David Collins had asked for permission to return to England in December 1792, to attend to 'urgent private and family affairs', but with his knowledge of the courts and the workings of the colony he would have been very hard to replace and Grose, who disliked writing letters, was very dependent on him. His second child with the convict Nancy Yeats, named George Reynolds Collins, was born in June 1793 and Collins stayed in the colony until September 1796, by which time Hunter was settled in as governor.

Collins arrived back in England nine months later to find his wife Maria 'ill and weakened beyond anything I could have imagined'. He wrote to his mother: 'I trust in God she will soon be restored to her former health, which I fear my absence robbed her of. All that I can possibly do shall be done to make her forget that I was absent.'

Collins seems to have been badly treated by the Admiralty. Because he accepted the civil appointment as judge-advocate he missed out on promotion in the Marine Corps; when his term as judge-advocate ended and he went back to England in 1796 he sought reinstatement on full pay, but was refused on the grounds that he had accepted a civil appointment and was left on half pay. Rather than accept a lower rank, he remained on half pay while pleading his case with naval and colonial officials, including Lord Sydney.

However, his situation would have been improved by the publication in 1898 of his book, *An Account of the English Colony in New South Wales*. Collins's book was full of detailed information and provided a comprehensive overview of the colony's first eight years. It was particularly informative about the Aboriginal people and their customs and relations with the white settlers, a subject of great fascination in Europe.

Collins's *Account* was based on a journal which he kept to relieve 'the tedium of many a heavy hour', and included some information supplied by King and Hunter. The text was supplemented by more than 20 illustrations showing views in the colony and Aboriginal ceremonies, probably copied in England from sketches and drawings by Thomas Watling, who is thought to have worked for Collins after White left the colony in 1794.

The book was well reviewed and sold well. As a result, Collins produced a second volume in 1802, mainly from information supplied by his friend John Hunter, governor of the colony from 1795 to 1800.

Collins returned in 1803 as lieutenant-governor of the proposed new settlement at Port Phillip, the present site of Melbourne, but within a month had decided that it was not a suitable site for a settlement and, with Governor King's approval, moved to Tasmania, where he established the settlement at Hobart in 1804.

He had two more children there with Margaret Eddington, the wife of a convict named Powers and daughter of the First Fleet convict Thomas Headington. Collins died in Hobart in 1810. The bill for his funeral was £507 8s 3d and his widow, Maria, who never came to Australia, was left with a captain's pension of £36 per year, increased to £126 in 1815.

Maria herself had produced, in 1804, a shortened version of Collins's *Account*, edited for 'the general class of readers'. It was highly praised; she also wrote several novels under a pseudonym.

The Reverend Richard Johnson was not the happiest of souls when Phillip was governor, and his outlook did not improve while Francis Grose was in authority. Phillip seemed to care little for religion but did not discourage it; Grose disliked 'the evangelicals' and deliberately undermined the clergyman, reducing the number of servants he was allowed and limiting the number of services he could hold.

Johnson and his wife Mary had lost a child in 1788, but they had a daughter, named Milbah Maria, in March 1790 and a son, Henry

Martin, in July 1792. Johnson did not suffer hardship gladly, but with a lot of help from Mary he continued to do the best he could with the limited resources he had, raising cattle, growing crops and establishing a large garden, starting schools in Sydney and Parramatta and looking after the sick, in addition to his work for the church—they must have been a very capable couple. By 1799 they had an estate of about 350 acres in the Petersham area, most of it providing produce for the colony.

By 1800 his health had started to suffer and Johnson took leave in London. At first, he may have intended to return to New South Wales, but he resigned as chaplain of the colony in 1802. The following year, the Johnsons' daughter, Milbah Maria, died. Johnson continued to work for the church in London for many years. He died in 1827, survived by his wife and son.

On 22 October 1792, Grose had written to the Under-Secretary for War, Matthew Lewis, complaining that Phillip 'does not feel himself authorised to indulge with grants, such as would wish either for comfort or amusement to cultivate a small quantity of ground'. This was in effect a request for permission to make grants of land to the officers of the New South Wales Corps, and Grose implied that Phillip may have neglected to take the matter up with colonial officials. But Phillip had not forgotten; permission to grant land to the officers arrived by the *Bellona* in January 1793. By that time, as George Mackaness wrote in *Admiral Arthur Phillip*, 'Grose had succeeded temporarily to the command and within a few months had parcelled out to most of the officers substantial areas, including much of the land around Sydney and Parramatta'.

John Macarthur received a grant of 100 acres at Parramatta in February 1793 and named it Elizabeth Farm in honour of his wife. A visionary, ambitious and volatile character, Macarthur spent 12 years in England on various business and legal matters between 1790 and 1817. During this time Elizabeth had seven more children and was often left to manage the family's growing farming and trading ventures, which she did with considerable success. John Macarthur died in 1832 after a period of mental illness and Elizabeth continued to live at Elizabeth Farm and develop the merino sheep which her husband had introduced. She died in 1853 at the age of 83.

George Barrington was granted a conditional pardon in November 1793 and in 1796 Hunter, in recognition of his good behaviour, gave him a full pardon and appointed him chief constable at Parramatta. He received several grants of land and after his retirement acquired a 90-acre farm on the Hawkesbury. He died in December 1804. Like many others of the time, he is said to have been insane towards the end of his life—his condition may have been what is today known as Alzheimer's disease.

Richard Atkins, despite bouts of heavy drinking which are frankly described in his diary, served in various responsible positions, taking over from John Macarthur as inspector of public works in 1796, becoming deputy judge-advocate in 1800 and being appointed judge-advocate in 1802. Atkins later had a blazing row with Macarthur, telling him in a letter that his behaviour was 'only worthy of a dastardly coward'. He was called back to England in 1811 as a witness for Bligh in the trial of George Johnston but he returned to Australia and died in obscurity in 1820.

When White left New South Wales in 1794, the artist Thomas Watling apparently went to work for David Collins; the views in Collins's *Account* are thought to be based on drawings by Watling. He had hopes, which he did not realise, of publishing an illustrated account of the colony in his own right. Watling was pardoned by Hunter in 1797 and returned to Scotland, but in 1806 he was again tried for forgery. He was discharged and later moved to London. The date of his death is not known.

The eccentric Henry Brewer was probably one of the first settlers to find that he preferred things the way they were in Australia, with its lack of formality and hierarchy, and that he did not want to go back to England. He owed his appointment as provost-marshal, a position of some status, to Phillip, and he had been on Phillip's staff for five years, doing whatever needed to be done; apart from his duties as provost-marshal, which involved making sure that the judgments of the court were carried out, Brewer directed the night-watch and planned and supervised the construction of some of the colony's early buildings, including the first Government House. He was probably also Phillip's artist-in-residence, copying charts and providing sketches and paintings of plants, animals, views and events for Phillip to send home to officials and acquaintances.

But when Phillip went back to England, Brewer stayed; he was a man of some consequence in New South Wales, but he would not have found a similar role in England, where his eccentricities might not have been so readily accepted by those in authority. In December 1793 he was given a grant of 50 acres at Concord (where there is still a Brewer Street); however, by this time the years of heavy drinking had made their mark and his health was failing. He died in July 1796, probably aged in his mid-50s.

The British seaman Edward Spain wrote of Brewer that he 'sailed with his old captain to New South Wales, where he was appointed provost-marshal, and there he died. Peace to his shade. If honesty merits heaven, Harry is there'.

The cattle that disappeared from Sydney Cove in 1792 were found at Cowpastures (near Camden) in November 1795, their numbers having increased to more than 60 head. When this came to Phillip's notice in England, the former governor wrote to King, who was also in England, on sick leave, telling him that, as two of the five cows originally lost were his (Phillip's) property, he therefore 'had an undoubted claim to a share in the cattle found to have increased in so extraordinary a manner'. Phillip gave his interest in the cattle to King 'to dispose of as you may judge proper'. In March 1798 Collins reported that 170 head had been seen in the area, and in 1804 a party sent to the area by Governor King counted more than 800 wild cattle.

John Hunter left the colony in the *Waaksamheyd* in March 1791 and spent much of the time on the long voyage working on his book. They arrived in April 1792 and *An Historical Journal, 1787–1792* was published the following year. When Hunter heard that Phillip had resigned, he immediately applied for the post of governor, and in September 1795 he arrived back in the colony. Hunter tried to continue the cautious, rational and fair policies of Phillip, but administration and politics were not his strengths and he was opposed and undermined by the military, many of whom regarded their service as a way of increasing their own wealth and influence.

He was recalled in 1800, replaced by King, and continued his service in the navy. He was promoted to rear-admiral in 1807 and vice-admiral in 1810, and was superannuated soon after. Hunter died in 1821 at the age of 83. Although he had no family, he kept in close contact with relations in England. Under his will his estate was divided among his nieces and nephews, with small sums to his male relatives and larger amounts to 'the great number of female relations which my brothers and sisters have left wholly unprovided for'.

Philip Gidley King and his wife Anna left Norfolk Island and went back to England in the *Britannia* in 1796, but they were back in the colony four years later, when King replaced John Hunter as governor of New South Wales in September 1800.

Despite his conscientious efforts to keep order and develop the colony, King's term as governor was difficult. The New South Wales Corps constantly undermined his authority and although he avoided the open rebellion faced by William Bligh, who followed him in

Bennelong in European dress, *from Collins's* Account of the English Colony in New South Wales. *Probably engraved in England from a drawing by Thomas Watling.*

1807, he left the colony in poor health and died in England in 1808, aged 50.

The Kings had a son, born on Norfolk Island in 1791, and four daughters over the next six years. In 1832, 25 years after she had left the colony with her husband, Anna King returned to New South Wales and lived with her eldest daughter Anna Maria at 'The Vineyard', looking onto the river three miles from Parramatta. She died in 1844, leaving 26 grandchildren in the the colony.

King's two sons with Ann Inett, fathered during his first term on Norfolk Island (from 1788 to 1790) both went to school in England and, like his son with Anna Coombe, they became officers in the navy.

Ann Inett and the Second Fleet convict Richard John Robinson, who were married in November 1792, had no children, but they were apparently successful in the colony: they received several grants of land, were listed in 1800 as owning 25 pigs, and opened an 'eating house', the Yorkshire Grey, in Pitt's Row (later Pitt Street) near the corner of Hunter Street, in 1804. In 1806 Robinson was employed as overseer of mills, and in 1809 Ann held a wine and spirit licence. He returned to England in 1819 and she followed him a year later. Whether they were still together then is not known.

When they sailed to England with Phillip in December 1792, Bennelong was probably about 28 years old and Yemmerrawannie was about 10 years younger. During the voyage, according to an account published in 1803, given by an Ensign G. Bond of the New South Wales Corps, Bennelong was 'treated with the greatest attention, made a companion of the captain and officers and was amassed with everything which they could afford to render his time agreeable and pleasant. When he arrived in England he was humanely introduced to the King at St. James's'.

In March 1794, when the storeship *William* arrived at Sydney Cove with supplies and equipment for the colony, Collins wrote: 'We learned that...the natives Bennelong and Yemmerrawannie were well, but not sufficiently divested of the genuine, natural love for liberty and their native country to prefer London with its pleasures and its abundance to the woods of New South Wales. They requested that their wives might be taught to expect their return in the course of this year.' By the *Surprize* in October 1794 they were told that the 'two natives in England were said to be in health and anxious for the governor's departure, as they were to accompany him [Hunter]. They had made but little improvement in our language'.

There is little record of their activities in England. They apparently lived 'in the European manner' but were badly affected by the cold. One of the few references is in a letter dated 5 August 1794, to the Home Office from Hunter, who at that time was living in London but was still active on behalf of the colony. It referred to bills which had been sent to Hunter for Bennelong's and Yemmerrawannie's expenses in England, for £63 'at Eltham' in Kent and £96 'in town', presumably London.

'The bills', Hunter wrote, 'are made out in my name as if payable by me, a circumstance which I by no means approve...The order given to supply them with what was necessary whilst in England...did not originate with me; that business began with Governor Phillip and should, in my opinion, have continued with him until finally settled.' In a second letter, written a few days later, Hunter wrote that Bennelong's disappointment at delays in returning to his home 'has much broken his spirit and the coldness of the weather here has so frequently laid him up that I am apprehensive his lungs are affected'. Yemmerrawannie died in England of a chest complaint and was buried in Eltham. Bennelong returned with Hunter in HMS *Reliance* in November 1795.

Collins   On his first appearance, he conducted himself with a polished familiarity toward his sisters and other relations, but to his acquaintances he was distant and quite the man of consequence. He declared, in a tone and with an air that seemed to expect compliance, that he should no longer suffer them to fight and cut each other's throats, as they had done, that he should introduce peace among them and make them love each other. He expressed his wish that when they visited him at Government House they would contrive to be somewhat more cleanly in their persons and less coarse in their manners, and he seemed absolutely offended at some little indelicacies which he observed in his sister Carrangarang, who came in such haste from Botany Bay with a little nephew on her back to visit him, that she left all her habiliments behind her.

Bennelong had certainly not been an inattentive observer of the manners of the people among whom he had lived; he conducted himself with the greatest propriety at table, particularly in the observance of those attentions which are chiefly requisite in the presence of women. His dress appeared to be an object of no small concern with him and everyone who knew him before he left the country, and who saw him now, pronounced without hesitation that Bennelong had not any desire to renounce the habits and comforts of the civilised life which he appeared so readily and so successfully to adopt...

His inquiries were directed immediately on his arrival after his wife Goroobarrooboollo, and her he found with Caruey. On producing a very fashionable rose-coloured petticoat and jacket made of a coarse stuff accompanied with a gypsy bonnet of the same colour, she deserted her lover and followed her former husband. In a few days however, to the surprise of everyone, we saw the lady walking unencumbered with clothing of any kind, and Bennelong was missing. Caruey was sought for, and we heard that he had been severely beaten by Bennelong at Rose Bay, who retained so much of our customs that he made use of his fists instead of the weapons of his country, to the great annoyance of Caruey, who would have preferred meeting his rival fairly in the field armed with the spear and the club.

Caruey being much the younger man, the lady, every inch a woman, followed her inclination, and Bennelong was compelled to yield her without any further opposition. He seemed to have been satisfied with the beating he had given Caruey, and hinted that, resting for the present without a wife, he should look about him and at some future period make a better choice. His absences from the governor's house now became frequent, and little attended to. When he went out he usually left his clothes behind, resuming them carefully on his return before he made his visit to the governor.

In March 1796 Collins reported that Bennelong was badly beaten in a fight with Colbee:

> On his coming among us again, he appeared with a wound on his mouth which had divided the upper lip and broke two of the teeth of that jaw. His features, never very pleasing, now seemed out of all proportion, and his pronunciation was much altered. Finding himself badly received among females...and not being able to endure a life of celibacy, which had been his condition from the day of his departure from this country until nearly the present hour, he made an attack upon his friend's favourite, Booreea, in which he was not only unsuccessful, but was punished for his breach of friendship, as above related, by Colbee, who sarcastically asked him, 'if he meant that kind of conduct to be a specimen of English manners'.

Bennelong died in 1813 and was buried at Kissing Point, on the Parramatta River near Ryde. There is a tiny park named Bennelong Park at

Colbee, *pencil drawing by Thomas Watling.*
Natural History Museum, London.

Kissing Point, where a large stormwater drain runs into the river, but there are still mangroves, a small beach and a very old, broken-down fig tree near some rocks that run down to the water. Bennelong may have sat under the same tree—fig trees live for up to 300 years—and perhaps he sharpened his spear on the rocks and caught fish off the beach. There is a sign bearing the park's name but no other information, either about the park or the person it was named for.

Although he lived rather dangerously, Bennelong's erstwhile friend Colbee outlived him by many years. Collins records that in 1797 Colbee was involved in a fight with Yeranibe, who dropped his shield; when he stooped to pick it up, Colbee struck him on the head with a club. Yeranibe died from the blow several days later and Colbee had to face Yeranibe's friends in a contest which was fought in front of the soldiers' barracks. Collins wrote that Colbee 'was overpowered and, falling beneath their spears, would certainly have been killed on the spot, but several soldiers rushed in and prevented their putting him to death where he lay'.

Colbee must have become assimilated to some extent; he received a grant of land near Windsor in 1816 as a reward for good conduct, and he was given a second grant near Bathurst in 1819. It is thought that he died about 1830.

Nanbaree, who was found with smallpox in April 1789 and adopted by Surgeon White, is said to have been White's 'gamekeeper and hunter'. White named him Andrew Snape Hamond Douglas White, although, not surprisingly, he continued to be known as Nanbaree. Later he served for a time on HMS *Reliance* as a seaman, and during 1802–3 he was with Flinders on the *Investigator*. Nanbaree died in 1811, aged about 40 and is said to be buried in the same grave as Bennelong.

In 1796, in an appendix to his *Account*, Collins wrote:

> Their spears and shields, their clubs and lines etc are their own property; they are manufactured by themselves and are the whole of their personal estate. But, strange as it may appear, they have also their real estates. Bennelong, both before he went to England and since his return, often assured me that the island *Memel*, called by us Goat Island, close by Sydney Cove, was his own property; that it was his father's, and that he should give it to Bygone, his particular friend and companion. To this little spot he appeared much attached and we have often seen him and his wife Barangaroo feasting and enjoying themselves on it. He told us of other people who possessed this kind of hereditary property, which they retained undisturbed.

If Bennelong's remarks to Collins about property had not been made until after his return from England, they might be regarded as made in light of knowledge he had acquired about English law and custom. In pointing out that Bennelong also told him *before* he went to England, Collins seems to be making sure it is understood that the Aboriginal people had a form of ownership of land before the Europeans came.

This was written after Grose had 'parcelled out to most of the officers substantial areas, including much of the land around Sydney and Parramatta', and in the face of ever-increasing demand for grants of land from settlers and soldiers alike; perhaps the colony's first judge-advocate had some misgivings about the fact that the Aboriginal people's relationship with the land was being ignored.

⁂

Soon after Phillip returned to England, he resigned his commission as governor of the colony in New South Wales. His resignation was accepted and he was granted a pension of £500 a year in recognition of his colonial service.

In 1793 Phillip was living at Bath, presumably receiving treatment for his illness and continuing to provide advice about the colony to the British government. He was married again, to Isabella Whitehead, in May 1794, and he returned to active service in 1796, initially in command of HMS *Alexander*, which he had joined as first lieutenant in 1778, then in the 74-gun ship *Swiftsure* and the 90-gun battleship *Blenheim*.

This was his last command at sea, but he continued to work for the Admiralty, being put in charge of the Hampshire Sea Fencibles, a shore-based defensive force trained as protection against an invasion by the French, which earned him a salary of £547 in addition to his pension. He also conducted an enquiry into the navy's unpopular and often brutal methods of recruitment.

He had risen to the rank of rear-admiral in 1799 and by 1806 he was living in retirement at Bath, where the Phillips bought the lease of No. 19 Bennett Street, a 'commodious and gentlemanly dwelling house' of three storeys, with additional rooms in the attic for staff and a large basement containing the kitchen, housekeeper's room and a butler's pantry.

Although he had apparently recovered from the illness and pain suffered in New South Wales, by 1807, at almost 70 years of age, his health was failing. Early in 1808 he suffered a stroke.

In May 1808 he received a visit from Philip Gidley King, who had succeeded Hunter as governor of the colony. King wrote to his son, 'I was with Admiral Phillip a week; he is very much altered, having lost the entire use of his whole right hand side, arm and leg; his intellect and spirits are as good as ever. He may linger on some years under his present infirmity, but, from his age, a great reprieve cannot be expected.' King saw him again later the same year and reported that he was 'much better than I could possibly expect'. King himself died suddenly, aged only 50, a week after the second visit.

Admiral and Mrs Phillip continued to entertain naval friends and Phillip maintained links with the colony, providing, for example, a

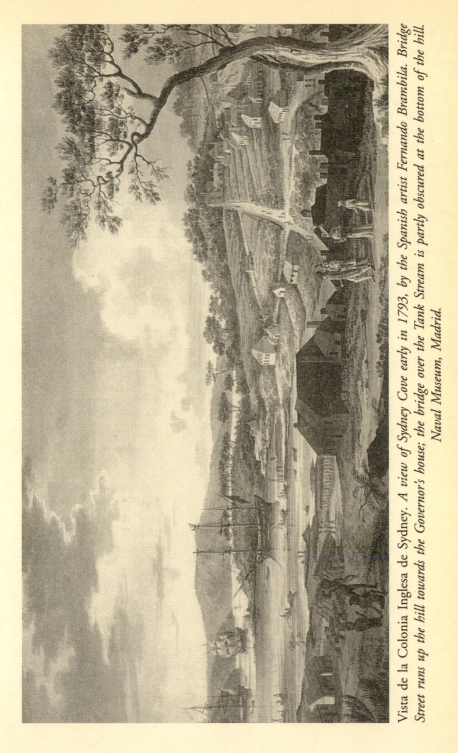

Vista de la Colonia Inglesa de Sydney. A view of Sydney Cove early in 1793, by the Spanish artist Fernando Brambila. Bridge Street runs up the hill towards the Governor's house; the bridge over the Tank Stream is partly obscured at the bottom of the hill. Naval Museum, Madrid.

reference to Governor Macquarie for a young convict, an architect from Bristol named Francis Greenway who had been sentenced to transportation in 1812 for forging a building contract.

Arthur Phillip died at his home in Bath in 1814. The cause of his death is not known; it was rumoured that he committed suicide by throwing himself into the courtyard of his house from an upstairs window, but there is no definite evidence of this. His funeral in the small church of St Nicholas at Bathampton was attended by a handful of friends. High up on the north wall of the church is a small stone with the inscription: 'Near this tablet are the remains of Arthur Phillip Esq., Admiral of the Blue, first Governor and Founder of New South Wales, who died 31 August 1814, in the 76th year of his age.'

Phillip's estate was worth £25,000 and included a number of drawings made in New South Wales, which were sold immediately after his death. Isabella Phillip died nine years later, aged 70.

◦

In July 1788 Major Ross wrote to Evan Nepean of the Home Department, 'I will in confidence venture to assure you that this country will never answer to settle in'. Later the same year the Reverend Richard Johnson said in a letter to Mr J. Stonard that 'Government would act very wisely to send out another fleet to take us all back to England'. In 1790 Surgeon White wrote that the government 'must soon know...how necessary it becomes to relinquish a scheme that in the nature of things can never answer'.

During the first few years, some of the senior men in the colony clearly thought it would not survive. Moving the settlement would have required resources that England would have been very reluctant to commit, but it is possible that, without Phillip's determination, wisdom and compassion, the colony might have descended into chaos and the pessimists might have been proved right. It may not be making too much of Phillip's influence and ability to say that the course of history, for better or for worse, and the mix of cultures which inhabits the continent today might have been quite different if a man lacking his qualities had been the first governor.

By the time he left Port Jackson in 1792, the settlement was firmly established, and no doubt Phillip took considerable pride in his public achievements.

Privately, he may have had some regrets. Phillip's second marriage, like his first, was childless. Bennelong, the man who called him *beanga*, or father, had died in New South Wales a year before him. Arthur Phillip had wanted to use Bennelong to reconcile the Aboriginal people to the coming of the Europeans. He may not have known of Bennelong's death, but he kept in touch with events in the colony and he would have known that his efforts at reconciliation had failed, that Bennelong's later years had been marred by quarrels with his own people, and that his death was being hastened by the alcohol which had become the currency of the European settlers.

Conversions

Length
1 inch = 25.4 mm
1 foot = 30.5 cm
1 yard = 0.9 m
1 fathom = 1.8 m
1 mile = 1.6 km
1 league = 5 km approx.

Mass
1 ounce = 28.3 g
1 pound = 454 g
1 hundredweight = 50.8 kg
1 ton = 1.02 t

Volume
1 pint = 568 ml
1 quart = 1.1 L
1 gallon = 4.6 L
1 bushel = 36.4 L

Area
1 acre = 0.4 ha

Temperature
To convert degrees Fahrenheit to degrees Centigrade, subtract 32; multiply the result by 5, and then divide by 9.

Currency
There are 12 pennies (d) in one shilling (s), and 20 shillings in one pound (£). A guinea was £1 1s.

Bibliography

In *Admiral Arthur Phillip*, George Mackaness wrote in 1937: 'Though we do not possess all the original documentary evidence—for example, the original journals of Governor Phillip and the Reverend Richard Johnson —through the energy and foresight of David Scott Mitchell, William Dixson and other patriotic Australians, we have preserved sufficient to provide the historian with the details of most of the important events, and of the careers of most of the men who have played more or less distinguished parts in our not uneventful history.'

Although he was born in New Zealand, Rex Nan Kivell's name should be added to those of Dixson and Mitchell. His collection, now held in the National Library of Australia in Canberra, is a unique resource for the study of the settlement and development of Australia and New Zealand.

Eyewitness accounts

Atkins, Richard. 'Journal 1791–1810'. Manuscript held by the National Library of Australia.

Barrington, George. *An Account of a Voyage to New South Wales.* M. Jones, London, 1803.

Bowes, Arthur. *The Journal of Arthur Bowes Smyth: Surgeon, Lady Penrhyn, 1787–1789.* Australian Documents Library, 1979.

Bradley, William. *A Voyage to New South Wales, 1786–1792.* Ure Smith, 1969.

Clark, Ralph. *The Journal and Letters of Lt. Ralph Clark, 1787–1792.* Australian Documents Library, 1981.

Collins, David. *An Account of the English Colony in New South Wales.* Reed, 1975.

Easty, John. *Memorandum of the Transactions of a Voyage from England to Botany Bay 1787–1793.* Angus & Robertson, 1965.

Fowell, Newton. *The Sirius Letters.* Ed. Nance Irvine. Fairfax Library, 1988.

Hunter, John. *An Historical Journal of Events at Sydney and at Sea, 1787–1792,* Angus & Robertson, 1968.

King, Philip Gidley. *The Journal of Philip Gidley King: Lieutenant RN, 1787–1790*. Australian Documents Library 1989.

Macarthur, Elizabeth. *The Journal and Letters of Elizabeth Macarthur, 1789–1798*. Historic Houses Trust of NSW, 1984.

Nagle, Jacob. *The Nagle Journal: A Diary of the Life of Jacob Nagle, Sailor, from the year 1775 to 1841*. Weidenfeld & Nicolson, 1988.

Phillip, Arthur. *The Voyage of Governor Phillip to Botany Bay*. Angus & Robertson, 1970.

Scott, James. *Remarks on a Passage to Botany Bay, 1787–1792*. Angus & Robertson, 1963.

Spain, Edward. *The Journal of Edward Spain*. St Marks Press, 1989.

Tench, Watkin. *A Narrative of the Expedition to Botany Bay and A Complete Account of the Settlement at Port Jackson*. Library of Australian History, 1979.

White, John. *Journal of a Voyage to New South Wales*. Angus & Robertson, 1962.

Worgan, George. *Journal of a First Fleet Surgeon*. Library of Australian History, 1978.

The books by Collins, Hunter, Phillip, Tench and White had been published by 1800 and Barrington was published soon after. All of the above except those by Barrington and Atkins have been published in recent editions, which were used in compiling this book. Atkins's manuscript is held by the National Library in Canberra. All contain first-hand accounts, except *The Voyage of Governor Phillip to Botany Bay*, which was compiled mainly from Phillip's despatches.

Daily records

Cobley, John. *Sydney Cove, 1788*. Hodder & Stoughton, 1962.

Cobley, John. *Sydney Cove 1789–1790*. Angus & Robertson, 1963.

Cobley, John. *Sydney Cove 1791–1792*. Angus & Robertson, 1965.

During the 1960s, Dr John Cobley of Forty Baskets Beach, near Manly, began compiling a series of books with the aim of providing a daily record of life in the early years of the colony. His method was to record, without comment or interpretation, every event from the original records 'under the date on which it occurred' and then edit out the repetitions. He compiled five books covering the period from 1788 to 1800 and several other books of historical importance before his death in 1989. The first three books of the series were used extensively for reference in this compilation.

Biographical records

Flynn, Michael. *The Second Fleet*. Library of Australian History, 1993.
Gillen, Mollie. *The Founders of Australia: A Biographical Dictionary of the First Fleet*. Library of Australian History, 1989.

These encyclopaedias of the first settlement provide details of everyone who came during the first three and a half years; births, deaths and marriages, the crimes for which they were transported, and their recorded activities in the colony. Among other things, they made it possible to give personal information and to cross-check references and they provided an authoritative source of names and spelling.

Art

Hunter, John. *The Hunter Sketchbook*. National Library of Australia, 1989.
McCormick, Tim. *First Views of Australia 1788–1825*. David Ell Press, 1987.
Rienits, Rex and Thea. *Early Artists of Australia*. Angus and Robertson, 1963.
Smith, Bernard and Wheeler, Alwyne (Editors), *The Art of the First Fleet*. Oxford University Press, 1988.

There are some 800 drawings dating from the first five years of the European settlement. They depict the views, buildings and events, the Aboriginal people, the flowers, plants and animals. Many of them are not signed. These books provide a representative selection, information about the known artists and a guide to the likely identity of the artists of the unsigned works.

First Views of Australia contains 'all the known topographic views of Sydney and Parramatta' to 1822 and much information about the paintings and the period; *Early Artists of Australia* is a history of art and artists from the first European contact to 1821; *Art of the First Fleet* deals in detail with the extensive collection of early Australian paintings held by the Natural History Museum in London. *The Hunter Sketchbook* contains 95 drawings by Hunter of birds, flowers, fish, animals, and the native people of Australia and other islands of the Pacific.

Historical records

Historical Records of Australia, Series 1 Volume 1. Government Printer, 1914.
Historical Records of New South Wales, Volume 1 Part 2. Government Printer, 1892 (Facsimile reprint Lansdown Slattery 1978).
Historical Records of New South Wales, Volume 2. Government Printer, 1893 (Facsimile reprint Lansdown Slattery, 1978).

These are based on Phillip's despatches to officials in England and their replies and instructions to him, as well as other official records and documents of historical interest. *Historical Records of New South Wales,* published first, contains more items of general interest; Volume 2, for example, includes the journals and letters of both Daniel Southwell and Elizabeth Macarthur and the *British Museum Papers, 1785–1795*, which contain many contemporary press cuttings. *Historical Records of Australia* includes documents found after the earlier publication and is more complete in respect of Phillip's despatches.

Biographies

Eldershaw, M. Barnard. *Phillip of Australia*. Harrap, 1938.

Frost, Alan. *Arthur Phillip, 1738-1814: His Voyaging*. Oxford University Press, 1987.

Mackaness, George. *Admiral Arthur Phillip, Founder of New South Wales*. Angus & Robertson, 1937.

Macintosh, Neil K. *Richard Johnson, Chaplain to the Colony of New South Wales*. Library of Australian History, 1978.

Other sources

Carter, Paul. *The Calling to Come*. Historic Houses Trust of NSW, 1996.

Crittenden, Victor. *A Bibliography of the First Fleet*. Australian National University Press, 1982.

Moore, John. *The First Fleet Marines, 1786–1792*. University of Queensland Press, 1987.

Nagle J. F. *Collins, The Courts and the Colony*. University of New South Wales Press, 1996.

Robinson, Portia. *The Women of Botany Bay*. Macquarie Library, 1988.

Troy, Jakelin. *The Sydney Language*. Australian Institute of Aboriginal and Torres Strait Islander Studies, 1994.

Australians to 1788. Fairfax, Syme & Weldon, 1987, esp. chs 18, 20.

Land Grants, 1788–1809. Ed. R. J. Ryan. Australian Documents Library 1981.

Acknowledgements

At Allen & Unwin, Patrick Gallagher backed the idea from the start, John Iremonger helped give the book direction and form, and Emma Cotter's editing and design skills were much appreciated.

At the State Library of New South Wales, Jennifer Broomhead, Copyright and Permissions Librarian, and Richard Neville, Curator of Pictures Research, gave me important information on the availability and provenance of text and illustrations.

Professor Oliver McDonagh and Stephanie Harris read early drafts and gave encouragement and advice.

My sincere thanks to all of them.

Jack Egan
Sydney, 1999

Index

Colour illustrations are indicated by entries in bold.
Black and white illustrations are indicated by entries in italics.